Out of Another @#&*% Crisis!

Also available from ASQ Quality Press:

Lean ISO 9001: Adding Spark to Your ISO 9001 QMS and Sustainability to Your Lean Efforts
Mike Micklewright

Learning Lean 5S: Quality Pocket of Knowledge (QPoK)
ASQ

Lean Kaizen: A Simplified Approach to Process Improvements
George Alukal and Anthony Manos

Lean for Service Organizations and Offices: A Holistic Approach for Achieving Operational Excellence and Improvements
Debashis Sarkar

5S for Service Organizations and Offices: A Lean Look at Improvements
Debashis Sarkar

Solutions to the Healthcare Quality Crisis: Cases and Examples of Lean Six Sigma in Healthcare
Søren Bisgaard, editor

The Executive Guide to Understanding and Implementing Lean Six Sigma: The Financial Impact
Robert M. Meisel, Steven J. Babb, Steven F. Marsh, and James P. Schlichting

Managing the Customer Experience: A Measurement-Based Approach
Morris Wilburn

A Lean Guide to Transforming Healthcare: How to Implement Lean Principles in Hospitals, Medical Offices, Clinics, and Other Healthcare Organizations
Thomas G. Zidel

Root Cause Analysis: Simplified Tools and Techniques, Second Edition
Bjørn Andersen and Tom Fagerhaug

The Certified Manager of Quality/Organizational Excellence Handbook, Third Edition
Russell T. Westcott, editor

To request a complimentary catalog of ASQ Quality Press publications, call 800-248-1946, or visit our Web site at http://www.asq.org/quality-press.

Out of Another @#&*% Crisis!

Motivation Through Humiliation

Mike Micklewright

ASQ Quality Press
Milwaukee, Wisconsin

American Society for Quality, Quality Press, Milwaukee 53203
© 2010 by Mike Micklewright
All rights reserved. Published 2010
Printed in the United States of America
16 15 14 13 12 11 10   5 4 3 2 1

Library of Congress Cataloging-in-Publication Data

Micklewright, Mike.
  Out of another @#&*% crisis!: motivation through humiliation / Mike Micklewright.
    p. cm.
  Includes bibliographical references and index.
  ISBN 978-0-87389-783-9 (hbk. : alk. paper)
  1. Total quality management 2. Organizational effectiveness. 3. Deming, W. Edwards
(William Edwards), 1900–1993 I. Title.

  HD62.15.M54 2010
  658.4'013—dc22   2010000567

ISBN: 978-0-87389-783-9

Publisher: William A. Tony
Acquisitions Editor: Matt T. Meinholz
Project Editor: Paul O'Mara
Production Administrator: Randall Benson

ASQ Mission: The American Society for Quality advances individual, organizational,
and community excellence worldwide through learning, quality improvement, and
knowledge exchange.

Attention Bookstores, Wholesalers, Schools, and Corporations: ASQ Quality Press
books, video, audio, and software are available at quantity discounts with bulk
purchases for business, educational, or instructional use. For information, please
contact ASQ Quality Press at 800-248-1946, or write to ASQ Quality Press,
P.O. Box 3005, Milwaukee, WI 53201-3005.

To place orders or to request ASQ membership information, call 800-248-1946. Visit our
Web site at http://www.asq.org/quality-press.

 Printed on acid-free paper

Quality Press
600 N. Plankinton Avenue
Milwaukee, Wisconsin 53203
Call toll free 800-248-1946
Fax 414-272-1734
www.asq.org
http://www.asq.org/quality-press
http://standardsgroup.asq.org
E-mail: authors@asq.org

Table of Contents

A Few Things About the Format of This Book

Perhaps because of the almost sick way I grew up—and many of us grew up—reaching the goal was always the most important thing, even if the process along the way to reaching that goal was usually a laborious chore. This mind-set has been prevalent even when I have read books, and I have read many books. It's hard for me to put a book down and stop reading it, even if it's a bad book. I feel like somehow, something very interesting will eventually come of the book, and I do not want to miss it. Plus, I want the credit, from myself, for completing the book. I can not give myself credit for a book only half completed. Also, I have other books waiting in queue and I want to get to them as quickly as possible, but I'm still reading the boring book and the possible good books will just have to wait.

So, with time I have learned that it is the process of gaining knowledge that is most important and not how many books have been completed. If I begin to read a book in which the knowledge gained is little compared to the time put into reading the book, I will put it down and start with a new book. This has been difficult to do because it goes against what I have come to expect in the form of a grade, gold star, diploma, degree, certificate, merit raise based on performance, and Black Belt.

Oftentimes, I find myself angry about the beginning sections of books. There are always sections like Contents, Acknowledgments, Preface, Foreword, Introduction, and Dedication. I want to tell the authors and publishers that if you want me to read those sections, then give me credit for reading those sections. It's not fair to number those pages with an extinct Roman numeral system. That's crazy. No one uses Roman numerals anymore except when counting Super Bowls. And even then, how many average football fans would know that Super Bowl XXXVIII was really Super Bowl 38? So why do we use Roman numerals at the beginning of books? If someone asks me how long a certain book was that I really enjoyed, I might say, "It was 322 pages, but if you count all the $@#* pages at the beginning that I did not get credit for, it was 351 pages." Now does that not sound so much more impressive than just 322 pages?

So, I feel like protesting, but I don't because my Roman Catholic upbringing makes me feel guilty for claiming that I read a book when in fact I did not read the opening sections with the Roman numerals. What a coincidence—the word Roman was used twice in the above sentence. So I read all the opening sections, with a great deal of reluctance and feeling a little pissy. Sometimes, though, I do not read all of the Acknowledgments and I feel a little better.

So, the good news is that in this book, you get credit for reading everything. No Roman numerals! (Now, perhaps the Super Bowl will be encouraged to change its numbering system?!) This should make you feel accomplished already.

Also, because I have grown up to be more goal oriented, I never really care about what page I'm on. I'm only concerned with how many *more* pages I have left to read. Also, I do calculations in my head to figure out what percent of the book I've completed toward the end goal. (For instance, if I'm on page 140 of a 350-page book, that's about 2/7 complete, which equates to about 28% done. In my mind, the important numbers are that I have 210 pages left to read and I am 28% done.)

Again, it's not the knowledge that counts in my sick world, it's how many books I've read, including the percentage of the book I'm currently reading.

So, the good news in this book is that each page has a page number that represents how many pages are left in the book and the percent of the book completed at that point.

Also, in the example above with the book that contained 350 pages, it officially had 358 pages, but the last eight pages represented the Index. No one reads the Index. I do not even feel the least bit guilty about not reading that section. So, the good news in this book is that the Index will contain the Roman numerals.

MOTIVATION THROUGH HUMILIATION—THE AMERICAN WAY

Why did I subtitle the book *Motivation Through Humiliation?* Quite simply, to speak the language of the leaders of our companies and our government institutions to motivate *them* to action through humiliation the way they believe people are motivated to perform better. The United States lacks true leaders. We don't even know what leadership qualities are. U.S. society and culture, as a whole, lacks leadership skills, and our culture of "me first" does nothing to promote leadership. But how do our leaders humiliate workers and students? Let me explain . . .

American corporate and governmental leaders (I use the word "leader" loosely, not to signify leadership qualities, but rather to signify those running companies and government) love to evaluate the performance of those who report to them, or those in school, as a means of motivating them. It's also easier to give annual performance reviews or report cards each semester than provide leadership day in and day out.

Corporate and governmental leaders, for the most part, probably received excellent grades in school and excellent evaluations moving up the ladder as they performed well working within the business system. That's how they got to the level of being a "leader." "Well then, how could this be a bad thing? Performance evaluations and management by objectives must be a good thing, right?" they think. After all, it worked for them and they are successful.

Prior to the Barack Obama administration, the Chicago Public Schools system had as its CEO a person named Arne Duncan. His title was truly "CEO," not superintendent, as is the case in most other cities, because the mayor of Chicago wanted the school system to be run like a "business."

Arne Duncan spearheaded a program in which high schoolers were being paid for grades: $50 for an A, $35 for a B, and $20 for a C. They would receive half the money when they received the grades and the other half when they graduated. The belief was that children could be motivated to get better grades if money was attached to the grade. The problem that Mr. Duncan did and does not see is that the *grade* becomes the goal, not the *education*. Students will do everything necessary to achieve the grade, including cheating on tests, bribing teachers, and copying tests of others. Other children, who are more honest, may study for the money but not for the sheer joy of learning. Teachers teach students how to take tests rather than how to learn. They teach only what is in the curriculum, and they don't teach about life and how to deal with success, failures, meltdowns, and heartaches. Children do not learn problem-solving skills or how to be creative. After graduation the former students, now workers in the workforce, will have been so accustomed to receiving something in return for learning that they will not feel motivated to learn on the job, or on their own, unless they receive money in return. Receiving money, or even grades or a gold star, are all forms of extrinsic motivation to learning. Wanting to learn on one's one for the sheer joy of gaining more knowledge is a form of *intrinisic* motivation and comes naturally to all children before they are corrupted with extrinsic motivators.

If you've ever watched an infant grow into a toddler and then grow into a child, you have noticed that the child wants to learn intrinsically. Intrinsic motivation to learning is natural, and we destroy that intrinsic motivation over the years and replace it with extrinsic motivators like gold stars, grades, and now even money.

Arne Duncan was promoted to secretary of education in the Obama administration. At some point he is more than likely to introduce a similar program nationwide. He is already promoting merit pay for teachers and incentives that encourage even more teachers to teach. Arne was replaced as the CEO of the Chicago Public Schools system by Ron Huberman, the former president of the Chicago Transit Authority. He admitted that he had no background in education. But then, who needs a background in education when all that matters are grades?

Don't Arne and Barack understand that the children who grow up in the Chicago Public Schools system may one day become governors of Illinois? Don't they see that "Pay for Grades" leads even more to "Pay for Play" politics, which Illinois has become famous for with its most recent governors, including ex-governor Rod Blagojevich, who attempted to receive favors in exchange for Obama's former senate seat? Isn't this just another form of extrinsic motivation that one has learned from the education, political, and corporate worlds? Are we all just idiots to allow these systems to continue?

It's no different in the corporate world. Employees are motivated to work within the system—never to challenge it—in order to receive the largest raise or bonus possible at their annual performance review. Managers do not have to lead employees throughout the year because they know that the objectives and goals are clearly stated and that the employee will be evaluated at the end of the year.

Since our "leaders" so strongly believe in report cards and evaluations, and since this book is targeted toward our corporate and business leaders, I thought it would only be appropriate to evaluate *their* performance in adhering to Dr. Deming's Principles, as I have done in Chapter 3.

SO WHAT IS A PREFACE?

I knew I had to write a Preface, because everyone writes a Preface to their book. I knew that I could not buck the system. I had to work within the system in order to be rewarded by the system—publishers publishing the book. Also, I could not imagine the embarrassment I would suffer if half of the readers who bought my book returned them to Barnes & Noble or Amazon.com with the complaint, "I was ripped off. This book does not have a Preface!"

But I was not sure what a Preface was. I knew the author wrote it, but what does it actually mean, I wondered. "Acknowledgments" is obvious, as is Introduction, Contents, and Dedication.

But what was a Preface? I had always thought a Preface was how someone looked prior to a face-lift and used in a sentence like, "You have such a pretty preface now, you don't need a face-lift." And then when s/he came out of surgery, s/he would have a Postface. Actually, there are two Postfaces. The immediate Postface, which looks like one has been just been mugged, and the longer-term Postface, which looks like one's face wrapped in cellophane.

Oh no, am I going to have to write a Postface also? No one else has, so I will not disturb the system within which I work.

And for that matter, do I need to write a Reverse if I include a Foreword? I won't include a Foreword. That way, I will not need to write a Reverse.

So, Preface is defined on www.answers.com as:

A preliminary statement or essay introducing a book that explains its scope, intention, or background and is usually written by the author.

Here's my Preface . . .

Preface

In 1982, Dr. W. Edwards Deming wrote *Out of the Crisis*. At this point in our great country's history, the United States was enduring a crisis of low quality and high costs. Our previous dominance in the provision of goods and services was being challenged, primarily by the Japanese. American consumers were becoming choosier in their product choices and when given two products of equal price, they were choosing the product with the higher quality levels, regardless of where it was built.

American companies were losing their competitiveness due to the production of lower-quality products. Adding fuel to the fire of lost American competitiveness was that foreign products, though being shipped halfway across the world, were also less expensive. Foreign products were less expensive *because of, not in spite of,* higher quality levels and less waste in both production and design processes. Of course, they were also lower in price because of lower labor rates.

The root causes to the crisis at hand in the early '80s are found in not following sound management principles, the same 14 Points (principles) that Dr. Deming defined in Chapter 2, "Principles for Transformation of Western Management":

1. Create constancy of purpose toward improvement of product and service, with the aim to become competitive and to stay in business, and to provide jobs.

2. Adopt the new philosophy. We are in a new economic age. Western management must awaken to the challenge, must learn their responsibilities, and take on leadership for change.

3. Cease dependence on inspection to achieve quality. Eliminate the need for inspection on a mass basis by creating quality into the product in the first place.

4. End the practice of awarding business on the basis of price tag. Instead minimize total cost. Move toward a single supplier for any one item, on a long-term relationship of loyalty and trust.

5. Improve constantly and forever the system of production and service, to improve quality and productivity, and thus constantly decrease costs.

6. Institute training on the job.

7. Institute leadership (see point 12.) The aim of leadership should be to help people and machines and gadgets to do a better job. Leadership of management is in need of overhaul, as well as leadership of production workers.

8. Drive out fear so that everyone may work effectively for the company.

9. Break down barriers between departments. People in research, design, sales, and production must work as a team, to foresee problems of production and in use that may be encountered with the product or service.

10. Eliminate slogans, exhortations, and targets for the work force that ask for zero defects and new levels of productivity.

11. a. Eliminate work standards (quotas) on the factory floor. Substitute leadership.

    b. Eliminate management by objective. Eliminate management by numbers, numerical goals. Substitute leadership.

12. Remove barriers that rob people of pride of workmanship.

13. Institute a vigorous program of education and self-improvement.

14. Put everybody in the company to work to accomplish the transformation. The transformation is everybody's job.

By not following these principles, a crisis manifested itself in the form of low quality, high costs, and low competitiveness. These were the symptoms of unprincipled, or perhaps misguided principled, management practices,

However, just like when a company attempts to find the root causes to a defective product or service provided to a customer, it is important to understand that true root causes can result in many different types of problems, or crises. So, while at the time of this writing we may not be experiencing the same crisis of low quality—at least not as much as we did prior to the '90s—we are still experiencing many other crises resulting from not following the management principles defined by Dr. Deming.

WHAT CRISES DO WE HAVE TODAY?

At the time of this writing (2008–2009), the United States is experiencing multiple concurrent crises. Each crisis is easily attributable to leaders of organizations and government not following multiple principles defined by Dr. Deming. These crises include:

1. Skyrocketing oil and gasoline prices

2. The outsourcing of American manufacturing capability

3. The depletion of natural resources to the level of not being sustainable

4. The destruction of our planet and multitudes of different species

5. The credit meltdown in our financial system

6. Worldwide recession

7. The U.S. funding crisis resulting from the huge amounts of debt incurred by the U.S. government as it attempts to spend its way out of recession

8. Corporate greed

9. Healthcare crisis

10. Social Security crisis

We are certainly not lacking crises. The intent of this book though is not to dissect and analyze each of the varied crises to determine causation because the causes are simply not following one or many of the above principles.

The intent of this book is to dissect each of the principles and see how we rate as a society, as an economy, and as a country when compared to these principles that the very wise Dr. Deming defined for us in the early '80s.

Also, as a society, when we do not get to the root causes of our problems, we tend to mask them with band-aids. In the credit crisis of 2008/2009, the band-aids came in the form of government bailouts, increased regulation, and government control. These band-aids, however, will never ensure that the problems will not come back again without addressing one of the underlying root causes of the crisis—the lack of following principle #1: *create constancy of purpose toward improvement of product and service, with the aim to become competitive and to stay in business, and to provide jobs.* Fannie Mae, Freddie Mac, AIG, Lehman Brothers, Washington

Mutual, and so on, did not follow this principle, as so many other organizations did not.

Band-aids exist in many forms. To address the crisis of lower quality, higher costs, and lower competitiveness, many programs—or as people in the business community like to refer to them, "programs of the month"—have come and gone. These programs include quality circles, total quality management, zero defects, benchmarking, balanced scorecard, and reengineering, to name a few. In the '90s and the '00s, they morphed into ISO 9001, Six Sigma, and lean.

This book will show how these practices and tools either support or do not support the principles taught to us by Dr. Deming. This book will also show that the popular activity of copying tools and practices from other organizations will not resolve an organization's problems. Organizations need to determine what they stand for, why they exist, and what their principles and values are as an entity, and then build their own practices and tools around those principles.

From reengineering to ISO 9001 to Six Sigma, these are only band-aids covering up the root causes, which are having either no principles, wrong principles, or misguided principles. Dr. Deming gave us the right principles to succeed in the long term, and yet we continue to ignore them.

WHY WRITE A BOOK ABOUT HOW WE COMPARE TO WHAT WAS WRITTEN IN ANOTHER BOOK?

Why have so many people written books about the Bible over the centuries? After all, the Bible was just another book. The Bible contained wisdom and provided a road map to leading a successful and righteous life. *Out of the Crisis* contained wisdom and provided a road map to leading a successful and righteous organization. Principles are timeless. When correct and good for society, they stand the test of time, industry, culture, and technology.

We don't have to keep introducing new programs (although this will always happen because of the desire to sell something new to gullible and willing CEOs). We can just adopt Dr. Deming's principles and develop our own way, our own tools, and our own practices. As Thomas Jefferson said,

Be flexible in style, but unwavering, like a rock, in principles.

So Dr. Deming's principles pertain to today's world just as much as they did in 1982 and just as they will in 2082.

On page 154 of *Out of the Crisis*, Dr. W. Edwards Deming wrote, "It may be obvious to anyone, on reflection on the obstacles that we have seen, that a long, thorny, road lies ahead in American industry—10 to 30 years—before we can settle down to an acknowledged competitive position."

Out of the Crisis was first published in 1982—28 years prior to the publication of this book—which puts us into the latter part of the era that Dr. Deming referred to in his book. So, where do we stand today? Have we settled down to an acknowledged competitive position, 28 years later? Have we remembered Dr. Deming's words, his 14 Points, or have we forgotten all he taught so little time ago.

This book will explore just that.

I am an avid Deming fan and believer. This does not mean I have not personally struggled with one or two of his 14 Points for Management, because I have. I've had a difficult time understanding why he strongly suggested eliminating the annual performance rating system. Perhaps it's just because I am a suck-up. Afterall, I was the one who couldn't wait to get my report card. I'm the weirdo who would ask my supervisors for a review. I loved this stuff because I worked very hard and I *knew* I would receive good marks. However, if there were any comments that were even a little bad, I would get a little defensive, but I would also work to eliminate the bad mark. Though this might sound like a good thing, it was actually a negative because I was learning to work within the system, not challenge it.

Dr. Deming would probably have thought that I was an idiot for struggling with this Point, and perhaps he would have been correct. It took some deep thinking and soul-searching on my part, as well as a paradigm shift in my thinking, but I now see how destructive performance evaluations can be personally to many people, how giving an annual review is really just batch processing of one's performance rather than providing day-to-day leadership, and how the system itself may never be changed because of the rewards of working within the system. (I am literally inside a Panera Bread in Arlington Heights, Illinois, editing this paragraph, and I hear a teenage girl tell another teenage girl, "I never got a star or an A in school and I used to get so sad when the other kids got them." She then stuck out her lower lip as a young child would do. Performance evaluations did not do much for her self-esteem.)

Changing one's thinking habits is as difficult as changing one's physical bad habits (that is, smoking, drinking, overeating, gambling). I have personally worked hard to challenge my thinking, grow some new dendrites, so that I may fully understand all of his common-sensical points and the value of each. I now believe in everything he has taught, and I ask you to challenge yourself in your thinking and truly breathe in all that the great Dr. W. Edwards Deming taught us. Come join the Deming cult (definition from answers.com: an exclusive group of persons sharing an esoteric, usually artistic or intellectual, interest).

GOALS OF THIS BOOK

My goal with this book and other projects is to resurrect the Deming principles, because I believe that since his death in 1993, they have been in large part forgotten and replaced with other programs or processes that oftentimes conflict with what he taught us.

I also believe we have so many concurrent crises because we have not followed what he taught us.

My goal is to teach those who were not in the business world before the early '90s about a great man who had a profound affect in the world business environment, if not specifically in the United States, then in Japan. Japan's success has led to positive effects in other parts of the world, and thus some of his principles still reverberate to some extent throughout the world.

My goal is to create more Demingites, more avid believers, who will also preach and spread the word of Deming for the good of society.

My goal is to shock and tell it like it is, much like Deming would.

My goal is to sell lots of copies of this book so that I can become a keynote speaker at conferences and conventions, giving me the opportunity to spread the Word of Deming to even more people. (It is pretty much an unwritten law that in order to give a keynote presentation, one must first write a book.)

I have tried different avenues to spread the word of Deming including 1) a presentation that I call S.A.D. (Society of the Anti-Deming), which reverses all of his points as a management system, 2) a Deming evangelist Webcast (through *Quality Digest*'s online magazine), in which I act as a Dr. Martin Luther King–type preacher preaching the words of Dr. Deming (see an excerpt on YouTube.com), and 3) a very popular Deming impersonation, What Would Deming Say?, in which I give Deming's presumed views of today's quality movements, and which forms the basis for this book.

I will keep trying different things, even if I make a fool of myself, which I seem to do quite often, to get the word of Deming out to the masses and to help create real, sustainable change.

I am a student of Dr. Deming's principles, as he was a student of Dr. Walter Shewhart's principles. I will continue to learn more about Deming (through interviews, discussions, his books, and taped presentations) and his principles and will teach others the same, while challenging them to change and improve.

DR. W. EDWARDS DEMING AND MIKE MICKLEWRIGHT'S RELATIONSHIP

Personally, and unfortunately, I never met or saw Dr. W. Edwards Deming speak in person. The closest I got to Dr. Deming and his teachings was through my first professional boss in the work world.

In the summer of 1985, I was hired as a summer student by Jay Wetzel, the VP of Engineering of the Saturn Project at General Motors. Saturn was not yet a corporation at that time and was just a project name within the Pontiac Motor Division.

Jay had met with Dr. Deming along with other managers from the Pontiac Motor Division. Jay Wetzel, along with most of Saturn's first management team, came from the Pontiac Motor Division. In 1983, still three years before my graduation from college, William Hoglund, then manager of Pontiac and soon to be president of the Saturn Corporation, had invited Dr. Deming to speak to 350 people in management. Jay Wetzel's commitment to Deming's principles was quoted in the day's agenda along with several other future upper-level managers of Saturn, as is shown in a book written by Dr. Deming's long-time secretary Cecilia S. Kilian, entitled *The World of W. Edwards Deming.*

There were several ways in which Dr. Deming influenced Saturn's practices in the early days, including appreciating the importance of benchmarking, the need to understand and experience the customers' needs, the importance of making purchases not based on price tag alone (even if it meant going outside GM to purchase parts typically awarded to a sister GM facility), the importance of building long-term relationships with suppliers, and the importance of education.

I believe that Dr. Deming also influenced Jay Wetzel in many ways. Upon completion of my internship and return to the University of Illinois for my last semester of school, I asked Jay for a performance review. He begrudgingly gave me one. One of his pieces of advice to me was:

> *Work on leadership style, posture, and "take charge" methods . . . this comes only with experience. This will help your image; learn how to do this without losing sensitivity in working with the others, sharing credit, and motivating others to join you as partners.*

In Chapter 6 of *The New Economics*, Dr. Deming outlines 14 (why was 14 always the magical number?) characteristics of "(t)he new role of a manager of people after transformation." The seventh characteristic was written as such (please observe the overlap between Deming's words and Wetzel's words):

7. *He has three sources of power:*

   a. *Authority of office*

   b. *Knowledge*

   c. *Personality and persuasive power; tact*

   A successful manager of people develops "b" and "c"; he does not rely on "a." He has nevertheless the obligation to use "a," as this source of power enables him to change the process— equipment, materials, methods—to bring improvement, such as to reduce variation in output.

Now did Dr. Deming influence Jay's thinking and wisdom directly for him to provide me with such advice? I'm not sure, but I do know that when any of us learn of some piece of profound knowledge, it influences how we speak to others in ways of which we are not even aware.

Acknowledgments

First and foremost, I must thank Panera Bread for allowing me to spend so much time in your two stores in Arlington Heights, Illinois. You gave me my office away from the office that allowed me to write my first two books almost simultaneously. Yours is a wise business model that provides free Wi-Fi and an endless cup of coffee to those of us who need the background noise and activity and yet the privacy to do our own work without the kids or the TV providing distraction in our own homes. I always made sure I bought at least one meal, as do the other worker bees hacking away at their laptop computers, within your stores. It is a prudent business decision to encourage us to be in your restaurant because we give the appearance of activity within the restaurant even during those slow hours between 3 pm and 5 pm. A restaurant with people present will always encourage more patrons to enter. Smart move!

From a professional standpoint, I thank the following bosses and mentors at my first "real" job with the Saturn Corporation: Jay Wetzel, VP of engineering, who left an everlasting impression on me while working for him in the summer of '85 as a summer student, Ken Franklin for his idealistic practices and beliefs in what Saturn could be, Greg Glos for his trust in me to proceed independently in so much of my work as a manufacturing engineer, and Phil Ross for his mentoring me in the proper way of doing design of experiments (DOE). DOE would later become my springboard into my new career as an independent quality and lean consultant in 1994.

I also wish to thank my other mentors at my second job with Seaquist Valve in Cary, Illinois, including my direct bosses Rick Epstein and Rich Kaleckas, as well as Pat Dougherty, who once told me, "It's easier to ask for forgiveness than permission."

I wish to thank other professionals who have influenced me to write this book and other books, including Don Dinero, Jim Huntzinger, Dwayne Butcher, Nigel Clements, Dr. Tony Burns, and Mark Graban.

I thank certain clients who have had an effect on my continuing education, including Terry Schadeberg, Jim Brizzolara, John Ballun, and Kevin Meyer.

As an avid reader, I have been inspired by many famous writers, including Thomas Jefferson, Benjamin Franklin, Dr. Edward DeBono, John Stossel, Malcolm Gladwell, Ricardo Semler, Herb Kelleher, Howard Schultz, Paul Orfalea, Bill Waddell, Norm Bodek, Jeffrey Liker, Bill Hybels, and of course, my favorite of all, Dr. W. Edwards Deming.

I wish to thank Dirk Dusharme and Mike Richman of *Quality Digest* magazine for allowing me the freedom to be creative and challenging in my writing and videos. So much of the material for this book was developed as I wrote articles and had them published by *Quality Digest*. Without *Quality Digest,* I would not have known how many people actually liked my writing style and what I have to say, and I may never have had the confidence to go ahead and write a book.

I thank my Dad, who died 10 years ago, for giving me his sense of fairness and making me understand "respect for people" many years before business people even heard of this principle as being one of the core principles of the Toyota Way.

I thank my Mom for her care and warmth. I thank my children Marissa, Erika, Cassandra, Ryan, and Samantha for who they are and who they will be.

And I especially thank my dear wife Donna for all of her support, ingenuity, creativity, drive, and patience with me as I put this book together. She is one of the root causes to the content of this book and she is my rock!

1

Who Was Deming and What Shaped His Life/Principles?

As this book is being written, the U.S. is suffering through the greatest recession since the Great Depression. To a great extent, the recession was caused by corporate greed and other shortsighted policies and practices in the financial and mortgage lending world. Dr. Deming would have been pissed at the many corporate leaders that led us into this financial mess. Before we delve into why this happened, we need to understand the man and what motivated him.

GOD OR THORN?

Dr. W. Edwards was a God. He was the:

    God of Quality Assurance

    God of Lean

    God of Common Sense

    God of the Common Worker—the frontline employee

    God of Wise Purchasing Decisions

    God of Continuous Improvement

    God of Eastern Management

    God of Japanese Industry

    God of Process Orientation

On the other hand, Dr. Deming was a Thorn. He was the:

Thorn of Quality Control (Inspection)

Thorn of Wasteful Practices

Thorn of the Illogical

Thorn of Top Management

Thorn of Wall Street

Thorn of Greed

Thorn of Outsourcing

Thorn of Western Management

Thorn of Fear

Thorn of Departments

W. Edwards Deming was a U.S. statistician, educator, and advocate of quality control methods in industrial production. He received his PhD in mathematical physics from Yale University, and he subsequently taught at New York University for 46 years.

From the 1930s he employed statistical analysis to achieve better industrial quality control.

In 1950 he was invited to Japan to teach executives and engineers. His ideas, which centered on tallying product defects, analyzing and addressing their causes, and recording the effects of the changes on subsequent quality, were eagerly adopted there and eventually helped Japanese products dominate the market in much of the world. In 1951 Japan instituted the Deming Prize, awarded to corporations that win a rigorous quality competition. Deming's ideas were taken up by U.S. corporations in the 1980s, particularly under the rubric of *total quality management*.[1]

W. Edwards Deming has been revered as virtually a god in Japan, and he was oftentimes referred to as a capitalist revolutionary.

Deming was relatively unknown in the United States until NBC broadcast a documentary in June 1980 titled, "If Japan Can, Why Can't We?" Many people credit this broadcast with igniting the quality revolution that swept the United States in the '80s.

QUALITY VERSUS LEAN

Most people associate Deming with the *quality* movement and would probably have no idea of his effect on today's current *lean* movement. In *Out of the Crisis,* Deming states, "The greatest waste in America is failure to use the abilities of people."[2] As if it's a new discovery, Americans have now come to recognize the 8 process wastes, up from the 7 process wastes, with the addition of the most recently recognized waste of not using employees' minds and skills. Deming preached this over 25 years ago.

Deming spoke relentlessly of the costs associated with waste and the relationship between low quality leading to more waste leading to longer throughput times leading to less profitability. The way to become lean and less wasteful is to first improve quality.

Many organizations today still do not see this relationship. They see no or little relationship between quality and lean efforts. In company after company, case after case, the quality professionals are leading and managing the quality management system and the manufacturing professionals are leading the lean effort, as if they are two separate and distinct programs requiring uniquely different skill sets. This is just pure ignorance.

This is just one of the many paradoxes that will be pointed out in this book. There is a great deal of waste in the multitude of continual improvement processes instituted within an organization. Each of one these processes, whether it is based on ISO 9001, Six Sigma, TQM, lean, balanced scorecard, or a homegrown process, has the same goal: to continually improve processes, products, and systems. Yet, because these processes are all attempting to do the same thing, these processes, when done together, are full of waste themselves as their leaders or champions (that is, management representative, Master Black Belt, value stream manager, sensei) fight for resources and attempt to out-duel each other to show which process is of the most value to the head honchos. Deming claims that infighting between different parts of organizations for resources is one of the most destructive forces in modern organizations. He credits Japan's lack of competition for its phenomenal success.[3]

Deming would most probably roll his eyes and shake his head in disgust as he wondered why people just can't think of the entire system rather than suboptimizing their little kingdoms, whether it is a management representative suboptimizing the quality management system or a Master Black Belt suboptimizing the Six Sigma program. Deming's Point #9 of his 14 Points for Management states: *Break down barriers between staff areas.* He meant break down barriers between functional areas or departments. Today, we have new functional areas like the lean group, the Six Sigma group, or the (ISO 9001–based) quality system group, and these areas now have just as many barriers as typical departments do. We've gone backwards, as more and more specialized departments are born and more and more barriers between functional groups are erected. What a joke!

DEMING AS A SPEAKER

Deming was a teacher to CEOs, middle managers, and educators. His public courses were filled with some of the best and brightest minds throughout the world. Up until the time of his death, he kept a consulting and teaching schedule that would tire a person a quarter of his age. He was known as a curmudgeon (an ill-tempered person full of resentment and stubborn notions) with little tolerance for those who didn't, or wouldn't, understand his concepts.

He oftentimes ignored questions from the audience, especially those questions he did not understand or he felt were ignorant. He once asked an audience member what he did for a living. The person responded that he was the director of IT, to which Deming responded, "So you do nothing." He refused to take on consulting assignments unless the CEO was present because he fully believed that quality starts at the top.

Dr. W. Edwards Deming died in 1993 at the age of 93. I realize that many readers know not who he was or are only vaguely familiar with his name. I would encourage these readers to take a few minutes, go to www.YouTube.com, and type in "Dr. W. Edwards Deming" and listen and watch this *dynamic* speaker at his best. Actually, I jest in referring to Dr. W. Edwards Deming as a *dynamic* speaker; nothing could be further from the truth. However, when Dr. Deming spoke he was inexplicably mesmerizing with what he had to say in his low baritone voice and monotone cadence.

Once hooked by watching the clips from his speeches and interviews of the past, and after reading this book, it might be wise to read either of Dr. Deming's most popular books, *Out of the Crisis* or *The New Economics.*

DEMING'S PAST AND WHAT SHAPED HIS LIFE/PRINCIPLES

When I impersonate Dr. Deming, I take care in ensuring that I do so with a great deal of respect. I also try to give the audience a sense of who he was, how he thought, the diversity of his being, and how he developed into the man he was and cultivated the principles he taught.

To obtain more detail about Dr. Deming's life story, one might be interested in reading his long-time secretary's book entitled, *The World of W. Edwards Deming.* Some of the information and facts given below originate from this book. The information given below is primarily pertinent to the relationship between his upbringing and his teachings.

William Edwards Deming was born in Sioux City, Iowa, on October 14, 1900. William had two younger siblings, Bob and Elizabeth.

In 1907, the family moved to what is now Powell, Wyoming. Their first dwelling was a shelter, rectangular in shape, like a railroad car, covered with tar paper. They pumped water from a well. They had little protection from the harsh weather. The family was oftentimes cold, hungry, and in debt. There was little tolerance for waste of any sort whether it was food scraps, clothing, or shelter. Cash flow within the family organization was very critical to survival.

William always worked from the time he was just a lad through grade school, high school, University of Wyoming (BS in electrical engineering), University of Colorado (MS in physics and mathematics), and Yale University (doctorate in physics and mathematics).

As a lad, he worked at Mrs. Judson's hotel. William would empty the boiler in the morning before school and again in the evening. After school, he would bring in kindling and coal for the next morning, along with other tasks. Mrs. Judson paid William $1.25 per week. He would hold on to the money except for contributions to the family for necessities. Once in a while he would treat his family to Sunday dinner at Mrs. Judson's hotel at a price of 25 cents per meal.

Growing up poor or in difficult times (the Great Depression, postwar Japan) can be a huge motivator in eliminating waste. It is why Deming spoke of waste elimination long before the term "lean" was ever invented.

COMPOSING MUSIC

William's mother played the piano at church and gave music lessons on the Kimball grand piano in their house to supplement the family cash flow. As William's mother provided lessons, William would lie on the floor and scribble with his pencil on a piece of paper and proclaim that he was writing music. After the student left the house, William's mother would place the piece of paper on the piano and play something and declare that William had written great music.

William was proud of his work. His mother made him feel proud of his work. Pride in work is extremely important for continuous improvement of one's life. Deming's 12th Point is to "remove barriers that rob people of their right to pride of workmanship." I'm sure this early life experience had a profound effect on his teachings and his 12th Point.

William went on to play several instruments, compose two masses and several canticles, and write poetry. When one feels proud of their work, one feels compelled to do better, to do more, to excel, to improve. Most of us seem to understand this when it comes to raising our own children, but then we tend to forget about the concept of allowing people to feel proud of their work when it comes to the business world. We should all question why this is.

SUMMER CLOTHING

William and his younger brother Bob, oftentimes during the hot summer months, would enjoy running barefoot on the farm they grew up on. To be sure, their clothes would be dirty and sweaty. Their mother, for simplicity's sake, had contrived one-piece pajama-like jumpsuits for the two boys to wear throughout the summer. Each boy had two jumpsuits. Every morning the boys would put on a clean jumpsuit and their mother would wash the jumpsuit worn the day before.

In this system, there was little to no waste. There was no excess inventory of clothes, because the finances were nonexistent. Today, we would call their laundry process "single-piece flow." Single-piece flow was not a goal of the family organization. It was a necessity. Waste increases rampantly when financial strength grows.

The United States has been a country of wealth and great financial strength for a number of decades. It has also been a country a great waste because of this strength. Single-piece flow (and the associated waste reduction), for the entire system and not just a work cell or department, is foreign, strange, and still not completely *necessary* in the United States because of our still-great financial strength. Our great financial strength, though growing relatively smaller on the global scene with each decade, apparently is still too strong to truly motivate the country and many companies into vast waste reduction.

Waste reduction and elimination will only truly come into fruition when there is a true crisis or a "true" perceived crisis. William grew up in a day-to-day crisis as he fought for survival. Toyota did the same. It's not surprising that constant waste reduction was one of Deming's key principles.

My father-in-law was born during the Great Depression. He still gets on my wife's case for not tearing those large paper towel sections in half when only a small piece is necessary to do the cleanup job. My wife and I might quickly glance at each other and snicker. And yet, he's right, and so was Deming.

Until such time that the United States runs headlong into another major crisis, each subsequent generation will become more wasteful than the previous. The key is to somehow, as a society, fight this propensity to waste when we are doing well as a family, as a community, or as a company.

WORK DURING THE COLLEGE YEARS—DR. SHEWHART AND VARIATION REDUCTION

During four summer months of 1925 and 1926, Deming worked at the Hawthorne Works Plant of the Western Electric Company in Chicago. He made $18.25 per week, cash, of which he saved $10 to $11 per week to attend Yale.

Deming said that what he learned at the Hawthorne plant made an impression on him for the rest of his life. One day, a group of men were talking about the uniformity of a telephone apparatus and about the teachings of a Dr. Walter A. Shewhart. They said that they did not quite understand completely what he was saying, but they knew that it was important.

This began a close relationship between Deming and his mentor Dr. Shewhart, as the two would get together frequently to discuss the need for statistics and the necessity to reduce variation.

Whenever Deming was asked to sum up in a few words the most important lesson of all that he taught, he would state, "reduce variation." This is why Deming would disagree with the main principle supporting a Six Sigma program. Six Sigma is about comparing performance data to specifications. What's the easiest way to achieve 3.4 defects per million opportunities? Open up the specifications. This does not improve quality. This does not improve consistency, reduce waste, reduce variation, reduce cost, or increase customer satisfaction. It only helps to achieve a certain defect level based on arbitrary definitions of opportunities and specifications. It only helps to achieve 3.4 defects per million—so what!

This experience and friendship with Dr. Shewhart had a profound affect on so much of what Deming taught us in his later years and became the basis for his 5th Point—Improve constantly and forever the system of production and service, to improve quality and productivity, and thus constantly decrease costs.

WORK DURING THE COLLEGE YEARS—SELF-IMPROVEMENT

Lose no time; be always employ'd in something useful; cut off all unnecessary actions.

—Benjamin Franklin

A Hawthorne plant associate and good friend of the young Deming, Dr. Hal Fruth, assured Deming that when he finished his degree at Yale, Western Electric would offer him a job, maybe at $5000 per year. He explained to Deming that it was not difficult to find men *worth* $5000 per year, but that was not what they were looking for. Dr. Fruth said, "If we offer you a job, it will be because we think there is a possibility that you may develop into a man worth $50,000 per year, and such men are hard to find." The conversation stayed with Deming for a long time. He learned that a company does not need good people; it needs people that are constantly improving; it needs people with knowledge.

This experience once again had a huge effect on what Deming taught us, specifically his 13th Point—*Institute a rigorous program of education and self-improvement.* Both management and the workforce will have to be educated in new methods, including teamwork and statistical methods. What an organization needs is not just good people; it needs people who are improving with education.

This goes for both work life and home life. This is how Dr. Deming was able to write over 170 papers and two important books while consulting for many major companies. This is how he was able to travel the world. This is how he was able write masses, canticles, and poems while mastering several instruments. He always grew as a person and in his knowledge. He stayed away from wasteful activities like watching TV or reading the newspaper. Cecilia Kilian, his long-time secretary, claimed that she could only recall Dr. Deming watching TV on four occasions.

Deming did not waste time and he constantly sought to improve himself and gain more knowledge. The beneficiary of who he was is society as a whole, as he helped to markedly improve Japanese industry and improve quality of life. He was 80 years old when industry within the United States finally started to listen to him. While most people at the age of 80 have long been retired, he gave 13 more years of his life to society through his two publications and through the teaching of over 10,000 people per year in his four-day seminars.

Because of this and his dedication to improve himself and improve society as a whole, Dr. W. Edwards Deming is a true American hero.

2

Tools versus Principles

*Be flexible in style, and unwavering, like a rock,
in principles.*

—Thomas Jefferson

Oftentimes to pull ourselves out of a crisis, we find band-aids to place over the wounds. In 2008–2009, the U.S. government and other governments around the world attempted to buy their way out of a major recession due to a financial meltdown in the credit markets, which was due to many other factors. Printing money is a short-term fix. It is a band-aid that helped the economy in the short term, but not the long term.

When a company wishes to improve its performance, even in good economic times, most often it will not determine root causes to its problems, but will decide to buy its way out of poor performance by investing in band-aids, the very same band-aids every other company has bought into— names like TQM, quality circles, zero defects, benchmarking, reengineering, balanced scorecards, and more recently Six Sigma, lean, offshoring, Lean Six Sigma, and ISO 9001. These band-aids are also known as tools, or as Thomas Jefferson referred to them, *style.*

Dr. Deming intentionally did not offer the style. He did not offer the tools. He offered us *principles* (definition: a basic or essential quality or element determining intrinsic nature or characteristic behavior) in the form of his 14 Points. Nowhere will one find a step-by-step, cookbook approach to implementing Deming's principles, at least not offered by Dr. Deming himself.

A step-by-step cookbook would be too easy, and *easy* is not how his principles should be deployed throughout an organization. A company must develop its own *style,* its own *tools,* its own *methodologies,* its own *systems,* in order to be able to truly *buy into* the program and improve the program, whatever it may be.

Deming believed that people should think. He would say that there is no such thing as "instant pudding" when it comes to running a business, though many business leaders continue to buy instant pudding whether it's in the form of Six Sigma, lean, or offshoring. He stressed that "there is no substitute for knowledge." One (person or company) should always seek to become more knowledgeable. With knowledge comes power. With knowledge comes a greater ability to think. With increasing ability to think comes the ability to develop a company's own style, tools, methodologies, and systems based on sound principles.

"Leaders" in the United States do not like to take the time to think. They would rather *buy* the styles, tools, methodologies, and systems. They are more concerned with the short term and meeting this month's shipping numbers or this quarter's financial expectations from Wall Street or ownership.

Why would a leader concern herself with developing new systems when it is so easy to buy a Six Sigma program that has already been developed?

Why would a leader take the time to learn on his own about the principles behind lean, when it's so easy to buy a five-day Value Stream Mapping Kaizen Event from any local Manufacturing Extension Program (MEP) or community college?

Why would a leader want to develop their own ISO 9001 quality management system when a consulting company with ties to a registrar is guaranteeing the development of an entire QMS and certification to ISO 9001 in 90 days?

Why would a leader try to eliminate or minimize the waste and costs in their processes when they can simply outsource the manufacturing of a product or service to the likes of China or India? They know that if the decision to outsource a product or service to an overseas country is made based on price tag alone, then everyone will buy into it. Who would be dumb enough to question such a *wise* decision? They'll come out smelling like a rose, record on their resume how much money they saved the company, and be off working at the next company that bought into their BS story of grandiose short-term results well before the problems and increased wastes start hitting the fan at their former company. This is what Ignacio Lopez did, after all, as the purchasing czar of General Motors, where he was credited with saving GM $4 billion from 1992–1993, while causing irreparable harm to the long-term supplier relationships that were key to GM's future competitiveness. These were some of the same relationships that I helped to build while working with Saturn in the late '80s. Was this Lopez's fault? Of course not. It was GM's, because GM did not adhere to the principle of developing and maintaining long-term supplier relationships and basing purchasing decisions on *long-term* costs.

The prevailing theme in most U.S. companies is that developing one's own unique culture, processes, and tools, based on your own principles, *takes too much time.* Leaders of U.S. companies don't have this kind of time. They need to be able to demonstrate big short-term success stories so that they can move on to the next company that has been targeted by their somewhat exclusive headhunter. In their eyes, it's best to simply buy what already exists out there because it is so quick and easy to do and everyone else is doing it. This way, leadership can concentrate on making sure the numbers look good. It's a win/win situation for all involved—in the short term—and that's all that seems to matter in the life of a nomadic leader.

Additionally, American managers can easily claim that they are *committed* to the process, committed to the tools, because they have committed the resources and the money to the tools. No one questions their commitment. They exclaim their commitment in a kickoff meeting so that everyone hears it loud and clear. They discuss how they have hired people and committed dollars to the new tool. And then they sit back and demonstrate no involvement. They think, "Why should we be involved? We do not have to change. We do not need to evaluate or, for that matter, determine our principles. We are good at what we do. This is why we are managers."

As Deming stated many times, quality starts at the top. It's not enough to claim commitment; there must be a very high degree of action and participation at the top. Management must be willing to change its ways and its organization, and must actively participate in constantly improving the processes and systems. It starts with determining the principles.

Deming claimed that a full 94% of all manufacturing problems are due to special cause variation, or, in other words, the system, or, in other words, those things within the system that only management has control over, or, in other words, management, or in other words, a lack of principles and supporting processes. How can management *not* be fully involved if they control the causes to 94% of the problems? If management personnel are not involved beyond the simple acts of committing people and money to a movement, to a continual improvement process, to the principles upon which the company is based, then they might as well save their energy and watch the cash spiral down the toilet bowl.

Dr. Deming did not teach us the tools; he taught us the principles. It is up to an organization's management to understand the intent behind these principles and develop the culture, processes, and tools to support them.

BUT WHAT IS A PRINCIPLE?

Principles are fundamentally accepted rules of action or conduct that are generally inarguable depending on one's purpose or goal, such as raising a family, playing a sport, or building a business.

Dr. Stephen Covey, in his landmark book, *The 7 Habits of Highly Effective People* wrote:

> *Principles are guidelines for human conduct that are proven to have enduring, permanent value. They're fundamental. They're essentially unarguable because they are self-evident. One way to quickly grasp the self-evident nature of principles is to simply consider the absurdity of attempting to live an effective life based on their opposites. I doubt that anyone would seriously consider unfairness, deceit, baseness, uselessness, mediocrity, or degeneration to be a solid foundation for lasting happiness and success.*[4]

I once wrote an article published in *Quality Digest*'s *Quality Insider* magazine entitled, "Society of the Anti-Deming," or SAD, for short. (See Appendix.) In the article, I wrote the opposite of each of his 14 Points and provided examples of how to live as an anti-Demingite, which in reality is the reality of many business practices today. I also presented this paper at a couple of conferences and the audience laughed hysterically at the irony in how we run our businesses versus how Deming suggested we run our businesses just a couple of short decades ago.

Here are the 14 principles as they are presented in Chapter 2 of *Out of the Crisis*. As Dr. Covey suggested, 1) determine in your mind if these principles are unarguable, and 2) think about how the opposite of these principles would affect good business practices.

DEMING'S 14 PRINCIPLES FOR TRANSFORMATION OF WESTERN MANAGEMENT

The following Points, and how U.S. companies stack up against these 14 Points in today's quality and business world, will be detailed in the next chapter.

1. Create constancy of purpose toward improvement of product and service, with the aim to become competitive and stay in business, and to provide jobs.

2. Adopt the new philosophy. We are in a new economic age. Western management must awaken to the challenge, must learn their responsibilities, and take on leadership for change.

3. Cease dependence on inspection to achieve quality. Eliminate the need for inspection on a mass basis by creating quality into the product in the first place.

4. End the practice of awarding business on the basis of price tag. Instead minimize total cost. Move toward a single supplier for any one item, in a long-term relationship of loyalty and trust.

5. Improve constantly and forever the system of production and service, to improve quality and productivity, and thus constantly decrease costs.

6. Institute training on the job.

7. Institute leadership (see point 12.) The aim of leadership should be to help people and machines and gadgets to do a better job. Leadership of management is in need of overhaul, as well as leadership of production workers.

8. Drive out fear so that everyone may work effectively for the company.

9. Break down barriers between departments. People in research, design, sales, and production must work as a team to foresee problems of production and use that may be encountered with the product or service.

10. Eliminate slogans, exhortations, and targets for the work force that ask for zero defects and new levels of productivity.

11. a. Eliminate work standards (quotas) on the factory floor. Substitute leadership.

    b. Eliminate management by objective. Eliminate management by numbers, numerical goals. Substitute leadership.

12. Remove barriers that rob people of pride of workmanship.

13. Institute a vigorous program of education and self-improvement.

14. Put everybody in the company to work to accomplish the transformation. The transformation is everybody's job.

One could also argue that if they were going to copy principles, why not copy the principles of Toyota, which were so well defined in Jeffrey Liker's book, *The Toyota Way*. This may not be a bad idea. However, there will be some principles that Dr. Deming preached to us that will not be covered in *The Toyota Way* principles, and vice versa. This is why a company should determine all of their principles, but make sure that none of Dr. Deming's principles are left out. It's important to understand that Toyota developed many of their principles based on the teachings of Dr. Deming, and that is why there is so much consistency between the two.

Again I ask you, as you read the Toyota principles below: 1) determine in your mind if these principles are unarguable, and 2) think about how the opposite of these principles would affect good business practices.

TOYOTA'S PRINCIPLES (AS DOCUMENTED IN *THE TOYOTA WAY*)

A strong relationship to Deming's Points is identified in parentheses at the end of each principle:

1. Base your management decisions on a long-term philosophy, even at the expense of short-term financial goals (Deming #1 and #2).

2. Create continuous process flow to bring problems to the surface (Deming #5 and #9).

3. Use "pull" systems to avoid overproduction (Deming #11).

4. Level out the workload (Deming #5).

5. Build a culture of stopping to fix problems to get quality right the first time (Deming #3).

6. Standardized tasks are the foundation for continuous improvement and employee empowerment (Deming #6, #12, #14).

7. Use visual control so no problems are hidden (Deming #8 and #10).

8. Use only reliable, thoroughly tested technology that serves your people and your processes (Deming #7).

9. Grow leaders who thoroughly understand the work, live the philosophy, and teach it to others (Deming # 7 and #14).

10. Develop exceptional people and teams who follow your company's philosophy (Deming # 9 and #13).

11. Respect your extended network of partners and suppliers by challenging them and helping them improve (Deming #3 and #4).

12. Go and see for yourself to thoroughly understand the situation (Deming #12).

13. Make decisions slowly by consensus, thoroughly considering all options; implement rapidly (Deming #9 and #14).

14. Become a learning organization through relentless reflection and continuous improvement (Deming #8 and # 13).

Toyota is a Deming-oriented company, as is evidenced in how the Toyota Production System was derived from Deming's 14 Points.

> *Every day I think about what he meant to us. Deming is the core of our management.*
>
> —Dr. Shoichiro Toyoda
> Founder and Chairman
> Toyota Motor Corporation

THE PILLARS UPON WHICH THE 14 PRINCIPLES OF TOYOTA ARE BASED

It is most commonly accepted by many lean experts that the two pillars upon which the Toyota Production System and its principles are based are:

The incessant focus on elimination of waste

The respect for and involvement of all employees

I prefer to call these the root causes to the success of the Toyota Production System, and I believe that there are two other main root causes. They are:

Self-reliance (part of principle #1 in *The Toyota Way*)

The incessant focus on and use of root cause analysis (part of principle #12 in *The Toyota Way*)

Much has been written about the first two root causes, but little has been written about the next two root causes, until now.

SELF-RELIANCE

We strive to decide our own fate. We act with self-reliance, trusting in our own abilities. We accept responsibility for our conduct and for maintaining and improving the skills that enable us to produce added value.

—The Toyota Way

My First Witnessing of Toyota's Self-Reliance

As a young engineer at Saturn, 10 percent of my performance evaluation was based on how well I had benchmarked my processes against other companies. Toyota was supposed to be Saturn's main benchmark and, ideally, if each person's process of responsibility was as good or better than Toyota's same process, we would probably be able to build a pretty darn good vehicle, or so that was the belief of some of the management personnel. My boss was Ken Franklin, a quiet, soft-spoken, yet humorous individual and teacher who had been a GM-er for many years. I always gave him credit, in my mind, for trying to live by the ideals of Saturn when so many other long-time GM-ers went about business as if they were working for traditional GM.

Ken docked me 10 percent on my first-ever performance evaluation because I could not show evidence of doing any benchmarking. Apparently that was one of Ken's requirements on the performance evaluation, and I had probably known about it but had chosen to ignore it for some reason. Saturn was teaching—and I was personally teaching later that year—that benchmarking was an essential step in the Total Development Process we had learned about from Toyota. Immediately after that review, I became the world's greatest benchmarker and crowned myself as such. I developed a questionnaire to obtain information/data that I needed to evaluate and compare the processes for which I was responsible with those of other plants so that I could come up with the best overall process.

I was responsible for designing, procuring, and working with the suppliers of all the fluid fill equipment. This included the equipment that would evacuate and fill the engine coolant system and the air conditioning system, as well as the equipment that would fill the windshield washer fluid, fuel, and power steering fluid. I went to different facilities to learn about their fluid filling operations based on my standard set of questions so that I could once again compare and determine best practices. I ended up designing a hybrid system and layout that had features of the many different sites that I visited. The sites I visited included of course many different GM plants. If

I knew of a person going to a Ford, Chrysler, or Nissan plant, I would give them my questionnaire and have them complete it. I also sent out surveys to many different sites to gain more information.

I had organized a group of about 20 Saturn employees to benchmark and walk through the Honda plant in Marysville, Ohio, which resulted in a basketful of useful information for all who visited, including myself.

Finally, I organized another trip for about six Saturn employees, all of whom reported to Ken Franklin, to visit the GM–Toyota joint venture plant in Fremont, California, called the New United Motor Manufacturing, Inc. (NUMMI) plant.

One of the questions on my fluid fill equipment survey had to do with the company information of the manufacturer of each piece of equipment. When I visited the other sites, I would simply read the nameplate on the equipment and record it on my survey. When we visited the NUMMI plant, I found no nameplates. The equipment did not even look like equipment because of its simplicity of design with its few hanging hoses and a few simple gages mounted onto a basic control panel. I was very *unimpressed* by what I saw when compared with the large, elaborate pieces of equipment, with the many bells and whistles, I had seen in all of the GM plants. These pieces of equipment were built by professional equipment builders, and it showed. The NUMMI equipment looked as if it was built by a garage mechanic. I was truly baffled and did not know what to do with the observations and information I had learned.

Though I took back some great information from the NUMMI tour that helped me design my area of responsibility, it never once hit me that if my area of responsibility was to be as good if not better than Toyota, we should be designing the equipment ourselves. We should be *self-reliant*. I did not appreciate what I had seen until many years later. I had always heard that Toyota's equipment was simple, but I always felt that this was archaic and a weakness of Toyota. It had never hit me that the reason for such simplicity was that by being so, they were self-reliant. They built their equipment themselves, and if there was ever a problem, they could fix it themselves. They did not have to call in the equipment supplier to fix the equipment.

It was not until recently that I realized that, as a company, we should not have been going to Toyota to evaluate and copy Toyota's equipment, or, for that matter, any other company's equipment; we should have been copying its principles, or root causes to success, with one of them being *self-reliance*. If I and so many other engineers would have been taught that we were seeking self-reliance and that it was a Saturn principle, my entire approach would have changed to understanding how to build equipment that will pull a vacuum on an enclosed system (when applicable), check for leaks, and dispense fluid to a known quantity or pressure. I would have, in essence, been performing more engineering work rather than sourcing work. After all, my degree was in engineering.

THE LEAN PARADOX

By trying to become more like Toyota, we are becoming less like Toyota. This is the paradox.

No one taught Toyota about value stream mapping, 5S, kaizen, quick changeover, jidoka, or gemba. These processes all resulted from good root cause analysis (see below), focus on elimination of waste, respect for people, and self-reliance. Toyota developed their own improvement systems because they are self-reliant. They didn't copy or buy someone else's processes. They developed their own processes internally, as a result of root cause analysis, and perfected these processes because they owned them.

As American companies copy the Toyota Way, they are doing exactly what Toyota would *not* do. Toyota allows visitors to its plants and shares information with the visitors because they know, for the most part, Western management will not change and no real improvements will ever be made until Western management changes its ways. The thought process is "go ahead, copy our work cells, copy 5S, copy single-piece flow, copy simplicity in equipment. None of it will be for the better, unless Western management changes its ways." Toyota would not have copied another company's processes. When a company copies another company's *style* or *tools,* it loses the ability to be self-reliant in the use of those processes. It does not vary or adapt the process to its own business. It has no ownership of the process, and many people within an organization resist those processes not internally developed.

THE INCESSANT FOCUS ON AND USE OF ROOT CAUSE ANALYSIS

The following is a made-up, but realistic, story of how 5S (sort, set in order, shine, sandardize, sustain) might have been originally developed by using the principle of getting to the root cause of a problem by using the tool of five whys analysis.

Let's suppose one day a defect on a vehicle was discovered and it was tracked back to a certain area in the assembly process. In the spirit of *gemba,* an often-used lean term that means "go see," an engineer went to the process area to discuss the issue with the operator in the area. Upon learning of the defect, the operator initially said that he just screwed up. However, the engineer and the operator had just finished learning about getting to the root causes of problems and they commited themselves to finding out why the mistake was made from a systemic point of view. They both determine that the operator will repeat the process for some time and the engineer will observe what he does. At one point, the operator nearly repeats the same defect and points this out to the engineer.

The engineer asks why the error was almost made. They begin to use the "five whys" process of root cause analysis. The operator states that he used the wrong tool. The engineer asks him *why* he used the wrong tool. The operator states that he picked up the wrong tool because it is nearly the same as the correct tool and he could not find the correct tool. The engineer asked him *why* he couldn't find the correct tool and the operator said, "Look at this place. Could you find what you needed in this pile of junk?"

So the engineer and operator began *sort*ing out all the stuff that hadn't been used for some time and that just seemed to get in the way of the stuff they did need. They identified what was absolutely needed in the area, outlined spots on the walls and pegboards and the floor, and identified what should be present in the area. They made it very obvious if anything was missing or out of place by *setting in order* anything that needed to be in the area.

After they cleaned up the area, the engineer then asked the operator, "*Why* did the area get so unorganized in the first place?" The operator said that there was nothing in the system to encourage him and the second- and third-shift personnel in the area to keep the place organized. The *system* was finally being blamed, not the operator. As such, this question was not really fair to be asked of the operator. He has no control over the system, so the engineer asked the same question of the plant manager. The plant manager stated that organization and elimination of waste was never important to the company. The engineer and the plant manager decided to build a system of organization to eliminate waste and minimize the possibility of human error. The engineer and operator had already developed the first two steps of *sorting* and *setting in order*. The engineer thought it was important to empower the employees to be responsible for their areas and equipment and how well it was maintained as part of being self-reliant. As such, they developed the third S: *shine*. The plant manager then stated that he wanted this methodology to be the same throughout the facility and so developed the fourth S: *standardize*. Both knew that their new system could fall apart without a system of discipline and accountability and so they developed the fifth S: *sustain*. They had blamed the system and developed a systemic solution, which they now called 5S.

The plant manager and operator were happy with their new system and thought they were done. The engineer, though, was not yet done. He asked the plant manager one last "*Why?*" He asked him, "*Why* was organization and the elimination of waste not an important part of the company?" The plant manager could not answer the question, and he suggested that the engineer talk to the CEO, which he did. The engineer told the entire story of what they had done as a team and then popped the question to the CEO. The CEO answered honestly, "It was not one of our principles because we had never thought of it and we never took the time to determine our principles." By the way, it was also never a stated principle of Saturn, at least in its early days.

From this one exercise, the CEO made the elimination of waste a principle of the company and determined all the other principles that the company's culture, internal processes, and tools would be based on from that point forward.

This story is why Dr. Deming stated that 94% of a company's problems are related to top management and broken or bad systems. One little case of a typical defect on the line, in which one could have easily blamed the operator, ended up being the responsibility of the CEO. And it all could have been figured out with a well-executed root cause analysis.

5S, quick changeover, kaizen, total productive maintenance (TPM), and Training Within Industry (TWI) are only solutions to good root cause analysis. They are Toyota's solutions, not necessarily your solutions. You could probably develop better solutions, better tools, better styles for your problems through the use of good root cause analysis.

In this made-up example, the style is 5S. Thomas Jefferson said, be flexible with it and change it to meet your needs. The principle is root cause analysis. Thomas Jefferson said, be unwavering, like a rock, in principles. Root cause analysis is the principle. Always use it and be unwavering with its use.

Many companies I have consulted for have asked me to present 5S training in an area and then apply it in that area with the participants. I try to redirect them and ask them why the training is needed. What is most important, I tell them, is to identify the problems in the area, pick out the most important problem(s), determine the root cause(s) to that problem, and determine a systemic solution, which might include 5S, a variation of 5S, or just as likely, something altogether different.

Before applying any lean tool, follow the above process. American management tends to apply tools to many problems without identifying the problem and executing good root cause analysis. Applying tools like 5S and TPM are the fun things to do, they are "in," but they do not change management. Applying tools needs to make sense for the given problem, and this is only known after doing root cause analysis.

PRACTICES/TOOLS THAT MAY NOT SUPPORT YOUR PRINCIPLES—SIX SIGMA

It is important to determine a company's principles first, because many of the tools and practices that organizations buy may conflict with their principles.

Many of the *practices* of Six Sigma management are directly in conflict with the principles of both Toyota and Dr. Deming. Examples include:

1. Having specialized Belt People resolve everyone's problems rather than everyone being involved in problem resolution and continuous improvement.

2. Setting goals of a) dollar savings, b) number of trained Black Belts, or c) number of Six Sigma projects completed, rather than focusing on the process. The goal becomes the focus and not the improvement.

3. Focus on projects (continual improvement) versus everyday improvements (continuous improvement).

4. Achievement of 3.4 defects per million, which has little to do with improvement.

5. Training in batches and wasteful training (using only a very small percentage of what is taught).

6. The Belt becoming the goal, not the knowledge.

To further explain how just one Six Sigma practice does not support one of Deming's principles, we will focus in on the fourth example above. One Six Sigma practice is based on reducing defects to a specific target of 3.4 defects per million opportunities. Deming would be very critical of this principle and would boldly state that it is a wrong principle. It is no different than the "zero defects" mantra that Phil Crosby preached. Both of these are flawed in that they compare the process performance to an arbitrary specification, tolerance range, and definition of "opportunity." The most obvious way to reduce defects is to change the specification. A broader specification means fewer defects. This may sound silly but it is exactly what was advocated by the founder of Six Sigma, Bill Smith. Deming's approach to quality was to reduce variation. Smith suggested that changing the specification "influences the quality of product as much as the control of process variation does." Six Sigma's basis in the product specifications is perhaps its most fundamental flaw.[5]

This principle does not support the focus on constant variation reduction—the key to continual improvement, customer satisfaction, and profitability. This principle flies in the face of Deming's 5th point: *Improve constantly and forever the system of production and service, to improve quality and productivity, and thus constantly decrease costs.*

SOME PRINCIPLES MIGHT HAVE NO BACKBONE—ISO 9001

ISO 9001 is said to be based on the following principles:

1. Customer focus

2. Leadership

3. Involvement of people

4. Process approach

5. System approach to management

6. Continual improvement

7. Factual approach to decision making

8. Mutually beneficial supplier relationships

Though all of these principles are sound, and yet vague, the translation of their meaning throughout the ISO 9001 standard varies tremendously. Some of the principles are supported well in the standard (for example, process approach, continual improvement); others are nearly nonexistent throughout the standard (such as, leadership, mutually beneficial supplier relationships). See Chapter 4.

WHAT'S A LEADER TO DO?

The leaders of an organization must:

1. *Determine, develop, and document the company's principles.*
   Start with Deming's principles, as so many Japanese companies

did, including Toyota, and further define them to suit your company's needs. This is the most recommended approach!

Or perhaps start with the four root causes to Toyota's success—the incessant focus on elimination of waste, the respect and involvement of all employees, self-reliance, the incessant focus on and use of root cause analysis—and further define your own specific principles to suit your company's needs.

Or, perhaps start with the eight principles of ISO 9001 and further define your own specific principles to suit your company's needs.

Understand that many of your company's practices may be inherently flawed and do not support the principles that your organization has now determined.

2. *Communicate to all within the organization what the principles are and that all processes, including those of continuous improvement, will be based of these principles.*

3. *Think and think some more!!* Develop, define, and implement a culture that encourages and allows all employees to think.

4. *Develop your company's own processes, style, methodologies, tools, and practices that support the chosen principles.* Learn from others, but don't automatically copy others. These methodologies, tools, and practices should be part of the quality management system, or better yet, your business management system. If you do copy tools from others, modify the tools to suit your company practices and culture (be flexible in style), as long as you continue to truly support the principles.

3

How Do U.S. Companies Rate Today against Deming's 14 Points?

On page 154 of *Out of the Crisis,* Dr. W. Edwards Deming wrote, "It may be obvious to anyone, on reflection on the obstacles that we have seen, that a long, thorny, road lies ahead in American industry—10 to 30 years—before we can settle down to an acknowledged competitive position."

This chapter will evaluate how U.S. corporations are performing when compared to Deming's 14 Points, which were published 28 years ago at the time of this writing.

Point #1: Create constancy of purpose toward improvement of product and service, with the aim to become competitive and stay in business, and to provide jobs.

Dr. Deming, in *Out of the Crisis,* also wrote of the *deadly diseases* that stand in the way of the transformation to the 14 Points. A cure for some of these diseases would require a complete shakeup of the Western style of management.

The first two deadly diseases, as outlined in Chapter 3, further explain the resistors to achieving constancy of purpose:

1. Lack of constancy of purpose to plan product and service that will have a market and keep the company in business, and provide jobs.

2. Emphasis on short-term profits: short-term thinking (just the opposite of constancy of purpose to stay in business), fed by fear of unfriendly takeover, and by the push from bankers and owners for dividends

Creating constancy of purpose is a high-level, almost spiritual goal that is contrary to most Western leaders' concerns of achieving the quarterly numbers, achieving this month's shipments regardless of quality, identifying it as shipped, and showing it on the books as an item in accounts receivable, where it will be counted as an asset at its full value (event though it may be flawed and shipped back next month).

American management, whenever possible, defers to next quarter any orders for material and machinery. They defer research, education, and training as long as possible.

In company after company that I work with, I am never scheduled to provide training of any sort during the last couple of days of the month as the company attempts to ship as many orders as possible. In my 15 years as a consultant/trainer, I have never seen nor heard of any company willing to train during the last couple of days in a given month, especially if it involves manufacturing, servicing, or shipping.

Just as the credit meltdown was beginning in late 2007, one of my clients, a homebuilding company, rushed to complete as many houses as possible and get them closed before the end of the year. Customer complaints skyrocketed, and customer satisfaction plummeted in January.

Wall Street is still king. Operational decisions and investment, for the good of the long-term survival and profitability of the company, are oftentimes put off to the next quarter or next year for fear of a falling stock price and the potential takeover of a publicly held company.

The key to this point is the CEO's answer to the question, "What is the purpose of your business?"

The wrong answer would be, "To make money. To increase shareholder value."

The right answer would be, "To build products (or provide services) that improve the *quality of life* for our customers, that improve society as a whole, and that provide jobs to our communities."

By not following Point #1, our country and some companies have experienced severe crises.

The Mortgage Meltdown. The mortgage meltdown of 2007–2008 basically boils down to lenders making money too easily available to too many consumers. Lending guidelines and lending criteria became way too loose and relaxed for the better part of the previous decade, housing values continued to rise extremely quickly because of the easy money and the low interest rates, and too many consumers bought way more home than they could truly comfortably afford because lenders would approve them for that much. Combine all of the above factors at the same time and doom was bound and determined to find its way into the real estate economy. This is how we ended up in this mortgage meltdown.

Even though homeownership had reached all-time high levels, the number of foreclosures reached all-time high levels as well. Homes were being foreclosed on at a record pace. RealtyTrac Inc. states that there was a 93% increase in foreclosure filings from July of 2006 to July of 2007. So why did so many people default on their home loans in 2009? Many areas around the nation were experiencing stagnant or depreciating housing values at this time. With lending guidelines becoming much tighter, it was making it harder for everyone to be able to buy a home. This added to the problems of sellers already having a difficult time selling their homes. There were already not enough buyers for as many houses as there were for sale, and with fewer borrowers being approved for mortgages, this created a serious buyers' market. In a buyers' market, many sellers end up dropping home prices even lower or putting extra money into their homes that they may not have otherwise. In 2007, there were over 2 trillion dollars worth of ARM (adjustable rate mortgage) loans that expired and experienced rate increases. This created a lot of problems for the consumers who were not able to refinance because their credit got worse since they took on their ARM loan, their home values decreased, and/or because of tightened mortgage lending guidelines. Again, add all these factors together, along with the fact that they probably bought too much home for their finances, and it spelled doom to these homeowners and to the economy as a whole.

Because of this mortgage mess, or mortgage meltdown, the stock market was very inconsistent, the economy went through rough times, and the housing market really took a turn for the worse. When the number of foreclosures increased, it cost the taxpayers extra money, caused depreciation of surrounding homes, devalued communities as a whole, caused banks to tighten lending guidelines so that money was not as easily available, and caused possible financial disaster to investors. Therefore, the mortgage meltdown had a significant affect on society as a whole, not just the lenders who are losing money directly, but on consumers, cities, states, and the country's economy as a whole.[6]

Lending companies had previously made out like bandits as long as housing prices kept rising and interest rates remained low. The combination of these two factors, *the focus on short-term gains* and *abundant profits,* along with the establishment of loose lending criteria and the need of the American homeowner to continually desire more home than their friends have, led to this disaster.

Enron Collapse. In December 2001, the Enron energy trading company declared Chapter 11 in the biggest bankruptcy filing in U.S. history. Enron was the seventh largest corporation in the U.S. at the time.[7]

The collapse had many causes. Enron made failed investments in fiber-optic networks, a power plant in India, and water distribution in the U.K.

Top executives in the company behaved unethically as they enriched themselves and formed partnerships designed to hide $500 million in losses. These are serious problems, but corporations have survived worse, and Enron could have been fixed with new management committed to reform. The fatal blow was the collapse in the price of energy and the sudden end of the California energy crisis, which drained cash and ruined Enron's credit. Enron was mainly a trading company, a business that depended on good credit and customer confidence.

There were other causes that allowed for the unethical behavior to occur, including allowing Arthur Andersen to provide both consulting and auditing services, a practice that we in the quality world have also experienced and witnessed when a company hires another company to provide both consulting services and auditing services when attempting to become ISO 9001 certified.

Enron and Arthur Andersen executives were only concerned with the short term, and greed overtook their senses and any sort of respectful constancy of purpose. They did not care about the long-term viability of the companies, improving the quality of life for their customers, improving society, and providing continued jobs to their employees as well as maintaining their retirement dollars. They cared only about how Wall Street viewed their financial situation in the short term and lining their own pockets with their employees' savings.

The End of the U.S. Automakers. The news from Detroit just gets grimmer. Chrysler files for bankruptcy. GM files for bankruptcy. The government begins to produce cars as it basically buys two car companies with bailout money. With gas prices soaring, sales of fuel-guzzling SUVs, Hummers, and trucks are plummeting. The Big Three that once ruled the industry—General Motors, Ford and Chrysler—are cutting costs, shuttering plants, and laying off workers.[8]

Detroit's troubles can be attributed to several factors. One is the new energy environment: the surge in gas prices seems to have taken the U.S. automakers by complete surprise. And one wonders, how could they not see it coming, with global demand for oil skyrocketing and peak oil, the year in which the most oil will ever be produced, occurring in 2005, as proclaimed by several respected commentators. From 2005 on, the world will be producing less and less oil each year, and global demand will be increasing each year.[9] Short-term thinking obviously prevailed and led to the demise of the U.S. automotive industry. The U.S. automotive executives had private counsel with Dr. Deming and yet years later they were sunk because they ignored Deming's first point.

Another factor was a cultural resistance to change: unlike their more nimble Japanese rivals, managers at the American auto giants have traditionally required a strong business and financial case even to consider new vehicle development. (Stronger fuel-efficiency mandates might have made such a case, but U.S. automakers also lobbied loudly, and successfully, against them.)

Finally, the U.S. giants were hobbled by a focus on the short term: while Toyota began in the 1990s to develop a car for the 21st century (it eventually became the Prius), companies like GM were happily building highly profitable trucks and monster-size SUVs and ignoring the smaller-car market. As a result, foreign carmakers were able to infiltrate the market. Today, 40% of cars "made in America" are assembled by foreign companies. It was tough for the Big Three to quit the habit. Selling SUVs in the '80s and '90s, says George Maglione, an analyst at Global Insight who covers the North American car market, "was a license to print money—a gravy train, and they rode it."

Dr. Deming even warned U.S. automakers of the first two deadly sins:

1. Lack of constancy of purpose to plan product and service that will have a market and keep the company in business, and provide jobs.

2. Emphasis on short-term profits: short-term thinking

Yet his messages and warnings were largely ignored soon after his death.

It brings back memories of waiting in long lines at the gas pump in the back of our station wagon as my family tried to venture out on a family vacation in the '70s. This was the first time that Americans really started to buy Japanese vehicles en masse as consumers clamored for more fuel-efficient, smaller cars.

It also brings back memories of my first real job with the Saturn Corporation as GM tried to make one last stand to build a profitable small vehicle before giving up the market altogether.

History repeats itself in a culture that does not learn from its past mistakes.

History repeats itself when the only purpose of a company is short-term profits.

History repeats itself in a company that does not invest in the future.

What About Providing Jobs? The last point to the "right answer" above regarding providing jobs to the community should be a purpose for the existence of the company. It's about not thinking selfishly, just for your own sake, and for your own wallet. It is thinking about your children's and grandchildren's future. Are their futures being outsourced as record numbers of outsourced products and services leave the United States, many times needlessly and at an overall higher *total cost?*

As stated in Chapter 2, another style or tool that is in vogue is the rampant outsourcing of products and services to China and India. Many organizations feel that they must do this in order to compete. When a simple comparison is made of the prices of a product made internally within an organization—domestically versus internationally—it is easy to see that there is an apparent huge cost differential and it is best and easiest to outsource internationally. The problem lies in the fact that oftentimes only piece part cost is computed, rather than total cost. This topic will be discussed more in Point #4.

The big problem lies in the fact that U.S. leadership is sacrificing its manufacturing capabilities and security for short-term profits. The purpose of many U.S. companies' existence in today's world does not even seem to be concerned with the importance of providing jobs within the community or country in which it exists. What will happen in a generation or two when manufacturing jobs have nearly completely left the country? What will happen to our security when a military arsenal is difficult to manufacture within this country?

Outsourcing internationally runs counter to one of Toyota's root causes to success: self-reliance!

> *Remote from all other aid, we are obliged to invent and to execute; to find means within ourselves, and not to lean on others.*

—Thomas Jefferson

I provide the following grade to American CEOs for their overall adherence to Point #1 of Dr. Deming's Principles:

F

Point #2: Adopt the new philosophy. We are in a new economic age. Western management must awaken to the challenge, must learn their responsibilities, and take on leadership for change.

Americans are still too tolerant of poor workmanship and sullen service.

Businesses seldom learn of their customers' dissatisfaction. Customers still do not complain. They merely switch suppliers.

Dr. Deming said, "Point #2 really means in my mind a transformation of management. Structures have been in place in management that will have to be dismantled."[10]

There are two main parts to Deming's 2nd Point:

1. Americans need to stop accepting low quality levels.

2. American management must change its ways and organizational structures.

I Was Nearly Fired for Trying to Improve Quality!

Top management should publish a resolution that no one will lose his job for contribution to quality and productivity.

—Dr. W. Edwards Deming
Out of the Crisis

To illustrate the first part, I tell this story. The COO of a long-time client of mine wanted to fire me one day. He was very upset with me because I was spending too much of his employees' time trying to resolve a big issue when he thought the issue had already been resolved.

The customer service manager had asked me to assist him in completing a corrective action form. He had received one because he had entered an order in the sales order system and forgot to include an option that the customer wanted on five products. To appease the customer immediately, the optional items were air-mailed to the customer with instructions on how to install the optional items.

The customer service manager wanted assistance in getting to the root cause as was required on the corrective action form. So we began to talk about the process and he demonstrated to me the process he used to enter the order. At one point, he got a little frustrated and said, "Mike, I just screwed up. Why do we even have to do this?"

This was the first indication of the company's culture of accepting low quality levels.

I convinced him to continue on with the root cause analysis. We did, and we eventually concluded that the root cause of the problem had to do with a very confusing part numbering system. This inadequate part numbering system was not only the root cause of this customer complaint but was also the root cause of many other customer complaints.

So, we set up an hour-long meeting with about six other stakeholders, copied two senior staff members, defined the customer complaint, explained the analysis used to get to the root causes, and then asked for possible solutions. As a team, we defined the criteria for choosing solutions. Their assignment was to bring back up to four different possible solutions to the inadequate part numbering system, which we would compare and evaluate systematically against each criterion. The next meeting would be scheduled in two weeks.

One of the team members attending the meeting typed up meeting minutes and sent them to each team member. He also sent a copy to the COO. The COO read the minutes and walked into a VP's office, fuming with anger. He wanted to fire me. He believed that I was taking up way too much time on a problem that was already resolved when the optional parts were air-mailed to the customer. He believed that the customer was happy with the company's immediate response and that it only cost the company the cost of the premium freight.

The COO had no concept of how the identified root cause was causing his company so many other problems and costing so much money.

The COO was absolutely perfectly content with accepting a certain level of poor quality.

Why Are Complaint Rates Dropping? Recent surveys reveal a decline in complaint rates. One would initially think that this is a good thing. Could it be that customers complain less because we are resolving more and more problems very well? Yeah, right!

In reality, customers complain less because of a phenomenon known as "learned helplessness." There is growing cynicism that complaining does not do any good. Customers state:

"It won't do any good."

"It's not worth the trouble."

"I don't know where to complain."

"I am afraid of retribution."

We have come to accept poor quality more than ever before. Or we just move on to a new supplier, a new restaurant, a new attorney, a new phone, a new computer, and in some cases, a new spouse, without working with the supplier to resolve the problem together.

And yet, companies continually talk about their commitment to customer satisfaction. But when it comes to correcting customer complaints and getting to the root causes of the problems that resulted in a customer complaining, we treat our customers like idiots.

Mistreatment of a complaining customer and incompetence of customer service personnel in understanding root cause analysis results in five times more damage to loyalty than monetary concerns. Does this not just beg of opportunity? Is opportunity not just knocking, but pounding?

A customer who complains and is satisfied with the corrective action is:

- 30% more loyal than one who did not complain

- 50% more loyal than one who complained and is dissatisfied with the corrective action

The first statistic begs for us to actually go out and solicit complaints proactively.

Most companies set an objective to reduce customer complaints. "Well, hell, that's easy to do," customer service personnel think to themselves. "I just won't report that many complaints received from customers this year. I'll just fix them, and no one has to know that there were that many problems at all. We'll attain our department goals and I'll get a good review."

I have encouraged many clients to establish an objective of increasing the number of customer complaints so that there is an incentive to report all complaints. Very few clients have taken me up on this suggestion. Ignorance truly is bliss!

The second statistic above, regarding the customer who complains and is satisfied with the resolution being 50% more loyal than one who complained and is dissatisfied with the resolution, is a direct reflection of good root cause analysis and providing immediate, permanent, and preventive corrective actions, as will be discussed in Chapter 6.

But Is American Management Changing Its Ways and Organizational Structures? No! There have been no such changes.

Oh sure, they've introduced new programs along the way, including TQM, focused factories, benchmarking, reengineering, ISO 9001, and more recently Six Sigma and lean. But for the most part, there have not been any real changes with regard to management's methodologies and organizational structure.

Process Orientation. Dr. Deming encouraged process orientation. ISO 9001 and lean encourage process orientation as well. Many companies state that they are process oriented. They may even have process owners or value stream managers. Yet very few companies actually are process oriented. This is due to the structure of the company not changing. Most companies are set up as collections of functional departments, each with their own objectives and goals. As long as each department meets

its own objectives and goals, even if it hurts another department meeting its objectives and goals, it's believed to be perfectly acceptable, and the process suffers.

As long as a company's main organizational structure is one that is based only on departmental functions, it will:

- Not be process oriented

- Have gobs of waste

- Encourage internal competition

- Focus on attaining departmental objectives, not the process

- Encourage individual performance appraisals

- Have a difficult, if not impossible, time performing effective root cause analysis

Years ago, as an employee of Seaquist Valve (now known as Seaquist Perfect Dispensing) in Cary, Illinois, I experienced a major organizational change to focused factories and process orientation. It consisted of many positive changes, including the division of the plant into three main product families and the cohabitation of all support personnel (quality engineering, quality technicians, manufacturing engineering, design engineering, production team leaders, and supervisor) for those three families. I was the senior quality engineer. I reported to the quality director but also had a dotted-line reporting relationship to the production supervisor of one of the product families. This is not unlike the principles of lean. It was a major organizational change to become more process oriented, and it worked very well.

Too many companies speak of process orientation and do nothing with the organizational structure to actually encourage it.

Leader Standard Work. In company after company, in my 15 years as an independent quality and lean consultant, the same issue of a lack of accountability and discipline creeps into the conversation. This is obviously a reflection of top management not doing *its* job. If a child does not do his or her chores and yet still gets to go to a party, play with friends, or borrow the car, is this the parents' fault or the child's fault? It's the parents' fault for not following through just as it's top management's fault for not following through.

In lean endeavors, some companies—not nearly enough though— attempt to create a lean culture to help support their (real or fake) lean success stories. One aspect of creating a lean environment is to create *standard work*. This is pretty much an accepted practice for those who do repeatable work, such as an operator or a customer service representative. In David Mann's excellent book entitled *Creating a Lean Culture,* the concept of developing *leader standard work* is introduced. Though 95 to 100% of an operator's day is made up of standard work, perhaps only 75% of a team leader's day is occupied by standard work, 50% of a supervisor's day is occupied by standard work, and maybe only 25% of a value stream manager's or process owner's day is occupied by standard work. But they *all* have standard work! Leader standard work may consist of following up on actions, ensuring that resources are available to complete actions, watching the process and identifying waste, ensuring that production tracking boards and other monitoring boards are being kept up to date, ensuring that standard work and kanban quantities are being adhered to, training staff, and improving the process.

This helps to create the lean or continuous improvement effort. This is an example of a positive change to the organizational structure that promotes accountability and discipline. Developing a culture based on Deming's principles to encourage this transformation is too often not addressed in American companies, and the focus continues to be placed on the tools of 5S, total productive maintenance, quick changeovers, value stream mapping, and Six Sigma.

Annual Performance Reviews. There's still no change here. They are still done, as much today as they were when Dr. Deming was alive. This is one management practice that Deming strongly encouraged companies to eliminate, yet 100 percent of the many companies I work with still do annual performance reviews.

Shipping Everything Out at the End of the Month. Perhaps the biggest telltale sign that management has not changed in virtually every company I have worked with is the focus on shipping as much product out as possible just before the end of the month or year.

As a trainer, I experience this frequently as company after company avoids scheduling any training, to be provided by me, during the last week of the month.

Am I the only one who sees this as completely idiotic? Do we not see that by shipping as much as possible during the last week of the month, we are only hurting the numbers for the next month? And since we hurt the numbers for that month, it's only fair to borrow from the next month and ship out as much as possible during the last week of the month once again. It's a vicious, endless cycle.

And meanwhile, in the rush to ship out as much as possible in a couple of days, quality suffers.

The homebuilder discussed earlier, who rushed to close out as many homes as possible before the end of the year before the mortgage meltdown, experienced huge levels of dissatisfaction in January. I'm sure a damaged reputation only added to their sales woes once the meltdown began.

Does anyone not see that the entire cycle of rushing to ship product before the end of the year could be easily stopped in just one month? Take a hit the first month—don't worry about setting another record month—bite the bullet, and stop the silliness and creating the environment for low quality. It just takes one month to start it.

I provide the following grade to American CEOs for their overall adherence to Point #2 of Dr. Deming's principles:

F

Point #3: Cease dependence on inspection to achieve quality. Eliminate the need for inspection on a mass basis by building quality into the product in the first place.

I have seen no change here whatsoever.

In my early consulting days, I would teach organizations about value engineering/value analysis. I would oftentimes refer to a book entitled *Understanding and Applying Value-Added Assessment,* written by William Trischler (ASQC Quality Press, 1996). I liked the book because it provided a dictionary of non-value-added verbs, along with the rationale as to why the actions did not add value, synonyms, and other related actions.

Two of the words in the NVA (non-value-added) dictionary are "inspects" and "tests." The rationale given as to why the word "inspects" does not add value is stated as, *"Inspection is typically performed to identify and eliminate defective work. Even if the inspection is done at the customer's request or is required by a regulatory agency to document proof of compliance, it does not add value to the product or service."*

I still reference this book when I now teach about waste and lean. I challenge those in the audience about the words *inspect* and *test,* and most people say that they agree that the words are non-value-added. I then challenge them to reduce the amount of testing they do on their products. With several clients who might produce large valves or motors or control boards, 100 percent test is the norm. When challenged to improve their operations to perhaps get to the point of testing fewer products and perhaps employing control charts, several people laugh or scoff at the idea, and some will state that the president or CEO would never consider the idea.

Again, it's the acceptance of low quality as the norm, the acceptance of not continuously improving processes to get rid of wasteful operations, and the acceptance that quality will be "inspected in" no matter what the cost to the company.

Of course, the acceptance of low quality does not only pertain to the manufacturing environment. I've seen countless companies make order entry errors. Their solution is to have a checker of the person who entered the order. When this does not work, they add a checker's checker. Entropy, the law of disorder, sets in as the process gets more and more complicated and quality levels stagnate or get worse.

"Inspection with the aim of finding the bad ones and throwing them out is too late, ineffective, and costly," says Dr. Deming. "In the first place, you can't find the bad ones, not all of them. Second, it costs too much." The result of such inspection is scrap, downgrading, and rework, which are expensive, ineffective, and do not improve the process. "Quality comes not from inspection but from improvement of the process."[11]

In fact, it seems that there is less and less use of control charts since Six Sigma's popularity spiked. That's going backwards.

I provide the following grade to American CEOs for their overall adherence to Point #3 of Dr. Deming's principles:

F

Point #4: End the practice of awarding business on the basis of price tag. Instead minimize total cost. Move toward a single supplier for any one item, on a long-term relationship of loyalty and trust.

> *Outsourcing is not an aspect of lean manufacturing. It is quitting.*
>
> —William H. Waddell and Norm Bodek,
> *Rebirth of American Industry*

When I worked at Saturn, the focus was just this: we were going to select the best suppliers based on defined criteria, regardless of any previous affiliations. Dr. Deming had surely had an effect on Saturn's top management, including Jay Wetzel and Bill Hoglund, the then-president of Saturn, in this department anyway. All components were to be sourced based on the best supplier from an all-around standpoint, including *total* cost—not just piece part cost: cooperation, location of the facility, R&D efforts, capacity, and innovation.

I remember very well the uproar within General Motors when Saturn selected a Japanese manufacturer to supply the air conditioning compressor rather than its own vertically integrated GM sister company with UAW employees.

In my own little corner of the world, I was a manufacturing engineer in charge of designing, procuring, and optimizing all of the equipment that will fill fluids in the vehicle (freon, engine coolant, transmission fluid, power steering fluid, gasoline, windshield wash fluid, and so on). Our focus was to pick one fluid fill equipment supplier—the best supplier—based on many factors, only one of which was cost. This is exactly what we did, and a relationship was truly built based on loyalty and trust.

Unfortunately, most American top managers misheard Dr. Deming. Instead of hearing "loyalty and trust," they thought Dr. Deming said that the relationships should be based on "royalties and cost."

This is what Ignacio Lopez believed during his residency as GM's purchasing czar between 1992 and 1993. Any supplier relationships built before then, some as a result of Dr. Deming's influence, came to a screeching halt as Lopez enacted polices that gained him a reputation of aggressive cost-cutting and an antagonistic attitude toward suppliers. Depending on one's point of view, Lopez was either a hero or a devil. He was a hero to top management, shareholders, and Wall Street, because he saved $4 billion dollars, and all they cared about was the short term, which suited Lopez's tenure perfectly as he left GM tumultuously after just one year of destruction. To the suppliers and to the eventual customers, Lopez was the devil. Long-term partnerships and relationships, which had taken years to develop and were still developing, were thrown out the window as Lopez mandated that every part was subject to being resourced to the lowest bidder, regardless of quality.

Relationships suffered tremendously, and quality levels dropped drastically. It takes years to build a community and a neighborhood, but a tornado can destroy all of that in seconds. Lopez was the tornado; he came, he destroyed, and he left, eventually hurting GM's reputation even more in the marketplace.

Millions of U.S. Jobs Outsourced to China. The rise in the U.S. trade deficit with China between 1997 and 2006 has displaced production that could have supported 2,166,000 U.S. jobs. Most of these jobs (1.8

million) have been lost since China entered the World Trade Organization in 2001, an act that was supposed to reverse this trend. Between 1997 and 2001, growing trade deficits displaced an average of 101,000 jobs per year, or slightly more than the total employment in Manchester, New Hampshire. Since China entered the WTO in 2001, job losses increased to an average of 353,000 per year—more than the total employment in greater Akron, Ohio. Between 2001 and 2006, jobs were displaced in every state and the District of Columbia. Nearly three-quarters of the jobs displaced were in manufacturing industries. Simply put, the promised benefits of trade liberalization with China have been unfulfilled.[12]

American manufacturing, and the jobs that go along with it, has been going overseas to China, India, Vietnam, and so on, in record numbers. The temptation has been too great for top management of American companies to resist. When such massive disparities exist between Chinese-made products and the same products made either domestically or internally within the company, top management directs its buyers to go ahead, full steam ahead, don't look back, don't consider total cost, just do whatever it takes to buy from China as quickly as possible. They feel that the cost is so cheap that it doesn't really matter if the Chinese manufacturer does ship 20% defectives. The defectives can be thrown away and it will still be much more cost-effective to buy from them. What they do not realize is that the variation that exists within the 80% of "good" parts is extreme and causes many, many headaches, heartaches, backaches, and gut aches within the American manufacturing facility and for the manufacturers' customers. The variation within the good parts is high and costly. American managers do not see this as a cost because they think that quality is "being within specifications," not about reduction in variation.

Time after time, company after company, when I talk to the production and quality employees, it's the same story. They all complain about the junk that they get from China and what they have to do to make it work, to rework it, or to find a way to use the product in some other capacity (that is, regrading, selling it at a lower cost, passing it off to a less discriminating customer). In most cases, they have no leverage against the supplier because they need the product now for an order and can not wait for another container to be shipped. The internal costs are enormous as the waste in the system mounts and the quality decreases.

Decisions were made based on piece part cost alone. Many companies are paying for their product before it leaves China's shore—six to eight weeks before its arrival at the plant. This allows for no leverage when the product is deemed to be unacceptable. So many sourcing decisions are made based on price tag alone. They should also be made based on other factors such as the cost of:

- Money, especially when paying for product before it leaves China

- Lower cash flow

- Not investing in the future because of less cash flow

- Lead times

- Delays

- Rework

- Repairs

- Recalls

- Warranty work

- All transportation, especially with the recent escalation in oil prices

- Tolerating defective products

- Scrap

- Travel expenses for senior executives to find sources and establish relationships with potential suppliers and government officials

- Travel expenses for employees to visit China for troubleshooting

- Not having those employees at the home office working on improvements

- Not being able to build a relationship based on loyalty and trust

- A different culture, language, and values

- Product not outsourced after overhead costs are reallocated to them, after outsourcing of other products

- Additional safety stock to ensure uninterrupted supply of product

- Expedited shipments

- Additional QC labor

- Lost sales due to out-of-stock conditions

- Obsolete goods or scrapped stock due to carrying higher levels of inventory

- Vendor becoming a competitor[13]

All of these expenses are real, and some can be extremely costly.

Lean Offshoring—An Oxymoron. What I find most interesting is America's supposed focus on and obsession with both lean and offshoring, when offshoring is so anti-lean and flies in the face of Toyota's focus on being self-reliant. And yet, American companies are trying to emulate Toyota? Come on!

Offshoring has led to *defects* that have to be used, *overproduction, waiting* for parts, *not using employee's minds* on how to get rid of waste at home so that outsourcing is not necessary, excessive *transportation,* large amounts of *inventory,* and *excess processing.* This paragraph lists seven of the 8 wastes in italics. Outsourcing is not lean! It is quitting!

And yet American companies continue to outsource and offshore, oftentimes when it is not financially justified to do so, but the decision makers are ignorant to this fact. Why? Many reasons!

Some feel the peer pressure to do so, whether it's the neighbor who is offshoring, the customer, or the competition. If everyone's doing it, it must be OK and it has been proven to be OK by all the other companies doing it.

Many decision makers do not have a financial decision-making model that allows the organization to consider all costs—they only consider the price tag, which oftentimes looks like a 50 percent price reduction. "How can one go wrong with that?" they think. "Hell, we can even accept a whole bunch of bad ones at that price," they think, not realizing that the company is accepting a huge amount of variation that tremendously increases costs.

Many decision makers are short-term focused and realize that they can save the company a ton of (short-term) money, look like a hero, claim thousands of dollars in savings on their resumés, and move on to the next job.

Many decision makers have no appreciation for all of the "invisible costs" that Dr. Deming taught us about associated with accepting waste and inferior product. Those invisible costs are unknown, but are huge.

And finally, many decision makers have no appreciation for the cost of variation and the associated lack of quality, and how it can go beyond negating any perceived cost savings based on price tag alone.

Vendor Becoming a Competitor. Mark Graban, creator of the LeanBlog, interviewed Norm Bodek for a podcast (http://kanban.blogspot.com/2006/07/leanblog-podcast-1-norman-bodek.html).

Norm later wrote:

> *China does represent a short-term labor savings, but in the long term we are giving away our companies to them. This week I was watching parts of the Tour de France bicycle race on television and saw one of the leaders on a Giant bike.*
>
> *At one time over fifteen years ago, Schwinn was probably America's leading bicycle company. They went to Taiwan to*

manufacture their bikes to take advantage of the low labor cost. The company in Taiwan was Giant. Initially, Schwinn wanted to reduce their assembly costs, but Giant convinced them to also save money on engineering and every other phase of manufacturing and design. After 10 years or so when the initial contract was over, Giant told Schwinn, "We don't need you anymore. We know how to make great bikes, you taught us how. All we have to do is learn how to market the bikes." Shortly thereafter, Schwinn went bankrupt and sold their "name" to another American company.

Unfortunately, we are great in short-term thinking.

The Biggest Cost. Perhaps giving away our manufacturing capability and our technology is the biggest long-term cost. By outsourcing at the current rate, we are giving up our children's standard of living, our country's security, and our dominance and influence in the global marketplace. This is a huge cost!!

And as we do so, and as we focus on short-term profits, and as we struggle with the nearly impossible task of developing relationships with Chinese suppliers based on loyalty and trust (because of the distance, different cultures, values, and beliefs), we will continue to receive lead-tainted Thomas the Tank Engine toys, adulterated toothpaste, melamine in pet food, and fish riddled with antibiotics.

I provide the following grade to American CEOs for their overall adherence to Point #4 of Dr. Deming's principles:

F

Point #5: Improve constantly and forever the system of production and service, to improve quality and productivity, and thus constantly decrease costs.

American companies would definitely state that they have made real progress in this particular area and might be disappointed if I was to state that we are also missing the boat on this point. With all of the most recent efforts and huge dollar commitments to ISO 9001, Six Sigma, and lean, it would seem that American companies have tried to "improve constantly and forever the system of production and service, to improve quality and productivity." These efforts, however, are misguided in the following ways:

1. Quality is still not being designed in.

2. Quality is still perceived as a Quality Department thing.

3. Americans still love the firefighter, the hero, the problem solver. We need much more focus on the problem *preventer.* When was the last time you read "good problem preventer" in a job description?

4. Americans still focus on meeting specifications as the main quality goal rather than reducing variation.

5. American companies are still departmentally focused.

6. American companies have multiple continuous improvement systems that are wasteful.

Quality Is Not Being Designed In. A company I was helping recently had a major recall and numerous complaints from customers regarding one of its new products. Previous to this, I was trying to convince the client that their quality planning process was very weak and that it could definitely be improved by implementing some of the recommendations I was making. The director of engineering had thought it was unnecessary to make any changes to their process, even though they had many instances of other product recalls.

Time after time, company after company, the process of quality planning, predicting problems, testing and experimenting to ensure a robust design, and reducing variation is weak or, in some cases, not understood at all.

A president of a hydraulic valve company proudly told me that design engineers are not allowed on the production floor. He then proudly tells me how many designs they kick out each week. His focus for the design engineers is all about the quantity, the production of designs and has nothing to do with the quality of the designs. The design engineers could design crappy products and they would have no accountability to the production environment. There is no feedback system. This company is only process-focused on the production floor—not in the office-to-production-floor processes. The design engineers do not have to worry about the effects of their poor designs or the difficulty in building certain products because they will never hear about these problems, and besides, by then they will have designed several more products, perhaps the same way.

I find it rare that production floor employees or manufacturing engineers are involved in the product design. Quality planning tools such as failure mode and effects analysis (FMEA), the sole purpose of which is to predict failures, evaluate them, prioritize them, and take actions, are rarely performed as a cross-functional team effort, even though it's required. They are usually completed by a single employee in a vacuum.

Designs and design reviews should be conducted by teams of people representing departments or processes affected by the design. This, however, would take time up front, and would take away from engineers designing larger quantities of products. If design engineers are evaluated on the number of designs they produce, which is a frequent occurrence, it's easier to not involve manufacturing and other departments in the design process.

Quality Is Still Perceived As a Quality Department Thing. ISO 9001 uses words such as *quality management system, quality policy, quality objectives, quality manual,* and *quality planning.* Of course, in most companies, employees interpret this word "quality" to be the Department of Quality rather than the adjective describing a management system.

I have convinced several companies to not use the word quality in describing their system. Instead of a *quality management system,* they have a *business management system.* Instead of quality objectives, they have business objectives, and so on.

It's the same thing with other continual improvement processes. Brand-new departments have sprung up along with new positions—the Six Sigma Group, the Lean Department.

A lean event does not happen unless the Lean Department does it. In many companies I've seen, they schedule once-a-month Kaizen Events headed up by the Lean Champion, Guru, Sensei, Leader, or whatever the latest cool title is. Six Sigma projects do not take place without Black Belts. Improvement efforts made by any individual in which the effort is not called a Six Sigma Project do not "count." It's no different than Quality owning the quality management system.

In my stand-up comedy routine, I state that one of my clients is doing so well with their lean initiative, they just doubled their Lean Department.

I taught a seminar at an electronics manufacturing services company recently on how to make the company's quality management system more effective and lean; it was only attended by quality department personnel.

I taught three classes of root cause analysis to 20 people each. I noticed that all of the attendees were from manufacturing. It was obvious that the company believed that since manufacturing personnel created all of the defective products, they should be taking the class and learning how to get to the root causes of problems. I convinced some people that the root causes of the vast majority of manufacturing problems originate with management and other departments (for example, engineering, sales). Two more classes were held with people from the other departments and a couple of top managers.

Americans Still Love the Firefighter, the Hero, the Problem Solver.
I have read many job descriptions and want ads for certain jobs. I have seen the request that the job applicant be an excellent problem solver, many times. I have never seen the request for an excellent problem preventer.

We literally honor our firefighters, our fallen soldiers, and rightly so, for they perform a necessary and vital function for our country. But do we honor enough the ability of leaders and other people to prevent fires, to prevent terrorism, to prevent wars? We do not.

Problem solvers within companies are oftentimes hailed as heroes. The more problems there are, the more job security they have, which is really probably the least of their concerns. The efforts of these problem solvers are very much noticed, and praises are sung their way from the top management voices at the highest levels in company-wide meetings. The problem preventer is never recognized at company-wide meetings.

Deming tells the story of attendance at an awards ceremony. The highest award went to a man who had discovered that the labels were not on the bottles of vaccine that were ready to be shipped. Identification was still possible. A few minutes later, that would not have been the case. The man saved the company $250,000. The second award went to a man who discovered contamination in a shipment before it went out. The shipment was of course condemned.[14]

If I was to be recognized or rewarded for catching a major problem just before it was shipped, I might be tempted to let a problem occur or progress and then plan on catching it later. Would you? The lesson learned is that people are rewarded more for catching bad stuff just before it leaves the facility.

Six Sigma is in itself not a continuous improvement approach; it is a problem solving approach. It does not challenge and change the system; it is a methodology for fixing problems. It is not necessarily a system of encouraging problem prevention, just problem solving.

The awards described above only put out large fires, but did not improve the system or quality.

Americans Still Focus on Meeting Specifications As the Main Quality Goal Rather Than Reducing Variation. Six Sigma is based on achieving 3.4 defects per million opportunities. This is no different than what Phil Crosby preached years ago about achieving zero defects.

Both concepts are based on attaining a defect level that is relative to a specification. The easiest way to do this is to open up the specifications. Bill Smith, the founder of Six Sigma, suggested that changing the specification "influences the quality of product as much as control of process variation does." Changing the specification does not improve quality. Improving quality is about reducing variation.

Genichi Taguchi introduced many people to the loss function. The loss function is simply a function that quantifies in dollars the cost of variation at any point away from the target value. Most Americans believe in the "goal post" theory in that there is no cost related to any product within specifications, and any product outside of the specifications has the same cost (scrap, and so on). In essence, a product barely in spec costs the company $0 and another product barely out of spec costs the company, as an example, $10—the full cost to scrap the product. Yet these products are not that different from each other. Perhaps the real cost of the product barely in spec is $9, not $0, because there might be problems with assembling this product to another product that is also barely in spec.

As more and more Americans jump on the Six Sigma bandwagon, there seems to be less and less interest in variation reduction. This is not constant improvement of production or service.

American Companies Are Still Departmentally Focused. Departments are anti-system, anti-process. And yet most companies are set up as functional departments. Improving the systems of production and service is very difficult to do when a company is organized solely by department. Few companies are organized by process. Customer service personnel sit near other customer service personnel. Engineers sit with other engineers. Lathe operators work near other lathe operators. Nurses sit near other nurses. Accountants sit with accountants. Quality sits with quality. As companies grow, so do their departments. The distance between departments increases. The communication decreases. Department focus grows, and process focus decreases. Tension increases between departments. Waste and inventory increase between departments, stagnating process flow.

When performing true root cause analysis, the root cause is usually found in a different department from where the problem was discovered. If there is tension between departments and a lack of communication, good root cause analysis can not be performed and the system can not improve. For more information regarding the reasons as to why root cause analysis is not done well within American organizations, see Chapter 6.

American companies are set up as departments just as much today as they were 20 to 30 years ago. Departments have departmental goals. Departmental goals oftentimes are in conflict with each other, so as one department tries to improve in an area by taking action, another department is negatively affected and may not achieve its goals. Resentment, competition, and poor communication take place. The system suffers!

This is compounded even more today because we now have quality departments, lean departments, and Six Sigma departments who compete for resources and attention when they should all be working together, literally and figuratively, as one. Not doing so is a distraction to improvement of production and service.

American Companies Have Multiple Continuous Improvement Systems That Are Wasteful. The quality department runs the ISO quality management system (QMS). The Master Black Belt runs the Six Sigma program. The lean "Sensei" runs the lean program.

There are quality objectives for the ISO QMS. Six Sigma projects have their Big Y's and little y's. Lean has future value stream and associated targets. Top management uses a balanced scorecard, which may or may not reflect what is recorded in the business plan.

The ISO QMS has a corrective and preventive action system. Six Sigma has DMAIC. Lean has a bag of tools. Then there's 8D, 5P, five whys, Apollo root cause analysis, TQM remnants, and Kepner-Tregoe.

Every time something new comes along, someone adds it to the company as perhaps "the coolest thing ever." Nothing is replaced or eliminated or integrated. The new technique or methodology is added and people get confused as to what they should use. The system is confusing, and the people are confused as entropy, or disorder, kicks in at full gear.

The president of an ISO/TS 16949 company that remanufactures transmissions asked me for my opinion of his new "Waste Walk" form. It was intended to be used by anyone in the company as a means of identifying and eliminating waste. It had a "definition of the waste" section, a root cause section, a short-term action plan, a long-term action plan, and a section to verify effectiveness. I told him his "Waste Walk" form was wasteful. He got defensive. I told him the form was basically exactly the same as his ISO-based Corrective/Preventive Action Form, and people would be confused as to what to use.

Another company has two sites that assemble hydraulic cylinders. Between the two sites, there were 11 forms that addressed root cause analysis. How would anyone know what to use? How can a system improve when the continuous improvement systems themselves are so confusing to use?

I provide the following grade to American CEOs for their overall adherence to Point #5 of Dr. Deming's principles:

D

A "D" was given because there have been some misguided attempts at improving production and service and because the quality of some products has improved, but there's a long way to go.

Point #6: Institute training on the job.

When I worked as quality engineer for a company that assembled aerosol valves, I was asked to be a supplier auditor. I was given a checklist of questions. The supplier quality manager would schedule the audit, and we would conduct the audit together. The audit consisted of our asking questions from a script as we sat in the conference room the entire time.

I did not know how wrong this was until a couple of years later when I was taught properly. Since then I have taught many hundreds of people the art of effective auditing. At the beginning, I did not know better. The supplier quality manager also did not know better. She was not trained properly. This happens in many jobs. Those who train others oftentimes are not properly trained themselves. Bad habits get passed along to more people.

Training is an ongoing process, on the job, that is done daily until such a point that one's performance is in statistical control and there is no more to be gained.

Training and leadership go hand in hand. Those who lead best are those who can train best.

Trainers need to know how to train. They need training in how this must be done. See the "Training Within Industry" section in Chapter 4 for a good example of this.

When developing a lean culture, one of the best ways to train others is during what is known as the gemba walk. It's part of the lean lingo. *Gemba* means "go see." Team leaders, supervisors, and value stream managers should do gemba walks with those who work for them. It is a time to challenge the way processes are operating, challenge everyone to see the waste in the process and in the system, and challenge them to develop solutions to the waste. It is great training—done by a leader in the true essence of the word "leader"—that is done on a defined periodic basis when done correctly. Even though it is a process understood by companies attempting to "do lean," it is not practiced very often or very well.

Temporary Employees and Training. Temporary employees are used today more than ever before. According to the Bureau of Labor Statistics, there were approximately 1.2 million temporary help agency workers in February 2005. In 2004 alone, temp agency jobs increased by 205,000.

"Temps" require training. The training they get is oftentimes negligible. Companies do not want to invest the time in training a new temp when they have little confidence that the temp will show up for work the next day. If I ask an ISO 9001–certified company for the training records of a temporary employee, the answer is often, "We don't keep training records for temps." In other words, they've probably received very little, if any, training.

And yet, so often when a company experiences a customer complaint, the explanation as to why the problem occurred, or as they might call it, the "root cause" of the problem, is that "we used a temp that day," and the resolution is that "we trained the temp," as if that solution will work beyond one day.

Perhaps there has been an increase in some aspects of training stemming from lean, Six Sigma, and ISO 9001 initiatives, but then there has most probably been a decrease in other aspects (that is, statistical process control, teams). The type of training has changed over the years, given what is now considered to be the hot topic of the day.

The training process itself has not improved much, if at all, and evaluating whether the training provided was effective has not changed much over the last 20 to 30 years. ISO 9001 requires companies to determine training effectiveness, but most companies do the bare minimum to comply with the requirement, and the ISO 9001 registrar auditors accept whatever they're shown.

There is so much waste in training. It is a process, and as such it will have waste in it, especially those courses that are generic in nature and not specific to the company receiving the training itself.

I've asked many people who have attended Six Sigma Black Belt training, "What percentage of what you learned have you ever used?" I have never heard a response above 10 percent. There is a great deal of waste in training!

Before starting a course, most times I ask the client to detail what will be expected of each participant so that they understand that what they learn will have to be applied. Perhaps I feel so strongly about this requirement because in my early days at Saturn, and since then, I would attend a training class and force myself to use what I learned, and then I would teach it myself. It was a formula that worked. I also felt that I owed it to the company to use what I learned since the company invested so much time in my education.

At most, 30 percent of the companies take my advice and develop a list of expectations for the participants.

Overall, "instituting training on the job" has not changed much since Deming was alive. There have been some improvements and some steps backward.

I provide the following grade to American CEOs for their overall adherence to Point #6 of Dr. Deming's principles:

D

Point #7: Institute leadership. The aim of leadership should be to help people and machines and gadgets to do a better job. Leadership of management is in need of overhaul, as well as leadership of production workers.

In the fall of 1985, as I was completing my last semester in general engineering at the University of Illinois, I was not yet sure if I was going to be offered a full-time position with Saturn. So, like every other soon-to-be graduate, I endured the interviewing process with the companies that came to the U of I to hire new engineers.

One company was particularly interested in having me work for them. I was invited for a plant visit, and late in the fall of '85 I visited Seaquist Valve, a manufacturer of aerosol valves. I was interviewed only by the HR manager. The position was for a production supervisor. I liked the company and the location. The interview went well and an offer was made.

Though I received an offer, I was very tentative and unsure about the position. I was uncomfortable with the idea that I would walk into a facility and immediately supervise people in a production area of the facility. Many of these employees had worked for the company for decades. I knew that I was uncomfortable with the idea, but I didn't know why I was uncomfortable. Something just did not seem right. I knew I could do the job, but not right away. I had no real job experience besides the typical odd jobs during school as a newspaper boy, caddy, busboy, waiter, man-made lake weed cutter, construction site grunt, and my brief intern-like position with Saturn. I had never supervised or led people, with the exception of being the president of the Independent Student Organization at the U of I. I was unqualified. I thought I had some leadership skills, but not many. If I had not received other offers, I would have accepted this position and Seaquist would have hired an unqualified person to the position of production supervisor. I'm sure they hired a different unqualified person for this role.

A few days later, I was offered a position with the Saturn Corporation. I accepted the job with Saturn and I was very excited about it. I was excited about this great position with a new company, but I was also excited because I did not have to make a decision about the Seaquist position. As it turned out, I ended up working for Seaquist about three years later, as a manufacturing engineer, when I had to return to the Chicago area for personal reasons and, unfortunately, had to give up my position with the Saturn Corporation even before we were selling vehicles. Both jobs ended up being great experiences of different kinds.

The question to ponder, though, is why did Seaquist Valve, like so many other companies, want to hire me, a 22-year-old, fresh out of school, with no knowledge of its products, processes, and technology, and virtually no leadership experience?

Since it was not just me who they were interviewing but other soon-to-be college graduates, the common link between us was that we were about to obtain a degree. So what!

A degree does not make one a good leader or mean that one has the knowledge. I've met plenty of degreed idiots and recluses. I might be one myself. A degree is a piece of paper that shows that somehow you found a way to pay for and pass all of the classes.

A Black Belt does not make a leader or mean that s/he has knowledge. It means that s/he took a course and maybe performed one or two projects. I've met Black Belts that do not know how to complete a designed experiment. I've known of others who do not know how to complete a simple cause-and-effect diagram. But . . . they have a Black Belt and it's printed in bold on their resumé.

A lean Sensei certification does not make one a leader nor guarantee that they have great knowledge. It means they know how to obtain a piece of paper, just like the one they obtained in college.

A degree, a certification, or a belt does not make one qualified. See Chapter 5 for more information on this topic. An ISO 9001 certificate does not make a supplier qualified. No degree, certification, or belt is a true reflection of knowledge and/or leadership. However, degrees, certificates, and belts are an easy way of doing our job of hiring qualified personnel . . . with a gamble.

One former client who was released from her job asked me to tell her what Six Sigma was about so that she could reference it on her resume. I did not.

People who are in supervisory roles need to be taught how to lead and need to have hands-on knowledge of the process that they supervise. If a person is hired out of college because s/he has the potential to lead, s/he must work in the process for months or years, not on top of the process that they will supervise. S/he will be challenged by his/her supervisor and s/he will be taught how to lead.

They will not necessarily be problem solvers, but they will teach others—those who know the problems—how to solve problems. They will encourage their people to follow through on their ideas and how to think.

There have been no changes in leadership qualifications since the death of Dr. Deming. A truly great leader has the same qualifications today as s/he did centuries ago and as s/he will have centuries from now. They are constant!

Leadership Qualifications. The qualifications that a leader must have include, among others:

1. Treat everyone with respect and dignity

2. Set the example for others to follow

3. Be an active coach

4. Maintain the highest standard of honesty and integrity

5. Insist on excellence and hold your people accountable

6. Build group cohesiveness and pride

7. Show confidence in your people

8. Maintain a strong sense of urgency

9. Be available and visible to your staff

10. Develop yourself and those you lead to the highest potential

1. *Treat everyone with respect and dignity.* I first read *Leadership by the Book* because it was written by Willow Creek founder Bill Hybels and famed business writer and consultant Ken Blanchard. Willow Creek is a nondenominational mega-church based in South Barrington, Illinois, and a church that we frequent. Bill Hybels and the other pastors inspire me quite frequently to become a better person and leader. Ken Blanchard inspires me to become a better businessman and leader. One book written by the two, in conjunction with Phil Hodges, is a must-read, I thought, and indeed it was.

The book encourages managers and supervisors to become "servant leaders," serving and supporting those who work for them so that they can do their jobs effectively with pride and continuously improve their jobs and performance.

In the traditional and typical company, top management is at the top of the pyramid-like hierarchy structure. Communication and direction toward the vision of the company flow down through the company, all the way down to frontline employees who have direct or near-direct contact with customers. These people can be operators, shipping personnel, tech service personnel, waitresses, customer service reps, flight attendants, and so on.

As is shown in Figure 3.1, those at the lowest levels are responsive to the needs of their bosses. Those at the lowest level of the hierarchy structure—those who have the most contact with the customer—are more concerned with pleasing their bosses, those to whom they are responsive, than they are concerned with pleasing the customer. Those at the top are considered to be responsible for those who work for them.

Bill, Ken, and Phil suggest that the when it comes to taking action to improve processes and improve customer services, the pyramid needs to be flipped over, as is shown in Figure 3.2.

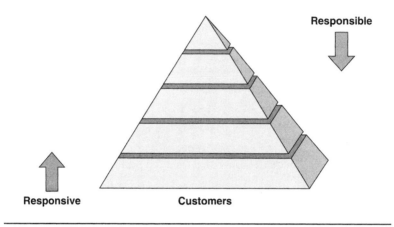

Figure 3.1 Traditional organizational hierarchy structure.

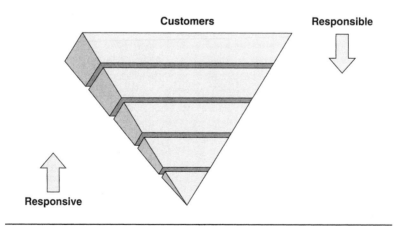

Figure 3.2 Hierarchy structure turned upside down.

When the pyramid is rotated, the higher levels are now responsive to the needs of those who work for them. The frontline employees are responsive to the needs of the customer and are empowered to make decisions for the benefit of the customer. They are more concerned with pleasing the customer than pleasing their boss. They are servant leaders. Responsibility to improve processes and increase customer satisfaction rests with frontline employees.

The benefits of becoming a servant leader and treating everyone with respect and dignity include:

- More immediate attention to the customer

- Quicker resolution to customer's problems

- Focus on developing the skills and responsibilities of the frontline employees

- Free up more time for supervisors and leaders to teach others how to solve problems rather than solving their problems

This requires leaving one's ego at the door. This is difficult to do for many American managers. American managers are typically an egotistical group who are proud of their accomplishments and ensure that many people know of their accomplishments. It's been my experience and observation that other cultures have a distinct advantage over Americans when it comes to being less egotistical and more humble. It is also perhaps why Japanese companies are so much more successful at practicing lean concepts, especially in the development of a lean culture, than American companies.

I've sat for several meetings with the VP of operations of a Texas manufacturing company. He dominated 95 percent of the meetings, in which three to five people were involved, including myself, oftentimes talking about how he saved so many companies with his "leadership." The irony is that the consultant is being paid to provide advice. In that case, I was being paid to listen to his stories. I guess I was his psychologist. He was a very egotistical man. And yet he promoted "lean," even though he knew and practiced very little of the principles behind lean. He thought he was a "lean" expert. He was not. He and his company practiced "fake lean." It was obvious in talking to him that he practiced "fake lean" because as he talked he used the word "I" exclusively and never used the word "we."

Though I have seen this egotistical behavior with many other top managers, it is obvious that the chance of seeing bigger egos increases exponentially the higher one climbs within an organization. This particular individual helped me to coin the phrase (as I am writing this):

The higher he go, the higher the ego!

And yet as Jim Collins proves repeatedly throughout his book *Good to Great,* humility is one of the two main characteristics of great leaders of great companies.

Can one be taught how to be less egotistical and more humble? Is there a system or methodology to encourage this type of behavior? Can a company hire individuals who treat others with respect and dignity?

These are important questions for the very top of an organization to consider and address. He or she must challenge him/herself to address this with regard to his or her own style of leadership. It is of the utmost importance in order to truly institute leadership.

2. *Set the example for others to follow.* A leader completes his or her tasks to support the completion of the tasks assigned to those who work for him or her.

A leader shows commitment to continuously improve the operations and support the people.

A leader is a servant leader.

A leader holds him/herself accountable—publicly.

A leader shares successes with the team and takes the blame when things do not go as planned.

A leader has standard work that may govern a small portion of his or her day. Standard work consists of activities that are performed on a consistent, scheduled basis that involve:

a. Training and coaching employees

b. Observing waste in the processes

c. Ensuring conformance of those who report to his or her standard work

d. Completing actions to improve the process

Standard work is generally recorded on a working document, and completion of one's actions is displayed for all to see. If an employee sees the completion of his or her boss's standard work, he or she is more apt to complete their own standard work accordingly.

David Mann discusses this concept wonderfully in his book, *Creating a Lean Culture* (Productivity Press, 2005).

An example of leader standard work is shown in Figure 3.3.

Nearly every company I visit has the same problem with completing corrective actions and preventive actions effectively and on time. And yet, so many company executives have never initiated their own corrective or preventive action nor perform corrective and preventive actions that are assigned to them. They do not use their own approved system, perhaps

O/P LEAD STANDARD WORK

Date: _____

Action Items

	Due	Done

To Do

Notes

Multiple Daily Tasks

	Prod bd	Sort PO's	Shop errors	FIBM's
9:00				
10:00				
11:00				
1:00				
2:00				
3:00				
4:00				
5:00				

Daily

Lead accountability meeting	8:00–8:15
Supervisor accountability meeting	8:15–8:30
Gemba walk	10:00
Gemba walk	3:00
PO scan checks	

Weekly

Time sheets	Mondays AM
L & L	Tuesdays 12:00–1:00
Recap week's training topics w/AI	

Monthly

O/P & Cust Serv meeting	2nd Wednesday
Power transmission training	4th Tuesday
Leadership meeting	3rd Wednesday

Figure 3.3   Leader standard work example.

because it is beneath them. They do not set the example to follow. No wonder so many corrective and preventive actions are weak and late. And they do not follow up with their people to ensure they are being completed.

3. *Be an Active Coach.* Coaching is the difference between giving orders and teaching people how to get things done. Leaders coach every day.

Leaders are out there on the front lines.

Leaders watch and study the process. They know that the results will come by focusing on the process. They are less concerned about the output (results) than the input (process focus).

Coaching, teaching, watching, studying, guiding are part of their leader standard work each day.

Leaders continuously challenge those who work for them to see and eliminate waste.

Too many American leaders lead from their corner offices and conference rooms, poring over data and not being *in* the process. Leader standard work is still very rare. We don't have many true leaders, but we sure have our share of micromanagers—the exact opposite of a true leader.

4. *Maintain the highest standard of honesty and integrity.*

Tell The Truth. All The Time. No one is pure evil.

—Randy Pausch,
The Last Lecture

Leaders don't hide mistakes or buy time to figure out a solution. They admit to problems openly so that the process-oriented team can get the problem resolved.

Leaders tell employees the good and the bad, and hold back as little as possible.

Leaders share company data and information with those employees who need the data or information to improve their job or processes.

Leaders do not cheat their employees out of recognition.

Leaders do not fudge numbers. They do not sacrifice quality for quantity.

They are true to the principles (if they exist) of the company. They do not sacrifice the long-term success of the company for short-term personal or company benefits. They believe in and uphold the company's constancy of purpose, if it exists. They are not like the leaders of AIG, Lehman Brothers, Washington Mutual, Freddie Mac, Fannie Mae, GM, and Chrysler.

Leaders do not cheat the company, the employees, and the customers like the "leaders" of the Enrons and Arthur Andersens of American business.

5. *Insist on excellence and hold your people accountable.* In the majority of the companies I visit, employees complain about the lack of accountability in their company.

In the majority of companies I visit, a very low percentage of corrective actions are completed effectively and on time.

Whose fault is this? It's management's fault. Better yet, it is the fault of the system that does not have methodologies to nurture leaders and leadership skills.

A leader's job is to ensure execution.

> *Execution is a systematic process of rigorously discussing the how(s) and what(s), questioning, tenaciously following through, and ensuring accountability.*
>
> **—Larry Bossidy and Ram Charan,**
> *Execution: The Art of Getting Things Done*

Execution is about challenging, questioning, following through, guiding, and ensuring accountability.

Execution is not micromanaging. Micromanaging is attending to small details in management: controlling a person or a situation by paying extreme attention to small details.

Micromanagers:

- Monitor and assess every step.

- Do not give general instructions on smaller tasks.

- Do not delegate.

- Are recognized easily as such by employees.

- Rarely view themselves as such.

- Refute such claims by citing their management style as "structured" or "organizational." This is part of the denial process.

Micromanagement:

- Tells an employee that their work or judgment is not trusted

- Creates apathetic and disengaged employees

- Affects productivity negatively

A leader's job is to ensure excellence.

Excellence is the constant elimination of waste, focus on the process, and reduction of variation.

More than 50 percent of presidents and COOs whom I have known well are excellent micromanagers (this is not a compliment). A far greater percentage of these "leaders" truly do not understand the importance of reducing variation because they are transfixed with just being in spec.

How many CEOs and presidents of "Six Sigma"–type companies would truly go to one of Dr. Deming's four-day seminars if they were in existence today? Not many, I can assure you, since this would be a task delegated to a lower level. And yet they would need it more than anyone else to understand more about the role of a leader and even to understand such mundane things as common cause variation and special cause variation.

6. *Build group cohesiveness and pride.* The first issue lies in the definition of what is a "group." If groups are defined as *departments,* group cohesiveness can be built in many departments but can be *detrimental* to the company as a whole as they compete against each other for resources and attention. This is usually the norm in most American companies.

If groups are *cross-functional teams,* focused on an entire process within a territory or a product or service family:

- Cohesiveness can be built more easily

- It can be most beneficial to the company

Dr. Deming taught us on page 125 of *The New Economics* that a leader fully understands the meaning of a system and ensures that his or her people understand the same.

Leaders teach their people the aim of the system and how the work of the group supports this aim.

Leaders help their people see how their goals must be in sync with the system's goals, that the people are key components in the system, and the need to work in cooperation with preceding stages and with following stages toward optimization of the efforts of all stages toward achievement of the aim.

Leaders ensure awareness within the group of the four stages a typical team experiences:

1. Forming

2. Storming

3. Norming

4. Performing

The leader helps to establish the aim of the group during the *forming* phase.

Leaders coach the team through the difficult times, or the *storming* phase, when resistance sets in after getting comfortable with working together.

Leaders challenge the team to get beyond the *norming* phase and into the *performing* phase, where the employees begin to think for themselves, lead themselves, and improve the process themselves.

Leaders demonstrate humility and check their *egos* at the front door of the building.

Most importantly, group cohesiveness must be built around cross-functional process groups, and it is not in most American companies.

7. *Show confidence in your people.*

> *If you always lean on your master, you will never be able to proceed without him . . . .*
>
> *Remote from all other aid, we are obliged to invent and to execute; to find means within ourselves, and not to lean on others.*
>
> —Thomas Jefferson, 1787,
> spoken to his daughter Martha Jefferson

> *Free, free, set them free.*
>
> —Sting, 1985
> "If You Love Somebody Set Them Free"

A leaders builds confidence in his or her people to be self-reliant. This is the same role a parent should have with his or her children.

Leaders drive fear out of the organization. Dr. Deming stated on page 26 of *Out of the Crisis,* "Top management should publish a resolution that no one will lose his job for contribution to quality and productivity."

Too many American companies drive fear into the organization with practices such as performance evaluations, writing people up for defective products or services, encouraging them to cover up errors or problems prior to an auditor's arrival, and management by objectives.

Leaders encourage calculated risk that is supported by data!

Leaders allow for failure, but demand reasons for and solutions to the failures. Leaders ensure that the system is improved so that the failures are not repeated by others within the organization.

8. *Maintain a strong sense of urgency.* Leaders build a culture of immediately seeing problems and working to resolve problems as they are happening, not a week or month later.

Even today in many organizations data from a process is input into a statistical software program and control charts are analyzed long after the product from that process has left the premises. An injection molding company—no longer in business—analyzed control chart data one to two weeks after the product was made and happily informed their automotive customer that they were doing SPC.

Generating control charts after the process has stopped is wasteful and defeats the purpose of control charts, which is to stop the process when an out-of-control condition first exists so that the process can be fixed prior to producing any defective products.

It's not just SPC data that needs immediate review and reaction—it's any data. Month-end reports detailing the performance of one's processes are wasteful, and yet most companies rely on these reports. It's too late to do anything about the data, and people do not remember the circumstances surrounding any problems.

Leaders need to ensure that visual controls and actions are openly displayed so that they create immediacy of action and urgency to complete actions on a timely basis.

Leaders stick to their schedule and ensure that employees stick to their deadlines.

If due dates are missed, leaders insist on knowing the reasons why they were missed and solutions to these reasons, as determined by the employees. Leaders may, along with the employee:

- Consider reassigning a task

- Determine a new due date, but keep the old due date visible

- Provide additional resources or assistance

American management relies on reviewing data at monthly meetings, in a conference room, way too late to drive effective actions.

9. *Be available and visible to your staff.* Leaders do not hide in their offices. They are out there where the action is and where the real work is performed. They see the processes for which they are responsible, all the time. They do the gemba (go see) walk, or in the office they do the *gemba sit* and watch someone work at their desk.

Leaders avoid not only offices, but conference rooms as well.

Leaders take an active role in daily accountability meetings to ensure that actions are being completed to improve the process and ensure that standard work is being completed, to ensure that the process is brought back to a level of stability when out-of-control conditions occur, and to ensure that the process has the resources required to minimize waste.

A VP of finance of a Wisconsin manufacturing company was embarrassed when, for the first time, he really watched closely as one of his employees proceeded through the "issuing credits" process. He had never really watched the process and he had no idea of the number of wasteful steps that were taken by his employees on an everyday basis.

In preparation for a lean culture class I was to teach for this same company, I *watched* a customer service representative, for 90 minutes, proceed through his job of entering orders into the system. I recorded any wasteful activities as I watched him navigate his way through a somewhat cumbersome process. I categorized the waste into the generally accepted eight categories of waste and used the document as an example when teaching others how to *watch* and *identify* waste. Figure 3.4 shows the waste that was observed during this time period.

American management still like their well-decorated offices.

10. *Develop yourself and those you lead to the highest potential.* Leaders continuously improve themselves through:

- Learning from their subordinates

- Learning from their customers and suppliers

- Benchmarking other processes or companies

- Gaining more knowledge through training and reading

- Learning from their mistakes and announcing them to others so that corrective action can be taken and others do not repeat the same mistakes

- Hiring more competent people than themselves

- Studying results to improve his or her performance

- Becoming diversified in interests and hobbies

- Becoming less wasteful at home and in their communities

- Supporting and encouraging all of the above with their employees

Too many leaders are found absent from training classes that I provide. They feel that learning about such things as root cause analysis is beneath them, though not knowing about and practicing root cause analysis is exactly why their company underperforms.

Summary. If these are the qualifications of a leader, or something similar to these words are qualifications of being a leader, what does your organization do to ensure that these qualifications are known and targeted?

Defects (Includes potential defects and lack of visual controls)
1. Building an adapter wrong first, on purpose, because the system won't build it; then swap out 14–15 parts; $260 order; prints 3 screens and highlights
5. The quote search identified two quotes with exactly the same quote number
7. Order write-up format and quote format look a lot different
11. Defaults on write-up form are oftentimes wrong and have to be changed
13. Stock versus reserved is difficult to read and can cause mistakes
17. Not enough space to type in long city names, so have to retype in notes or abbreviate
Overproduction
Waiting (Includes searching)
4. Quote search screen takes a while to upload
8. Spent time looking for e-mail address (his e-mail history and name recognition were wiped out with last week's system failure)
12. Waiting at the scanner
Not using employees' minds/skills
19. Mike has a lot of ideas about wasteful key strokes, etc. Not being used.
Transportation
6. Walk to printer at least 2× for each order.
16. Long walk to copier
Inventory
9. "Orders to release" slot (Mike's): 15
20. Parts hold slot (Mike's): 4
21. Pending slot (Mike's): 3
22. Orders to be entered (All): 54
23. FIBM to be checked (All): 0–25

Figure 3.4 Waste seen during a gemba "sit" of an order entry process.

Motion
2. Lots of head movements from computer back to paper on the table to the right side (18 times before paper moved). Also, moved head several times to see territory map.

Excess processing (Includes redundancies)
3. Inputs delivery code and then types out "UPS Ground Collect"
10. Type "F" for each line item to flush—happens 100% of the time
14. Double entering input adapter and ratio
15. RPM and torque should be generated automatically from the other inputs
18. Customer service code entered many times
24. Many keystrokes to find necessary files

Figure 3.4 *Continued.*

We know that Dr. Deming was completely against performance evaluations because of the harm they can do to individuals. Deming believed that performance evaluations should be thrown away and leadership on a day-to-day basis needs to be substituted. If, however, your company so strongly disagrees with Dr. Deming on this point, then perhaps you can meet him halfway and have the employees evaluate their supervisors on the above leadership qualifications, sort of like what I have done in this section and in this chapter. In this way, you will at least ensure that supervisors are responsive to their employee needs, as was shown in Figure 3.2.

Dr. Deming wrote on page 126 of *The New Economics* that a leader has three sources of power:

1. Authority of office

2. Knowledge

3. Personality and persuasive power; tact

He said that a successful manager of people develops numbers 2 and 3; he does not rely on no. 1. He nevertheless has an obligation to use number 1, as this source of power enables him to change the process—equipment, materials, methods—to bring improvement, such as to reduce variation in output. (Dr. Robert Klekamp).

I still see no change in this area. I still see those in authority—but lacking knowledge and personality—depend on their power. I see those in authority unconsciously filling a void in his or her qualifications by making it clear to everybody that he or she is in a position of authority. We know this when a subordinate might question an action or a direction and the supervisor provides the response, "Because I'm the boss."

The lack of true leadership is probably American management's greatest weakness.

I provide the following grade to American CEOs for their overall adherence to Point #7 of Dr. Deming's principles:

F

Point #8: Drive out fear, so that everyone may work effectively for the company.

> *Top management should publish a resolution that no one will lose his job for contribution to quality and productivity.*

> —W. Edwards Deming,
> *Out of the Crisis*

ISO 9001 Audit Fear. A chief operating officer of a company congratulates an internal audit team on not finding any nonconformities. The message he sends to the other auditors is that I am most happy when nonconformities are not found. So, you'd better not find them. The message he sends to the auditees is that they'd better make sure they do whatever it takes to avoid nonconformities. Or in other words, everyone continue to work on covering up problems and errors, hide them from the auditors, and make sure you do not use the audit process as a way to improve the processes.

The president of another company congratulates the entire company each time the ISO 9001 registrar auditor leaves the building after having issued one or two minor nonconformities. The president (and others) knows they have many more nonconformities than the auditor saw or chose to record, but he prefers to live in an "ignorance is bliss" world.

After suggesting to a management representative while teaching an internal audit training class that he should tell his registrar auditor that they would like to receive as many corrective actions and opportunities for improvement as he sees and not to hold back, he said he understood the reason for my suggesting this, but he could not do that because his performance evaluation was dependent on how many nonconformities were recorded. As Shigeo Shingo, co-creator of the Toyota Production System, once said, "No problem is big problem."

The message is quite simple: continue to hide the nonconformities from the auditor, and you will not get into trouble. The president does not want to hear about nonconformities. He only wants the piece of paper in the nice frame near the receptionist in the front foyer. He wants as few nonconformities as possible and wants them dealt with quickly so that they can get back to business as usual until the next audit.

Employees receive the message loud and clear. They are afraid that they will be the cause of a nonconformity and cause great anger in the president. About a week before the auditor arrives, they "prepare" for the audit: they do housekeeping, they get rid of or hide uncontrolled documents, they conduct last-minute audits, corrective actions, and management reviews, and they read their procedures and try to follow them for a change.

If any company has to prepare for an audit, the company is fooling itself and trying to fool the auditor. They are doing this out of fear, the fear that may exist when the president learns that there are more than the token one or two nonconformities.

Customer Complaints. Fear lies in the reporting of customer complaints. Customer service representatives or others who may receive complaints from customers oftentimes will not report them, especially if the problem was initiated by them and if they can resolve the issue with no one finding out about the complaint.

The fear lies with the company-wide objective of reducing the number of customer complaints to a certain level. Employee pay and bonuses may be contingent on minimizing the number of complaints. If one is the "cause" of another complaint that makes the company or department miss its goal, one fears scrutiny and scorn from his or her fellow coworkers and supervisor. The employee learns how to hide problems and not report them for fear of retribution due to a flawed system.

If companies feel they need to set a goal regarding customer complaints, I encourage them to consider setting a goal to *increase* the number of customer concerns or complaints, while still maintaining a goal of reducing the number of customer *returns*. Very few companies have taken me up on this recommendation.

Six Sigma Projects. Frequently, in many Six Sigma–oriented companies, after Black Belts have been trained, they are given projects and told that they must achieve a cost reduction of $500,000 or some number more suited to their organization. The bogey is set. The bogey is no different than a quota. Dr. Deming's Point #11 strongly recommends eliminating quotas of any sort.

The quotas are set anyway, and the Black Belt does whatever is necessary to reach that quota. As an operator may sacrifice quality of the product in order to achieve a certain production quantity, the Black Belt may sacrifice another process or departmental objective, or fudge the numbers, or shift numbers to other accounts in order to achieve the cost reduction target mandated by upper management.

The Black Belt is afraid of retribution. The Black Belt is afraid that his or her boss will look bad because he or she spent so much money in training costs, and a return on that investment must be shown and must be obvious. So the team sets out on a mission to ensure that the quota is met. Occasionally, it is legitimately met because there truly is so much waste within so many companies, but when the quota is not met the numbers are fudged or expenses are reallocated to different accounts, making it possible to show the achievement of reaching the targeted cost reduction.

It is truly a numbers game, and this is the problem with targeting a dollar quota. The focus turns away from variation reduction, waste elimination, and the process itself to a focus on dollars. If the focus is primarily on variation reduction, waste elimination, and process, the dollar savings will result naturally.

It's not just the Black Belts that feel the pressure and the fear. Oftentimes, the Champion or the leader of the Six Sigma movement feels the pressure and the fear because goals to train a certain number of Black Belts by a certain date and complete a certain number of Six Sigma projects have been established. This person in charge will now find people to train rather than train those people who want to be trained and will have the ability to use the material. Also, silly projects will be started, and many projects will be "completed" before they have reached the goal, all in the interest of attaining the quota. The goals become the focus, not the continuous improvement activity, all because of a system of fear.

Corrective and Preventive Action Systems. Earlier, I wrote about the COO who wanted to fire me as the company's quality and lean consultant. He never did. However, my work performance suffered as a result. I did not challenge the system and the methodologies nearly as much as I had. Fear prohibits employees from truly challenging the system. Fear forces one to work within the system and to never buck the system. I was told by other employees that I was becoming more like them. They had all pretty much become accustomed to being quiet when the COO talked and never challenging the system. They were rewarded by the organization by being allowed to keep their jobs and by receiving a small pay raise each year. They were rewarded for working within the system.

Another company had for many months attained a 20% to 30% completion rate for closing out corrective and preventive actions on time. The COO wanted to increase this rate and made it known that this was necessary.

The company did institute some nice improvements to their corrective/preventive action database and notification system to increase visibility and ensure accountability.

And these improvements did help the company to achieve an 80% on-time completion rate, a marked improvement. However, other factors played a role in achieving this improvement, including the fact that employees initiated many fewer corrective and preventive actions and the effectiveness of those that were closed out on time became less so. Once again, a sort of quota was established, and with this quota came the fear of not achieving the quota.

The very purpose of a corrective/preventive action system is to continually improve the process. This company's system of corrective and preventive actions actually caused it to regress in its own process. There were fewer corrective and preventive actions initiated and completed, and the quality of those completed took a nosedive, but they had a higher percentage completed on time. Big deal! This company's top management does not understand continual improvement. Their focus is still on the numbers game—how many are completed on time—rather than the quality of the system—how many are effective at eliminating the root cause. If this company wanted to measure something more appropriate regarding the effectiveness of the corrective/preventive action system, they would be better off measuring:

1. Percentage of corrective/preventive actions resulting in a systemic change

2. The ratio of preventive actions to corrective actions

3. The percentage of corrective/preventive actions resulting in less waste

Performance Evaluations. This is probably one of the biggest motivators of fear within the workplace. Annual performance evaluations are just as rampant as they were 20 to 30 years ago. They are further discussed in Point #11 below.

Fear within the organization exists just as much today as it did when Dr. Deming taught us. As long as there are quotas to be reached and performance evaluations to be given, and as long as there is no focus on variation reduction, fear will continue to thrive.

I provide the following grade to American CEOs for their overall adherence to Point #8 of Dr. Deming's principles:

F

Point #9: Break down barriers between departments. People in research, design, sales, and production must work as a team, to foresee problems of production and in use that may be encountered with the product or service.

I recently worked with a very good client (definition: one that is actually open to the possibility of truly changing its operations and management structure to increase focus on the process) and suggested that they go with an approach more focused on the process. This company, like many companies, has had a tremendous amount of infighting between departments. Root cause analysis was seldom done well. The root cause analysis of a problem was assigned to one person within a department. The analysis would take that person into another department. At this point, arguments and finger-pointing would ensue as one department felt they were being attacked by another department. Oftentimes, there would be a stalemate. Or, in many cases, the person assigned to do root cause analysis would stop before it got to another department, and the root cause would never be determined. The system would not be fixed, and the problem would recur.

This company, so typical in so many ways, needed to be more process-focused and less department-focused. A company set up as departments, and departments alone, can not do root cause analysis effectively, and problems will persist.

Specific suggestions were made on how to align the organization more territorially, with sales personnel, customer service personnel, order entry personnel, engineering, and drafting sitting and working together for customers within one territory. Additional suggestions were made with regard to setting up the manufacturing side of the operations to be more product family–oriented, with product teams consisting of machining, two different assembly operations, material handling, shipping, quality, and maintenance for each family of products.

In essence, the suggestions consisted of making one big company into three smaller companies that would be much more nimble in seeing and resolving problems and getting higher-quality products out the door, on time.

After much deliberation between those in top management, the president e-mailed me the results of their debates. Some of the excerpts within the e-mail included:

> *"As you can imagine, the meeting was quite contentious, with good arguments on both sides . . ."*
>
> *"The net result is that we will stay functional organizationally, but will implement cross-functionally when possible."*
>
> *"Instead of just doing assembly, we are including the production planner and inventory puller into the equation. The group lead for group 2 (newly created position) will essentially be the value stream manager for that piece of the overall value stream process . . ."*
>
> *"So it is a bit of a hybrid. We will see how it goes with the first implementation and go from there."*

The company did not take all of my suggestions, but it was a huge win because they debated and challenged their very structure, their very organization, and they are trying things in order to be more process focused. It's an ongoing process, and perhaps some of these changes will result in great improvements. And perhaps they will result in only minor or no improvements. The challenge for the organization will be to question and evaluate their changes and challenge themselves to make further changes in the organizational structure in the future if there is still a great deal of waste and a lack of process focus.

We Are Kings and Queens of Our Departments. Departments and functional departments exist just as much today as they ever have. It is very difficult to upend an organization for the sake of being more process oriented. Many years of holding a position, such as a VP of engineering, plant manager, or director of quality, with people reporting to them with the same interests and beliefs, and oftentimes personalities, will make one resistant to change. A certain camaraderie amongst each other will have built over the years, and they will be comfortable with each other, even though they all complain about each other to their real friends within the company.

These VPs, managers, directors, and otherwise, do not want to give up their kingdoms—their fiefdoms—over which they rule. They've worked hard to get to this point in their careers and they are now finally the King or Queen of their very own department. They can set their own departmental objectives, and they never have to worry about the overall company's success or the success of the overall system. All they need to worry about is how *their* department works. They continue to suboptimize their processes, oftentimes to the detriment of the other departments. But who cares? they think, as long as they keep meeting their objectives and keep receiving their bonuses.

VPs, managers, and directors always like to talk to the "troops" about the need for change to stay competitive, as long as it's not them who has to change.

The higher on the ladder you are, the harder it is to change your position and your ways!

Those who are most resistant to the change to a process-oriented company are the very CEOs, COOs, VPs, directors, and managers who preach change to the organization. In their minds, they do not have to change. They got to the position that they're at within the organization because they are really good at what they do, they think. Why would they need to change? Besides, that would not look good. Change is good as long as *they* do not need to change.

Dr. Deming preached to us the need for sweeping changes at the top. Sweeping changes at the top have not occurred, and one telltale sign that they have not is that most companies are still departmentally organized. The barriers between departments, including departmental objectives and the literal and figurative departmental walls, still exist today as much as they did when Deming was alive because leadership has not changed.

The president of a hydraulic valve company in Illinois proudly stated that design engineers were not allowed on the production floor.

The customer service group of a medical device company in New York intentionally did not release orders to the production floor until the last day or two of the month so that the production group could not meet their monthly numbers.

My Fortunate Experiences. I feel very fortunate that in my two "real" work experiences prior to becoming an independent quality and lean consultant, I experienced great attempts and successes at breaking down the barriers between departments.

At Saturn, UAW mechanics and operators were part of the production design process. For me, it was a match made in heaven. I was a new engineer, fresh out of school, and was given the responsibility of procuring and designing nearly all of the fluid fill equipment and then ensuring that the processes of filling the vehicles with the fluids was efficient, effective, and optimized.

I knew very little about these processes and had to learn quickly. I befriended UAW operator Denny Stafford and UAW mechanic David Fox who were part of our team. I learned a great deal from them and they benefited from me because I was an engineer that was allowing them to design with me—something very unusual within a GM facility They had great ideas, and the overall process benefited from our teamwork, which was only allowed because the barriers between the departments were collapsed.

When I first began working with Seaquist Valve, I worked in a very traditional organizational structure. As a manufacturing engineer, I sat with the other three to four manufacturing engineers. Later, as a quality engineer, I sat with the other three quality engineers.

Seaquist hired a consulting/training company to lead us through the transition to focused factories, as it was called then. The idea behind focused factories is to break down the barriers between departments by placing all of the support personnel near the manufacturing or service location for a particular product family. It's not really that much different than building a lean culture and work cells to eliminate transportation, inventory, and other wastes. We just didn't call it part of lean back then.

I was placed in the group that made female aerosol valves primarily installed on the top of spray paint cans. A new office area was constructed near the female valve assembly area. The new office team consisted of the production supervisor, production team leaders (one per shift), manufacturing engineer, design engineer, quality engineer (me), and quality technicians (one per shift). Our desks formed the outer perimeter of the open rectangular office structure. In the middle was a conference table. Anytime there was a problem, we converged on the table and worked on it together. When it came to signing off on new work orders, a process that would normally take a week as each order was reviewed in serial fashion was reduced to minutes as we sat and discussed them together and then approved or disapproved them together, as a team. Customer complaints were handled as a team, much more effectively and efficiently. Typical job descriptions and activities became more muddled and less clear as we worked on what was best for the process. As a quality engineer, I also helped to design new product enhancements. Customer service personnel worked on corrective actions. Production team leaders performed designed experiments, after I taught them how to perform them. And the design engineer began to understand the equipment more than ever before.

I indeed feel blessed that I worked for these two companies and experienced true success in breaking down the barriers between departments.

It is also why I say with confidence that the vast majority of companies have not made this transition. Top management needs to change its dependence on the organizational structure, its ownerships of kingdoms and fiefdoms, and do what's best for the processes as a whole, and yet they are the biggest resistors to change.

Because most companies are still organized by department and run their organization via departmental objectives, I provide the following grade to American CEOs for their overall adherence to Point #9 of Dr. Deming's principles.

F

Point #10: Eliminate slogans, exhortations, and targets for the work force asking for zero defects and new levels of productivity.

To be honest with you, I had to look up "exhortation" on www.answers.com because it is not a word I am accustomed to using.

Exhortation is defined as a _speech or discourse that encourages, incites, or earnestly advises._

With that defined, the following slogans and exhortations are in use today:

3.4 defects per million opportunities

Six Sigma quality

Lean

Lean Six Sigma

Lean and green

Kaizen

Voice of the customer

ISO 9001 quality

Zero defects (still around in some places)

Safety first

It is also quite common to see scenic motivational pictures encased in beautiful fake wood frames with words like Teamwork, Imagination, Achievement, Perseverance, Destiny, and Appreciation and an accompanying statement of wisdom, which are somehow going to encourage us to be more team oriented, creative, driven, persistent, forward thinking, and thankful, respectively.

These pictures do nothing to inspire one to be any of these things. The structure of the organization and the leadership capabilities of those at the top of the organization and throughout the organization are the only real difference makers.

The slogans and exhortations listed above can also suggest to some people that they are inadequate in the areas of teamwork, imagination, and so on, and management is telling them to try harder in these areas, as if it is their fault. These slogans can generate frustration and resentment.

> *When leadership determines that their employees need motivation, it is a sign that leadership has not been leading.*

Management oftentimes does not provide the means to achieve 3.4 defects per million or to be more team oriented or to be more imaginative, which it claims are the goals of the company. Goals without the means or plans or resources to achieve the desires of the company are meaningless.

Slogans and exhortations focus on the employee not doing something adequately enough. Why would one need to tell employees about *achievement,* unless management believed the employees were not achieving enough? It takes focus away from blaming the system.

I suppose that one test of how well we are moving past slogans and exhortations is to analyze the documented root causes in response to corrective and preventive actions. It would seem that today, as was the case when Dr. Deming was alive, people (as well as machines, computers, and tools) are still being blamed for problems, rather than the system.

I provide the following grade to American CEOs for their overall adherence to Point #10 of Dr. Deming's principles:

D

Point #11a: Eliminate work standards (quotas) on the factory floor. Substitute leadership.

An electrical assembler in Illinois still pays its employees by the number of pieces they assemble. They do deduct defective parts made from the total number of parts assembled, but the focus is clearly on quantity, not quality.

A cylinder client in Texas evaluates the performance of its employees primarily by the amount of product they produce. They are also negatively evaluated for the number of nonconformance reports written against them for defective products produced by them. The workers are being blamed for producing defective products while working within a system over which they have no or little control. In essence, a quota has been established—the quota is to achieve no more than zero defects, otherwise you will be written up. As a result, the workers find ways to avoid recording nonconformances and hiding them from the managers so that they will not be blamed for them. This internal process *drives fear* into the organization. The intentional disregard for recording nonconformances results in losing valuable opportunities to improve the system. But who can condemn the workers for withholding information and hiding problems when working in a system of blame?

Within the manufacturing and service industries, it does appear that, overall, pay for piecework has decreased since Dr. Deming's demise, but it does not appear that leadership has been substituted. Rather, micromanagement has been substituted.

Sales Commissions. Paying salespeople by sales commissions is another form of quota. It emphasizes quantity over quality. The more sales dollars a salesperson brings in, the more she or he will be paid. Generally, salespeople do not care whether production can handle the amount of orders brought in; that's for them to figure out. Planning is not an issue for them to worry about; that would take away from them selling more. Competition for internal resources and manufacturing/servicing time may ensue between sales personnel. This can oftentimes lead to late deliveries and poor quality. This is of no or little concern to the salesperson because it does not affect his or her pay, and any problem was *obviously* manufacturing's or servicing's fault.

Salespeople can be overly zealous with granting permission for customers to return goods and providing credits to their customers as long as it does not affect their commission, which it usually does not. One of my client's top salesmen granted permission to his distributors to ship back defective product and product that they did not sell—at will—above and beyond the agreed-upon conditions within the original terms and conditions.

Paying sales commissions to sales personnel is just as prevalent today as ever.

I provide the following grade to American CEOs for their overall adherence to Point #11a of Dr. Deming's principles:

C

Point #11b: Eliminate management by objective.
Eliminate management by numbers, numerical goals.
Substitute leadership.

For more than 14 years, I have helped companies establish objectives and goals. So it may not seem that I support Deming's 11th Point. However, what Dr. Deming was most adamant about was managing by objectives and goals *without a plan.* He stated on page 75 of *Out of the Crisis:*

> *Internal goals set in the management of a company, without a method, are a burlesque.*

I have always ensured that the company with whom I am working has a documented plan on how they will achieve the goal. A goal without a plan is useless. If there is no plan, there is no reason to expect different results.

ISO 9001 requires that quality objectives be established. It does not *clearly* require that a plan to achieve the objectives also needs to be established. This is, therefore, sometimes missing from companies' systems and plans.

Performance Reviews. Part of management by objective is to review the performance of individuals and departments in achieving the objectives through annual performance reviews.

I was the type of student who was excited when grade school report cards were distributed. I would run home and show my parents how well I did. I would do analyses on my overall performance where I would compare the results with the previous quarters and the previous years. In high school, report cards were delivered through the mail. I was disappointed if it was a day late.

During my first experience at Saturn, as a summer student, I repeatedly asked the VP of engineering for a performance evaluation, which he finally gave me. I always looked forward to my performance evaluations while working for Saturn and Seaquist Valve, and if my boss or supervisor was late in providing one to me, then I would remind him.

OK . . . so I'm a little weird . . . .

As a consultant, I have also requested evaluations. As a presenter, I always ask the hosting company or organization for copies of the evaluations. I like to receive them because generally they are very good. Occasionally, I do receive a bad evaluation, and since I am human it does bother me. But I compare it to the other evaluations and determine if it was from an overly critical person in the group or if there were other comments of the same nature, and I need to make an improvement to my delivery or materials.

I recall one time providing a complex design of experiments course in Pennsylvania using another organization's materials. I had one comment on an evaluation form from a student that stated I moved too slowly in teaching the class. He sat right next to another guy in the class and they frequently did talk to one another throughout the class. The guy he sat next to wrote on the evaluation form that I went too fast. I figured the average evaluation was just like the baby bear's bowl of porridge, "just right." You can't please everyone!

Another time I was teaching a class on Dr. DeBono's lateral thinking (creativity) material to a chemical company in California. One attendee was from top management. He was forced to attend by the president (not a good start) and he made it obvious throughout the class that he did not want to be there by his disruptive comments and by missing large portions of the class by not showing up for a long time after breaks. Others in the class apologized to me for his behavior. He tore me apart on his evaluation. All of the other evaluations were very positive. Did I have control over the circumstances of his presence in the training and thus my evaluation? No, I did not. And yet his evaluation was the only one I could remember. And since he was the highest-ranking member in the class, I never received more work from that company. This was an example of a very negative evaluation of my performance, over which I had no control, resulting from the circumstances surrounding his attendance at the training. He wanted to prove to the president that he wasted his time. Does this not happen to many people?

In both of these cases, I had to tell myself that there were extenuating circumstances beyond my control, just as most performance evaluations have extenuating circumstances beyond the control of the person being evaluated.

In other cases (that is, presentations), I have occasionally received a few bad evaluations and, as a result, I've changed the presentation or learned from it. In one case in particular, I gave a very *personal* presentation entitled "Living Lean" as a keynote presentation to a company full of scientists, engineers, and Black Belts. I received about six evaluations, out of about 70, that said it was way too personal for them. I received many positive comments as well. I changed the presentation slightly, reduced the length from 1.5 hours to 1 hour, and gave the presentation at an ASQ Audit Division conference to rave reviews.

I used the evaluations to improve my product—the presentation. Perhaps in my business today, as a presenter, I have more control over my product (service) than most people might have over their product or process, but there are still extenuating circumstances beyond my control.

Products that I have created for which I have received pretty consistent positive reviews include:

The ISO Auditors Are Coming! training video

Auditing Nuts and Bolts training video

What Would Deming Say? (a Deming impersonation given at conferences)

Lean Quality Management Systems workshop

Putting Your Internal Audit System on Steroids workshop

Perhaps one of the reasons I do not mind and, in fact, seek out evaluations, is because for some reason (perhaps due to my interest in acting) I do not mind making a fool out of myself, and so, therefore, I do not mind taking risks. Impersonating Dr. Deming was a big risk that has paid off well because the comments I receive from people have been very positive.

Other products or services that have had mixed reviews, going from one extreme to the other, include:

Batchin': Why Something So Wrong Can Seem So Right
(a training video that shows how we batch process so much and how to apply lean at home)

Shitsu-Kigeki: If It's Japanese, It's Got to Be Good
(Stand-up comedy)

Living Lean presentation

ISO 9001:2000 News Report video

After presenting my stand-up comedy routine, this time for the third time, to the ASQ Section of Chicago, I thought I had a new career in comedy because it went so well and the reviews were outstanding.

A few months later, I performed nearly the same presentation for the ISO International Conference at 8:00 a.m. in the morning, and I thought I would never do comedy again. It bombed. The year before at this very conference, after providing two 35-minute breakout sessions, I was told that I came in second for "Best Conference Speaker," finishing up behind the keynote speaker, Norm Bodek. After the comedy routine the following year, it was obvious that the organizers did not want me to come back to their conference and I have not since.

Again, there are a lot of factors that go into the success of my product, many of which are outside of my control (for example, 8 a.m. slot for comedy). This is true for all of us. Evaluations can sometimes become unfair, and the degree of unfairness varies tremendously. However, people's livelihoods depend on those evaluations, and sometimes people have very little control over their work environment, which can make their performance evaluations extremely wrong and unfair.

The evaluator him- or herself can have more effect on the product or service than the person doing the work.

The video referenced above entitled *Batchin!* is a good example of a product that has received very extreme reviews from the very positive to the very negative. For just over an hour, I act very excited, talking about lean, waste, batching versus single-piece processing, 5S, and how I improved my laundry process. My goal was to be as excited about lean as Steve Irwin, the crocodile hunter, was when he spoke of crocodiles.

I asked ASQ to review it for possible inclusion in their Quality Press publications catalog as an item they would sell, like they had done for a few other videos of mine. It was reviewed and rejected.

About a year later, I Googled my name and saw that *Quality Progress* magazine (an ASQ publication) had reviewed *Batchin!* and given a very positive review. I called ASQ and pointed out this discrepancy. They said that they would re-review it for possible inclusion in the Quality Press offerings.

I spent thousands of dollars creating this video. One evaluation has prevented me from making a profit; another person's review might allow me to make a small profit.

This is just another example of why evaluations are not fair.

So, Why Do We Still Manage by Objective and Give Performance Reviews? As Dr. Deming stated, on page 102 of *Out of the Crisis:*

> It (management by objective, numbers, fear, merit rating, annual review) nourishes short-term performance, annihilates long-term planning, builds fear, demolishes teamwork, nourishes rivalry and politics.

It leaves people bitter, crushed, bruised, battered, desolate, despondent, dejected, feeling inferior, some even depressed, unfit for work for weeks after receipt of rating, unable to comprehend why they are inferior. It is unfair, as it ascribes to the people in a group differences that may be caused totally by the system that they work in.

ISO 9001, Six Sigma, and balanced scorecards strongly imply management by objectives. These are hot topics, so why not do it, managers think. The system of management by objectives and performance evaluations never gets questioned as long as hot topics strongly encourage the use of these practices.

But if people are "bitter, bruised, battered, desolate, despondent, dejected, feeling inferior, some even depressed," why does *every* company that I have ever worked for in my 15-year consulting career give performance reviews?

It's quite simple. Those who run the company, the managers, have always finished above average, and a positive evaluation provides more fuel for the *ego*. I know! They have never experienced feelings of bitterness, dejection, and depression after a review because they have never received a bad evaluation. They are the overachievers. The rest of the company, by default a full 50 percent of the workforce, are the underachievers. It's good, the managers think, to remind them of why they are in this position and why the managers are the managers.

Top management has been selfish in instituting performance evaluation systems within their organization. This is not a form of leadership. It is a lack of day-to-day leadership.

It's ironic to me that those companies who practice "lean" are the same companies that perform "annual reviews" once a year, in *one big batch* at the end of the year, rather than provide a single-piece flow of leadership throughout the year, every day.

> *Annual performance reviews are batch processing of employee feedback.*

Grading and Ranking in School. Performance evaluations actually begin much earlier in life in the form of handing out grades in school and, in some cases, paying children for the grades that they receive. This is just as damaging, if not more damaging, to children. Read more about the ill effects of grades in school in Chapter 8.

I provide the following grade to American CEOs for their overall adherence to Point #11b of Dr. Deming's principles:

F

Point #12: Remove barriers that rob people of pride of workmanship.

The premise behind this principle is that most everyone wants to do a good job. Think about it. How many people have you dealt with in your career that did not really want to do a good job? There aren't many, are there?

If we all pretty much want to do a good job, what prevents us from doing a good job? They're called barriers. They are in the way of our doing a good job and slowly they eat away at our ability to be proud of the work we produce.

But what are these barriers? There are many barriers of a wide variety. When we speak of root cause analysis, we realize that many of the root causes to problems and defects are the barriers we speak of in this principle. Some barriers may be root causes (blaming the system after asking "why" about five times). We also may experience barriers by not getting to the root cause of problems because we don't dig far enough, (we ask "why" the problem happened perhaps two or three times. More on this topic will be discussed in Chapter 6).

In a transmission remanufacturing facility in Georgia, I was conducting hands-on root cause analysis training for a group of people. We were working on a serious problem that resulted in sending defective product to the customer. We kept digging deeper and deeper (repeatedly asking "why") as we went to *go see* each operation involved. It's extremely important to see everything when conducting root cause analysis and, ideally, see the problem or defect re-created. We traced the cause back to a dial caliper that was hardly legible. When we asked the operator if he'd ever misread the gage and why the gage was in such a state of disrepair, he stated that he had made mistakes but was getting better at remembering what the worn numbers and tick marks were. He said that they had requested new gages some time ago but were denied them because of budget cuts.

The operator had grown accustomed to using an inadequate gauge and almost couldn't care less if the reading was off because he had learned that management couldn't care less whether he read the correct dimension or not.

This is one example of a barrier. Other examples of barriers include:

Defective product from suppliers

Cheapest supplier chosen

Product shortage

Equipment that is not maintained

No instructions defining the job

Overly complex and redundant documentation

Inconsistent product acceptance criteria from person to person

No defined product acceptance criteria

No organization

Lack of adequate tooling

No leadership

Uncalibrated gages

Inadequate working environment

Inadequate training

Rush jobs (poor planning)

No technical assistance from engineering

Poor production start-ups

Poor area organization

No engineering document control (using old revisions)

Lack of communication with management

How Do ISO 9001 and Lean Address the Barriers? The good news is that ISO 9001 and lean efforts have tried to address many of these types of barriers. This is not to say that companies that are ISO 9001 certified or are on a lean journey are doing a good job at removing the barriers.

ISO 9001 has requirements for:

Maintaining the Infrastructure (including the building, transportation and communication equipment, and hardware and software)

Managing the Work Environment

Quality Planning

Work Instructions

Training to Ensure Competency

Calibration

Lean addresses:

Workplace organization (5S)

Standard work (beyond work instructions)

Visual controls to make standard work and acceptance criteria more clear

Equipment maintenance and effectiveness (Total productive maintenance)

Communication with management (Lean culture/accountability meetings)

Job breakdown sheets and training to ensure competency (as part of Training Within Industry's JI program)

A company's performance in truly addressing these requirements or practices varies as much as the product or service they provide.

With regard to ISO 9001–certified companies, the majority of the companies address the bare minimum of the requirements because they see them as ISO requirements, not as requirements to help eliminate barriers that will make it much easier for employees to do their work and regain pride in workmanship. So they play the game of seeing what they can get away with from the registrar auditor, much as a child plays the game of what he or she can get away with from his or her parents.

Most of us know that pulling the wool over the auditor's eyes is a game that can't be lost. The audit does not ensure that the practices are *effective* in eliminating the barriers that rob people of their pride in workmanship. The barriers still exist after they leave, for the most part.

Now, if a company is more concerned with living by the true spirit of ISO 9001, much of which is found in ISO 9004, and not worry about what the registrar auditors do, then that company will truly will be using the standard as intended and will begin to eliminate the barriers that prevent workers from being proud of their work.

As with ISO 9001, companies can practice *fake lean* or they can choose to truly remove the barriers to pride in workmanship by living by the spirit of the Toyota Production System as defined by the root causes of TPS success:

The incessant focus on elimination of waste

The respect and involvement of all employees

Self-reliance

The incessant focus on the use of root cause analysis

The majority of companies practice fake lean and do little or nothing to build a culture that will embrace true lean principles and the above root causes to TPS success. They practice tools.

One of my clients, counter to my recommendations, would require me to provide 5S (sort, set in order, shine, standardize, sustain) training to a variety of different people throughout a production environment. These people oftentimes had no interaction with each other. Then, randomly, the group (not team) would go "5S" an area of the plant that they may or may not be familiar with. This is fake lean. Fake lean usually consists of doing 5S, instituting work cells for an area of the plant (not the entire value stream), and perhaps some total productive maintenance (TPM). It focuses on suboptimizing a department, not eliminating the waste from the entire value stream. It does not address the difficult part of building a lean culture. Practicing lean tools (5S, moving equipment around) accounts for only about 20 percent of the lean effort that's required. Small gains achieved by practicing the lean tools will be realized and will help to eliminate the barriers to pride in workmanship, but they will not be sustained.

Every company practicing lean basically states the same thing: the hardest part is sustaining the lean successes. This is because they have not built the culture to do so. The culture has not been built because the principles have not been determined, documented, and communicated.

Offshoring. While a company living by the spirit of ISO 9001 and lean has a good chance of eliminating some of the barriers to pride in workmanship, these same companies, via purchasing more and more product from overseas sources, are creating even larger barriers in the form of:

Defective product from suppliers

Product shortage

Company after company in the United States struggles to make defective product and services from China and other overseas sources *work*. Shortages exist when product is delayed due to vast amounts of transportation. Inventory of the wrong product, some obsolete and becoming more defective as it sits on shelves, increases. Product that has been purchased based on price tag alone is inferior to product that was either formerly manufactured in-house or by a local domestic supplier. Workers are told to deal with it and make it work.

Any efforts to increase pride in workmanship by living by the spirit of ISO 9001 and lean quickly evaporate as workers deal with defective components from overseas suppliers. This will be discussed more in Chapter 4.

Salaried employees also experience many barriers to pride in workmanship, with the one most noticeable barrier being the annual performance review, as was discussed in Point #11.

I provide the following grade to American CEOs for their overall adherence to Point #12 of Dr. Deming's principles:

C

Point #13: Institute a vigorous program of education and self-improvement.

Knowledge indeed is a desirable, a lovely possession.

—Thomas Jefferson

During the summers, while the young Dr. Deming pursued his doctorate in mathematics and physics at Yale, he worked at the Hawthorne plant of Western Electric, just outside Chicago. While there, a Dr. Fruth assured Deming that when he finished his degree at Yale, Western Electric would offer him a job, maybe at $5000 per year. He explained to Deming that it was not difficult to find men worth $5000 per year, but that was not what they were looking for. Dr. Fruth said, "If we offer you a job, it will be because we think there is a possibility that you may develop into a man worth $50,000 per year, and such men are hard to find." The conversation stayed with Deming for a long time. He learned that a company does not need good men; it needs men that are constantly improving; it needs men with knowledge.

Dr. Deming challenged himself by writing canticles, masses, compositions, and poems. He played a number of musical instruments and he experimented in his garden. His long-time secretary Cecilia S. Kilian claimed that she only recalled Dr. Deming watching television on four occasions. He always kept his mind active and he kept busy until the day he died at the age of 93.

Dr. Deming believed that one should continuously improve oneself both at home and in the workplace.

Dr. Deming believed in continuously gaining more knowledge, and it was a company's responsibility to encourage all employees to do the same. He believed that top management should make it clear to all employees that no one would ever lose their jobs for attempting to improve quality and productivity.

He believed that education in simple but powerful statistical techniques is required for all levels of employees.

In concert with these beliefs, Dr. Kaoru Ishikawa democratized statistics by making them easy for the common person to understand. He promoted the use of the seven basic quality tools: check sheets, scatter diagrams, flowcharts, histograms, Pareto diagrams, cause-and-effect diagrams, and run/control charts.

Also in concert with these beliefs, Dr. Genichi Taguchi democratized performing design of experiments so that a technician or engineer could perform successful experiments without having to rely on a statistician.

Dr. Deming would not have promoted Six Sigma because the statistics that are taught are not simple, and therefore they are not powerful. Six Sigma is not for all employees; it is for the elite—those who are chosen to be Green Belts and Black Belts.

Lean training does filter down to all levels within the organization, and this has been a good thing for promoting education and self-improvement.

What is most important is to gain knowledge, not certificates. Earning a certificate or Black Belt is *extrinsic* motivation. One goes through a training program not for the sheer joy and pleasure in learning, but to gain a belt or certificate. This is wrong, and this is the wrong message to send to all employees and, more importantly, to human beings who naturally want to learn yet are learning to learn only when money or a promotion is tied to it.

Reading and gaining more knowledge for the sake of enjoyment alone is *intrinsic* motivation. It is more pleasurable because we do it for ourselves, not for the sake of showing others that we did it.

Companies should not be rewarding people with belts, certificates, and bonuses for completing a course.

As Dr. Deming quoted Alfie Kohn on page 113 of his book, *The New Economics,* "rewards motivate people to work for rewards," not for the company or the sheer joy in improving processes.

ASQ now offers 14 different certifications. I have four ASQ certifications myself (Six Sigma Black Belt, Quality Auditor, Quality Engineer, Manager of Quality/Organizational Excellence). I have to say that I was motivated extrinsically to obtain these certificates to demonstrate to potential clients that I was indeed qualified. I should not have felt compelled to receive a certificate to prove myself. I should feel compelled to always gain more knowledge.

There used to be a time when there were seven or fewer certifications available, and some ASQ members would try to get all of them. I'm sure there probably is someone out there today that has all 14 certifications.

I am always amused how these people with multiple certifications attend ASQ conferences and walk around the conference halls with their name tag and all the little multi-colored certificates attached to and hanging from their name tag, as if to loudly proclaim how smart they are. When I see them, I think to myself that they are not necessarily knowledgeable, rather they are good test takers, and they were compelled to take the tests for pure adulation, rather than knowledge.

Six Sigma has Yellow, Green, Black, and Master Black Belts. Some programs even have pink and white belts.

Employees can now work their way to a bronze, then silver, then gold lean certification through a program sponsored by the Society of Manufacturing Engineers (SME), Association of Manufacturing Excellence (AME), and the Shingo Prize.

All are extrinsic motivators, and the certification processes as a whole have increased dramatically since the time of Dr. Deming's demise.

Certifications are not driving us toward "self-improvement." They are driving us more toward "self-gratification." Companies must begin to back off extrinsic motivators, like certifications, rewards, belts, money, and other "resume-builders," and encourage "self-improvement" for the purpose of improving oneself.

I provide the following grade to American CEOs for their overall adherence to Point #13 of Dr. Deming's principles:

D

Point #14: Put everybody in the company to work to accomplish the transformation. The transformation is everybody's job.

Top Management. Top management within many companies attends overview training on the latest thing, tells everyone "we're going to do this" and "I'm committed," provides the resources in terms of time and trainers, and then is never involved again. Six Sigma or lean or ISO 9001 or balanced scorecards is delegated down toward a lower-level manager.

There was, however, a Wisconsin company's top management team to whom I was teaching root cause analysis. The president was converted to a huge believer in root cause analysis and came to realize that the reason problems were mounting within the organization was because no one was truly doing root cause analysis correctly. So the president began to evaluate each and every corrective action and preventive action form, after employees had been trained, to determine whether the root cause was truly determined. He chose to do this as a means of providing ongoing, daily training and mentoring in root cause analysis until people started to "get it." This is what a leader should be doing. Unfortunately, this behavior by a company president is rare.

The transformation is everyone's job, and the transformation process along with the continual improvement process should be processes that are internally developed. Even if a consultant or a trainer delivers a training program, that training program should be evaluated for effectiveness and efficiency. It should then be modified to suit your company's needs, integrated within your quality system, and internalized as a program that belongs to the company.

I recently provided a presentation to over 100 senior- and junior-level managers of a power transmission company in Wisconsin, entitled "Leadership's Active Role in Continuous Improvement." The company was beginning to train its employees in a modified and scaled-down Six Sigma program in conjunction with a community college. Essentially, the tools within the program that were being taught as part of the course were the seven basic quality tools. The company made no mention of Six Sigma or belts of any color. They were beginning to take *ownership* of the continuous improvement process as if it was their process. The next step would be to improve it! This needs to happen, along with leadership's active participation in the process.

Six Sigma is credited with being so popular partly due to the fact that the process made quality professionals and other problem solvers speak the language of the CEO—money. The positive aspect of this is that some people were learning a little more about the financial aspects of the company. They were gaining knowledge, and knowledge gained is always a good thing. However, they were also gaining the knowledge of how to manipulate the numbers to always make their project look like a winner.

So, quality personnel and problem solvers have now learned the language of the CEO. But I ask you . . .

> *Is it more important for quality professionals to learn the language of the CEO, or for the CEO to learn the language of quality?*

Most CEOs still do not know the language of quality and the importance of reducing variation.

Dr. Deming warned us with a list of the "deadly diseases" that afflict most companies in the Western world. One of the diseases is "Management by use only of visible figures, with little or no consideration of figures that are unknown or unknowable." Deming wrote on page 121 of *Out of the Crisis:*

> *But he that would run his company on visible figures alone will in time have neither company nor figures. Actually, the most important figures that one needs for management are unknown or unknowable (Lloyd S. Nelson, p. 20), but successful management must nevertheless take account of them.*

Six Sigma encourages management in the spreading and proliferation of this deadly disease.

I can remember, back in 1991 when I was working as a manufacturing engineer for Seaquist Valve, a story of just how silly it is to run a company based on visible figures alone. At this particular location, we were assembling aerosol valves on high-speed assembly equipment. For a particular product line, there were four subassembly machines that assembled two internal plastic parts to a spring. These subassemblies were fed into boxes and stored as a part number. The boxes of the subassembled parts would then be brought to the main assembly machine and dumped into a feeder bowl to be assembled into the valve itself on the much larger continuous-motion assembly machine.

I had initiated a project to eliminate the four subassembly machines by incorporating their functions into the main assembly machine, thus getting rid of machines, inventory, non-value-added transportation, mixed parts, waiting for components if planning was not accurate, and freeing up a lot of floor space.

It was a lean project before the word "lean" was used. It just made sense. And yet, my boss made me perform a very painstaking return on investment analysis. He not only made me perform studies to back up my claims, but he rejected my ROI analysis at least four times. Each time, I had to go back to the drawing board to redo my ROI analysis. After about three months, the project was approved and it turned out to be successful.

Still, most of the numbers were made up or projected. The entire project just made sense for the sake of the process and the elimination of a lot of waste. I believe my boss also believed the whole project made sense, but he wanted me to learn the world of the corporate return on investment analysis and how to justify a project. I learned, but I also learned that it was a complete waste of time and delayed the project for months.

The invisible figures—those difficult to quantify, including the cost of inventory, the cost of money, the cost of lead times, the cost of mixed and obsolete parts, the cost of storage and space, the cost of packing the parts in boxes, the cost of boxes, the cost of transporting the parts to and from the warehouse, the cost of parts spilling, the cost of handling, the cost of maintaining part numbers in the system, the cost of human frustration working within a difficult system—were huge. This alone should have justified the project without having to perform a costly ROI analysis.

Many lean-minded companies will do whatever it takes to improve the process without justifying the return. This needs to occur more in the United States. Management needs to understand the focus of continuously improving the process, and they can help to do so by eliminating the need to perform at least some wasteful cost analyses. This is part of their job in leading the transformation.

Dr. Deming recommended that management organize itself as a team to advance the other 13 points. Perhaps this was done when Dr. Deming consulted with U.S. companies back in the '80s and up until he died in 1993, but I can surely state today, without any doubt, that most of Dr. Deming's principles were never sustained and are hardly existent in today's business world.

The Rest of the Pack. ISO 9001 does very little to promote involvement by all employees, even though it is suppose to be based on the principle of employee involvement.

Lean promotes involvement by all employees, but most companies do not practice it with everyone's involvement.

Six Sigma does not promote employee involvement, but rather focuses on the work of specialized Black Belt people.

I provide the following grade to American CEOs for their overall adherence to Point #14 of Dr. Deming's principles:

F

4

What Would Deming Probably Think of Today's Movements?

Business and quality movements and processes come and go with the passing of great leaders and the introduction of great new revolutionary programs invented by imaginative people who want to suck you dry with these new programs.

It's much more inviting to introduce a brand-new revolutionary program that is really just a repackaging of other program(s) that existed years ago than to give credit to a true pioneer of the past who gave us what should have been enduring principles that could make any company successful in the long run.

I was interviewed by *Quality Digest* magazine and I was asked why Dr. Deming's teachings are still relevant today.

I told Mike Richmond, the interviewer, that Deming's principles are timeless. They were relevant in 1950 when Dr. Deming first began to travel to Japan on a regular basis, they were relevant in the '80s when American companies first started to listen to him after Japan's successful quality movements, they were relevant in 1993 when he died, they are relevant today, and they will be relevant in the year 2500. Principles of business are timeless; they will always apply, as long as there are people running businesses.

TQM, value analysis/value engineering, reengineering, and benchmarking are gone.

Deming, Crosby, Juran, Shewhart, Ishikawa, Shingo, and Taguchi are gone.

But are they? Or do they somehow still exist or partially exist in some new program of today that has been morphed, sometimes for the worse, sometimes for the better?

As I showed in Chapter 3, Dr. Deming's principles have largely been forgotten by American corporations. However, some of his principles do live on in some applications of today, including the principles of lean. The problem lies in whether American companies live by the principles of lean or only occasionally practice the tools of lean.

Six Sigma, lean, Lean Six Sigma, outsourcing, and offshoring are today's focal points for business improvement. What would Dr. Deming think of these focal points?

SIX SIGMA

When I write my bimonthly article for *Quality Digest,* I try to entice readers to open up the article, which they receive as an e-mail, by providing them with the first part of a joke. In order to see the punch line, they need to open up the article. Recently I asked:

> *Question:* What is the proper way of wearing a Black Belt once you've earned it?

> *Answer:*

I then wrote a popular article entitled "Black Belt for Sale," which went something like this:

I'm a changed man. I am an ASQ (American Society for Quality)–certified Six Sigma Black Belt. To obtain the ASQ Black Belt, I had to pass a test and then show proof to someone within ASQ that I had completed one project (I was exempt from showing proof of another project because I had years of quality experience).

Early in my career at the Saturn Corporation of GM and at Seaquist Valve in Cary, Illinois, I had performed hundreds of designed experiments, FMEAs, correlation studies, and process capability studies. These qualify today as major parts of a Six Sigma project, as long as they include a lot of the somewhat unnecessary paperwork associated with a Six Sigma project.

I felt that I did not have to study much or take a class because a good deal of what I had practiced and taught for years would be on the test. However, I wanted to know what to expect. So, like so many others, I purchased the *CSSBB (Certified Six Sigma Black Belt) Primer* from Quality Council of

Indiana. I took many of the practice tests provided with the Primer. When I did not understand something, I memorized answers. As I did this, I would find the location of the proper answer in the Primer and read it. Then I would record the topic on a little sticky note and attach it to the page of the Primer. By the time I took the test, the Primer was loaded with yellow notes sticking out in every direction. I had learned where topics were located in the Primer, not necessarily the knowledge behind the topics themselves. I was practicing my skills of knowing how to take a test.

If I had been gaining knowledge through this "study" methodology, it would have been worthwhile. But quite honestly, I gained very little knowledge. A *"primer"* is defined on www.answers.com as *"A book that covers the basic elements of a subject."* It is a book created to help one pass a test. This is what I was gaining. I was gaining the knowledge of how to pass a test so that I could become certified. I was not gaining much in the way of new knowledge. Of course, I had knowledge from my past experiences, but perhaps not enough to pass the test. The time I spent preparing for the test was not adding additional knowledge to my knowledge bank, it was just preparing me to pass the test. This is not the right reason for studying.

Once I passed the test, I had to show proof of completing a Six Sigma project. It is difficult for a consultant/trainer to do so because many of us are not involved in actual projects anymore. We are paid to consult, train, and facilitate. Even though I had performed hundreds of projects earlier in my career, I needed to show a brand-new project using the "Six Sigma methodology." I convinced one of my clients that we work on one together. It was a simple little project, but we made it more complex by incorporating as many of the Six Sigma tools and forms as possible to make it look more like a Six Sigma project. It was, of course, accepted. Much of the effort that was put into the project was wasteful. But, when it comes to certifications (ISO, Black Belts, and so on), the ends justify the means. I was an ASQ Certified Six Sigma Black Belt!

Why Did I Become a Certified Six Sigma Black Belt?

Believe me, I resisted becoming a Black Belt for a long time!!

When I first began my consulting career 15 years ago, my bread and butter was teaching and facilitating design of experiments (DOE). I also did a lot of work in the areas of SPC, FMEA, ISO, and lean. Eventually, my work became all ISO 9001 and lean related. I wondered why the market for doing proper designed experiments had dried up when there was so much interest in it in the '80s and '90s. The answer was that DOE, along with SPC and FMEA, had been swallowed up by Six Sigma along with many other tools, many of which are never used. Clients were no longer interested in receiving knowledge and an education in specific process improvement tools; they wanted the entire package and the right to call themselves a "Certified Black Belt."

When I informed clients and potential clients that I could provide the knowledge of improving processes without going through extensive Six Sigma training and that I had plenty of documented proof of successful projects, all they cared about was whether I was a Black Belt, that they receive Six Sigma training, and that they become a "certified" Green or Black Belt.

So I succumbed to the pressure and became a Black Belt.

Another DOE Expert Is Beaten by Six Sigma

A couple of years ago my former mentor at the Saturn Corporation, Phillip J. Ross, called me out of the blue and asked me how my business was. His business was very slow at the time. Phil is an expert in design of experiments and had authored the book *Taguchi Techniques for Quality Engineering*. Phil is great at resolving problems and preventing problems. I asked Phil if he had jumped on the Six Sigma bandwagon and, predictably, he said he had not.

Now, one might think that Phil should have kept up with the times and that it is his own fault for his business suffering because he did not change with the times. He may have resisted, like I did.

However, I prefer to think of it this way: Companies out there are big fools for not hiring an expert such as Phil to teach people the theory and knowledge behind designed experiments to truly resolve and prevent problems. Companies are big fools for climbing onto the Six Sigma bandwagon and setting targets for the number of Black Belts that they have trained (so that the Black Belts can record it on their resumes and jump ship), rather than obtaining the knowledge to do true process improvement.

Why Do I Want to Sell My Black Belt?

I am an avid reader of anything quality, lean, and business related, and so hopefully, as I continue to gain more knowledge, my viewpoints will change and hopefully improve.

I became a Six Sigma Black Belt, but I never pushed it or tried to sell it too much. At one point, I did update my Web site (www.mikemick.com) to include Six Sigma services. A couple of years later, I removed any reference to Six Sigma after coming to grips with the many problems of Six Sigma as a whole and as I became an even bigger fan of Dr. Deming (while impersonating Dr. Deming at conferences and corporate events).

At a couple of trade shows, as I tried to hawk all of my services with the tagline, "Continuous Improvement in a World of Standards," I also made fun of earning a Six Sigma Black Belt because there is no standard for how one is earned, and the qualifications of a Black Belt can vary tremendously. See below.

In this photograph is a stand with Black Belts hanging from it. Two signs read, "Earn Your Black Belt Easily" and "Take One." I gave away 300 black belts at a cost of $1000, attracted a ton of traffic to my booth, and generated a lot of laughter (but no business).

Seven Sigma?

In my stand-up comedy routine, I talk about how I am going to compete with Six Sigma by rolling out my Seven Sigma program, which would include no tolerances for supplier parts (everything has to be dead nuts perfect), a 50% cost reduction target for suppliers each year, and a process to get us there called DMAICB (define, measure, analyze, improve, control, bankruptcy). Who cares if your company is bankrupt; you'll be the first Seven Sigma company ever!

What Are the Problems with Six Sigma?

Here are just a few problems with Six Sigma. There are more.

1. *It is an elitist system.* Dr. Deming repeatedly stated that quality is everyone's responsibility. Now people wait for the Belts to do all of the improvement activities. Improvement activities can not happen unless it's a Six Sigma project handled by a Belt. Lean, in some companies, is also going this direction, in which the only people eliminating wastes are those who are lean experts, or Senseis.

From *Quality Digest* magazine, in a "Last Word" article published in 2000 and entitled "The Emperor's New Woes, Revisited," an anonymous trained GE industrial engineer writes:

> *I explained that while I was doing the (Six Sigma) project, I had found and fixed several other processes. I was immediately admonished by one of the Black Belts for doing so. She told me I should've turned these into Six Sigma projects. I explained that it made more sense to me to quickly make the fixes so we could start reaping the benefits right away. Her retort was, "If you didn't do it in Six Sigma, then it didn't happen." Of course, her metric of preference was dollar savings from Six Sigma projects. She couldn't care less that what I did was the right for the business. She, like many other Six Sigma "devotees," was only interested in managing her career.*

Do you remember my joke about how one of my clients is doing so well in their Lean Six Sigma initiative, they are doubling their Lean Six Sigma department? Whole new wasteful bureaucracies are being established in the name of getting rid of waste. How ironic.

2. *Six Sigma training is wasteful.* I talked with an acquaintance who works for a large company. He said they trained 800 Black Belts. I asked him how many of those Black Belts were actively using what they learned. He said about five percent (that's 40). I asked, of those 40, how much of what they learned in class do they actually use? He said about five percent.

Essentially, two out of 800 trained Black Belts were using everything they learned. That's 1 out of 400, or 0.25% effective, or 99.75% ineffective. Or, we could reverse the number and state this in Six Sigma terms and claim that the Six Sigma training for this company has 997,500 defects per million opportunities (if a defect is defined as not using what was taught or unused inventory of knowledge).

Need I say more? For more information, see my article entitled, "Lean Six Sigma: An Oxymoron" on my Web site (www.mikemick.com).

3. *It's the Black Belt that matters, stupid!* A lady called me from St. Louis about five years ago. She managed a department. She had five people

who reported to her. They all had Green Belts from different companies and different training sources. She wanted them to all be Certified Black Belts. She was mostly concerned with whether or not I could *certify* them as Black Belts (apparently she did not know that since there was no standard, my dog could certify them). I told her that since the training from different sources can vary tremendously, she should consider, at a minimum, a refresher Green Belt training session for consistency's sake so that all six people would have the same background and knowledge before moving on to Black Belt training. She disagreed. She was trying to keep costs down, she said.

So then I told her that I could provide training using my own materials for DOE, SPC, FMEA, and other tools at a much lower cost (rather than what I was doing then by purchasing expensive materials from another source and passing the cost of the materials along to the client). I asked her what it was that she really wanted: the knowledge of process improvement or the certificate. She snapped back, "What part of certification do you not understand?"

Knowledge is not important. Certification is all that's important (this goes for ISO 9001 as well). Becoming a Green Belt or a Black Belt or a Super-Duper, Triple Wide, Master Black Belt is a resumé padder. It is obtained by way too many people to promote themselves rather than promote continuous improvement. The company pays for the training, and the trainees leave the company with their new Black Belt for higher-paying jobs. Is it not crazy for top management to not see this?

It all starts early in life. As I proofread this article, I am watching the local news. Apparently at some of the Chicago Public Schools, they will start paying $50 to each child for each A they receive, $30 for each B, and $20 for each C they receive. This is ridiculous! These kids are not learning for the joy of learning and to improve themselves. They are learning for money. This is no different than employees learning Six Sigma for the Black Belt that will give them more money with another company.

The GE industrial engineer quoted above stated, *"No matter how well we perform our jobs or what our knowledge or contribution to the business is, we won't be considered for any promotions unless we are Green Belt–certified."*

I have seen many "Certified" Black Belts who have no idea of how to set up a designed experiment and some that do not even know how to complete a fishbone diagram.

I know of a former client who lost her job and asked me what Six Sigma was so that she could put it on her resume.

I keep having to remind myself of the world we live in, "It's the certificate, stupid, not the knowledge!"

4. *Open up the specs, stupid!* What's the easiest way to get to 3.4 defects per million opportunities (DPMO)? There are two options:

    a. Open up the specifications!

    b. Increase the number of opportunities that you count!

Specifications are arbitrary and so is the number of opportunities. Both of the options above will decrease the DPMO, but will not improve quality.

The focus must be on variation reduction just as Dr. Deming, Dr. Juran, Dr. Shewhart, Dr. Taguchi, and Dr. Shingo taught us. Six Sigma does not provide this focus.

5. *CEOs are still not learning the language of quality.* The founders and practitioners did accomplish one thing that could be considered somewhat of a success: they got CEOs to listen to them about quality—kind of.

Much of Six Sigma's success in attempting to deploy its methodologies within so many U.S. companies is due to the fact that goals and success stories are quantified in dollars—the language of the CEO. This success lies in the fact that the CEOs will now listen to these crazy quality and continuous improvement freaks or—as a client's president referred to a quality engineer—*quality puke!* Isn't that special?

Dr. Deming constantly reminded us that the drive to improve quality starts at the top.

> *It is much more important that CEOs learn the language of quality, than quality professionals learn the language of the CEO.*

Many CEOs still have not learned about quality and the necessity to reduce variation, and Dr. Deming's 14 Points. This is what is needed. Six Sigma is just another band-aid in the long procession of band-aids.

> *Six Sigma is a band-aid covering the wound of CEO ignorance of quality by disguising it with money.*

Are There Other Options?

    a. *Seven tools of quality.* Dr. Kaoru Ishikawa is known for "democratizing statistics" by making statistical analysis less complicated for the average person with the *seven tools of quality* (scatter diagrams, check sheets, flowcharts, histograms, control and run charts, Pareto diagrams, fishbone diagrams).

He said that good visual aids make statistical and quality control more comprehensible to the average person, and that as much as 95 percent of quality-related problems in the factory can be solved with these seven fundamental quantitative tools.

Ninety-five percent?? Is this not something one must wonder and think about? One can teach these tools effectively in about 16 hours.

What is more effective—teaching one Black Belt for 160 hours or teaching 10 employees the seven basic quality tools in 16 hours? This is the question that you and your organization must ask yourselves.

b. *The Toyota Way* (Jeffrey K. Liker, 2004, McGraw-Hill). There are no complex statistical tools that are referred to throughout this entire book, which explains the principles behind Toyota's success.

From p. 253, Mr. Liker writes:

> . . . *Toyota does not have a Six Sigma program. Six Sigma is based on complex statistical analysis tools. People want to know how Toyota achieves such high levels of quality without the quality tools of Six Sigma. You can find an example of every Six Sigma tool somewhere in Toyota at some time. Yet most problems do not call for complex statistical analysis, but instead require painstaking, detailed problem solving. This requires a level of detailed thinking and analysis that is all too absent from most companies in day-to-day activity. It is a matter of discipline, attitude, and culture.*

This is consistent with what Dr. Ishikawa claimed.

c. *Kaizen and the Art of Creative Thinking* (Shigeo Shingo, 2007, Enna Products Corporation and PCS Inc.). Dr. Shingo's *scientific thinking* mechanism provides insight into how creative ideas to problems are developed. In his book, there is no mention of statistical tools. This book is also very consistent with the comment made above by Jeffrey Liker.

d. *The Idea Generator: Quick and Easy Kaizen* (Bunji Tozawa and Norman Bodek, 2001, PCS Press). The focus of this book is on generating a culture and a system that encourages all employees to think up and generate easy improvement ideas and implement them themselves. There are no complex statistical tools referenced in this book at all. This is very consistent with all of the above.

This book is truly about continuous improvement (little improvements made every day by every person) rather than continual improvements (scheduled Six Sigma projects or five-day kaizen events).

There are many different alternatives. It all comes down to effectiveness of the improvement process. Six Sigma has proven to be ineffective at many companies.

e. *Develop your own way.* Big or small company, you can develop your own way by first determining your *principles*. It is strongly encouraged to copy the principles of Dr. Deming. From there, develop the culture and internal processes that support those principles. From there, your people will develop their own tools, some borrowed from other sources, some brand-new and unique to your organization.

Black Belt for Sale

So I am putting my Black Belt up for sale to the highest bidder. I have no use for it. It has watered down lean efforts when combined as Lean Six Sigma; it has watered down variation reduction efforts, it has created bureaucracies, it has isolated people.

I know that it is perhaps not the best time to sell my Black Belt because pretty much everyone now has one anyway, and they are so easy to get. It's pretty much like selling a house right now—not a good market.

But nonetheless, I know that there are still many people out there who need one and would like to obtain a Black Belt in the easiest possible manner. If you can buy a degree (basically), if you can buy an ISO 9001 certificate (basically, via easy audits of "barely there" quality management systems that are graciously accepted as being compliant by registrars eagerly awaiting your continued business), why can't one buy a Black Belt?

Six Sigma's Failure in the Marketplace

I am indebted to Dr. Tony Burns for this material and his inspiration as discussed in e-mails and in his article entitled "Six Sigma Lessons from Deming," March 2008, *Quality Digest.*

Six Sigma captured the imagination of CEOs around the world. There have been many claims of its successes yet these have at least partially been attributed to the *Hawthorne effect,* which implies that if enough money is thrown into any methodology, at least some short-term results can reasonably be expected. However, an increasing number of articles such as those in *Fortune,* the *Wall Street Journal,* and *Fast Company* suggest that Six Sigma companies are failing. The market share performance of many companies—including Ford, General Electric, Motorola, Delphi, Home Depot, 3M, Eastman Kodak, Xerox, and Larson—has fallen dramatically, and 91 percent of Six Sigma companies have trailed the S&P 500 since adopting Six Sigma.

Individual examples include the *Detroit News's* account of quality problems with the new Ford Edge, despite Ford Motor Co. having trained 10,000

Six Sigma Black Belts and spent hundreds of millions of dollars on the methodology. Quality problems caused Ford to recruit quality expert Kathi Hanley away from Toyota Motor Corp. Hanley pored over the Edge and found more than 70 significant issues and hundreds of minor concerns.

The Ritz-Carlton is the only service company to have won the Malcolm Baldrige Award twice, and its success is based on total quality management (TQM). This may be compared to Home Depot, a Six Sigma company with falling profits and what has been described in an investigative report by Los Angeles NBC affiliate, NBC4, as the "Worst Service Ever." What has gone wrong with Six Sigma and what lessons can be learned from the past, particularly from the great W. Edwards Deming?

From Ken Hunt, "The Big Idea: Six Stigma," September 27, 2007 (http://www.theglobeandmail.com/servlet/story/RTGAM.20070830. rmbig0830/BNStory/specialROBmagazine/):

> *Once-mighty proponents of the (Six Sigma) program have begun to scale back their involvement, if not abandon it outright. Two of the most recent dropouts: 3M and Home Depot. In fact, Robert Nardelli, the former CEO of Home Depot, was forced out in part because his Six Sigma program was blamed for plummeting customer satisfaction and employee morale. At 3M, management is rolling back many Six Sigma initiatives: the program, it decided, was not compatible with the spirit of innovation that had once made 3M great. Invention is an inherently risky, wasteful, and chaotic process—exactly the sort of stuff Six Sigma seeks to eliminate.*

From 1999 through 2003, Motorola lost 60,000 jobs and significant market value share to become more "agile" and "flexible," even though years prior to this they seemed to be the most agile and lean company on earth.

Six Sigma versus Dr. Deming's Principles

The following list briefly summarizes how Six Sigma violates Deming's 14 Points.

1. Create constancy of purpose toward improvement of product and service, with the aim to become competitive and stay in business, and to provide jobs.

   Six Sigma has been shown to stifle innovation (for example, at 3M). It's all about the bottom line. Wall Street loves it—need I say more? It is not about love of product and improving quality of life. Six Sigma companies continue to shed American jobs.

2. Adopt the new philosophy. We are in a new economic age. Western management must awaken to the challenge, must learn their responsibilities, and take on leadership for change.

   Six Sigma destroys most of what Dr. Deming taught us. His philosophy and principles died with Dr. Deming in most companies and have long been forgotten. Leadership has not changed.

3. Cease dependence on inspection to achieve quality. Eliminate the need for inspection on a mass basis by building quality into the product in the first place.

   Six Sigma supports mass inspection if it reduces defects per million going to the customer.

4. End the practice of awarding business on the basis of price tag. Instead minimize total cost. Move toward a single supplier for any one item, on a long-term relationship of loyalty and trust.

   Six Sigma pioneer GE has a stated goal of outsourcing 70 percent of all it does, with 70 percent of that going out of the United States. Six Sigma has oftentimes turned into a project of justifying outsourcing to the lowest bidder.

5. Improve constantly and forever the system of production and service, to improve quality and productivity, and thus constantly decrease costs.

   Six Sigma is project based. It is about continual *improvement,* not *continuous improvement (see Chapter 9). The word "constant" that Deming used is most similar to "continuous."*

6. Institute training on the job.

   Six Sigma offers training—to the elite. It's also about learning for a reward—a Belt. It does not encourage learning for the sheer joy of increasing knowledge.

7. Institute leadership. The aim of leadership should be to help people and machines and gadgets to do a better job. Leadership of management is in need of overhaul, as well as leadership of production workers.

   Six Sigma does not address leadership at all. It addresses management by objectives.

8. Drive out fear, so that everyone may work effectively for the company.

   Six Sigma encourages reaching a quota of dollars saved, number of projects completed, or number of Black Belts certified. If one does not, one is in trouble.

9. Break down barriers between departments. People in research, design, sales, and production must work as a team, to foresee problems of production and in use that may be encountered with the product or service.

   Six Sigma has created new departments of specialists. New barriers have been resurrected. A recent blog question I received was, "How do I get my industrial engineers and Black Belts to work together?" Need I say more?

10. Eliminate slogans, exhortations, and targets for the work force asking for zero defects and new levels of productivity.

    Six Sigma is a slogan. So is 3.4 defects per million opportunities.

11 a. Eliminate work standards (quotas) on the factory floor. Substitute leadership.

   b. Eliminate management by objective. Eliminate management by numbers, numerical goals. Substitute leadership.

   Six Sigma has imposed new quotas and resurrected management by objectives all over again, this time based on dollars.

12. Remove barriers that rob people of pride of workmanship.

    Green Belts and Black Belts are just new barriers that rob others of pride in workmanship. Employees can not resolve their own problems efficiently and effectively; they have to wait for a Belt to do it, with all of the fancy reports and analyses, in order for the project to "count."

13. Institute a vigorous program of education and self-improvement.

    Six Sigma only encourages getting a new belt and passing the test to get that belt, no matter how it is done. It does not encourage true education, self-improvement (unless that is measured strictly by salary and bonuses), and joy in learning.

    Two quality control (QC) personnel, working for a company that supplied menu boards for McDonalds, went through Six Sigma training, as encouraged by their customers, with other members of their company. They said, "The material was way over our heads and we felt completely stupid. It was a waste even having us there." This is a sentiment I have heard expressed by many people who have gone through Six Sigma training.

Are they getting further educated? Are they improving themselves? Or have they now lost their self-confidence?

For many people, Six Sigma training is demotivating.

14. Put everybody in the company to work to accomplish the transformation. The transformation is everybody's job.

Six Sigma only wants the Belts to make the improvements. The CEO is not necessary, the non-Belted engineers are not necessary, and the operators and line workers are not necessary to be involved in the transformation.

LEAN

Whereas the principles of Six Sigma and the principles of Dr. Deming are completely at odds with each other, the same can not be said when comparing the principles of lean to the principles of Dr. Deming.

It is understood that the principles of Dr. Deming were listened to and inhaled deeply by Toyota, affecting the very core of their management practices. From Toyota, we get the Toyota Production System and lean. The principles should be the same.

Where American companies fall flat, though, is in the execution of the lean principles. Lean practices within the United States, for the most part, do not comply with the lean principles.

On page 12 of *Out of the Crisis,* Dr. Deming wrote,

*A. V. Feigenbaum estimated that from 15 to 40 percent of the manufacturer's costs of almost any product that you buy today is from waste embedded in it—waste of **human effort,** waste of machine-time, non-productive use of accompanying burden. No wonder American products are hard to sell at home or abroad.*

*In some work that I did for a railway, study showed that mechanics in a huge repair shop spent three-quarters of their time **waiting** in line to get parts.*

The reader's own estimate of the cost of common practices in the United States, such as awarding business to the lowest bidder *and **robbing people of their right to pride of workmanship** (Points 4 and 12 in Chapter 2), would add a deplorable amount to Dr. Feigenbaum's estimate.*

*   ***Handling damage,** right in the factory, is in many places appalling, sometimes running 5 to 8 percent of the manufacturer's cost. Further loss occurs in **transit.** Then there is **shelf-wear**— further loss. Ask any grocer what his loses are from handling damage on his platform, platform to **storage** shelf, shelf-wear, mauling by curious customers.*

I've highlighted in bold all of the above words that relate to the eight commonly accepted forms of waste that are taught in any lean course.

When writing about Point #5, "Improve constantly and forever the system of production and service" in *Out of the Crisis*, Dr. Deming referred to "continual reduction of waste."

On page 53 of *Out of the Crisis,* Dr. Deming states:

The greatest waste in America is failure to use the abilities of people.

Throughout his book and throughout his life, Dr. Deming spoke of the elimination of waste. It is obvious from his writings that he helped to formulate the two pillars of the Toyota Production System:

The incessant focus on elimination of waste

The respect for and involvement of all employees

And yet, most people associate Dr. Deming with *quality,* not *lean,* as if there is a big difference. There are few lean promoters who attribute anything with regard to the lean movement to the principles and teachings of Dr. Deming.

(As I write this book and contemplate which publishers to approach, I struggle with determining if it is best to approach publishers of quality-related materials or publishers of lean-related materials. Publishers of quality-related materials will advertise this book to quality professionals in the quality world. However, it is my belief that those people in the lean world and in the databases of the lean publishers could benefit much more from a book such as this, but they may not know of Dr. Deming's name.)

Dr. Deming would ask production workers, "Why is it that productivity increases as quality improves?" Answers would include "less rework" and "not as much waste." Production workers understand this. But does top management?

Dr. Deming would write on the blackboard, while presenting to Japanese top management from 1950 onward, the following chain reaction:

Improve quality

Costs decrease because of less rework, fewer mistakes, fewer
delays, snags; better use of machine-time and materials

Productivity improves

Capture the market with better quality and lower price

Stay in business

Provide jobs and more jobs

It's the improvement of quality that greatly helps the effort to eliminate all
wastes and the drive toward single-piece flow rather than the traditional
batch and queue processes. There are many lean promoters within organizations that still do not understand this relationship.

One manufacturing company's operations manager led the lean efforts
within the organization. He provided no help to the quality department's
effort to build a quality management system and, in fact, he was an obstacle
as he purposefully and repeatedly got in the way of any progress. He was
practicing *fake lean* to drive up efficiencies while not improving quality.
Unfortunately, this is an all too common occurrence in American companies today.

This same company has two kaizen team leaders out of about 700
employees. There are no kaizen events unless they are involved.

Compare this to Toyota, where there are approximately 50 *lean change
agent specialists* out of 200,000 employees.[15]

This is the equivalent of one out of 4000 employees.

The focus is not on developing the skills of a specialist, rather it is on
developing the skills of the work team leader, of which there are tens of
thousands. The work team leader directly and dramatically affects quality,
cost, productivity, safety, and morale of the employees within the company.
This is also the focus of Training Within Industry, discussed later.

So, if the focus on developing lean specialists such as Senseis, value
stream leaders, or Lean Six Sigma Black Belts is one of the problems, what
are the other problems?

A large lean consulting and training organization insisted that their clients refer to them as Senseis. The term Sensei is a term of honor spoken by a student to a teacher as a show of respect. It is not supposed to be a term demanded by the teacher to promote his ego.

Humility is a characteristic of lean. Pride is not.

Top Ten Ways U.S. Companies Fail at Lean Implementation

1. We have not determined our *business principles.*

2. We apply tools (such as 5S, TPM) rather than define the problem, perform root cause analysis correctly, and apply solutions, which may or may not include the use of a tool.

3. We rely on specialists rather than respecting the knowledge and abilities of all the workers by getting everyone involved in the transformation.

4. We do not build a lean culture that requires management to change along with the physical lean changes.

5. We pretend to be process focused, but we are not. We are department focused. We call people value stream leaders, but they are not.

6. We would prefer to copy someone else's systems and ways rather than think and develop our own ways. Some at Toyota say that TPS really stands for Thinking Production System. Americans do not like to think; we like to take the easy way out and buy tools and consultants. We no longer believe in being self-reliant.

7. Our accounting systems are archaic and still treat inventory as an asset and hourly workers as a liability.

8. We still believe that to improve quality, we hurt efficiency, and if we improve efficiency, we hurt quality.

9. Some have lean tied in with Six Sigma, a problem-solving approach with faulty practices that do not support lean and Deming's prinicples.

10. There is waste in our continual improvement systems as we have lean people running the lean program, quality people running the quality management system, Black Belts running the Six Sigma program, and top management not really involved in any of them.

Lean Principles and Practices and Dr. Deming's Principles

The following list briefly summarizes how lean *principles* and *practices* within the United States relate to Deming's 14 Points:

1. Create constancy of purpose toward improvement of product and service, with the aim to become competitive and stay in business, and to provide jobs.

   Lean principles *support continuous improvement of products and services as well as the aim to provide jobs.*

   Lean practices *in the United States are mostly still focused on short-term bottom-line results. Lean experts are given dollar improvement quotas to drive short-term improvements.*

2. Adopt the new philosophy. We are in a new economic age. Western management must awaken to the challenge, must learn their responsibilities, and take on leadership for change.

   Lean principles *encourage building a culture that involves changing management systems, including the development of standard work for leaders, daily accountability meetings, visual controls, and true leadership and mentoring through the gemba ("go see") walk.*

   Lean practices *in the United States involve little or no management system changes.*

3. Cease dependence on inspection to achieve quality. Eliminate the need for inspection on a mass basis by building quality into the product in the first place.

   Lean principles *involve not passing on bad product to the next person. Each person becomes the inspector of the previous job, thus increasing pride in workmanship. There is no QC department performing mass inspections after huge amounts of inventory have been created. Mass inspection is a batch mentality. Lean is not.*

   Lean practices *in the United States are mixed. Inspections are done in smaller batches, but they are still being performed, oftentimes by the QC department.*

4. End the practice of awarding business on the basis of price tag. Instead, minimize total cost. Move toward a single supplier for any one item, on a long-term relationship of loyalty and trust.

Lean principles support minimizing total cost, including the cost of defects, overproduction, transportation, waiting for product, excess inventory, extra processing, and trips back and forth.

Lean practice in the United States is to continually increase the amount of offshoring, no matter what the total cost. There is no focus on developing relationships based on loyalty and cost; they are only based on price tag.

This is most appalling of all and directly contradicts Thomas Jefferson's advice of "Be flexible in style and unwavering, like a rock, in principles" and replaces the saying with:

Be flexible in principles and unwavering, like a rock, in style.

Many American companies claim to be going down the path of lean, proclaim the need to eliminate waste, and then offshore, which is riddled with waste. This is a prime example of being flexible in principles.

5. Improve constantly and forever the system of production and service, to improve quality and productivity, and thus constantly decrease costs.

Lean principles are synonymous with kaizen, *or continuous improvement, which is synonymous with improving constantly and forever.*

Lean practices in the United States are more geared toward continual *improvement.* Continual *implies recurrence at regular or frequent intervals, as in* kaizen events, *in which all involved do nothing but work on improvement activities for three to five consecutive days.*

Americans like to do batch process improvement activities to get rid of batch processing.

6. Institute training on the job.

Lean principles support on-the-job training, especially in the mentoring relationship of team leaders, supervisors, and upper management with their employees during a gemba walk.

Lean practices *in the United States do not see many team leaders, supervisors, and high-level managers truly mentoring those who work for them on a daily basis.*

7. Institute leadership. The aim of leadership should be to help people and machines and gadgets to do a better job. Leadership of management is in need of overhaul, as well as leadership of production workers.

Lean principles *support developing a lean culture that is dependent on developing leadership qualifications.*

Lean practices *in the United States have not changed the role of management. Micromanaging the process is still the role of management rather than coaching and teaching.*

8. Drive out fear, so that everyone may work effectively for the company.

Lean principles *support everyone's involvement in improvement as well as the open admission and documentation of one's own mistakes and errors for the purpose of improving the process.*

Lean practices *in the United States still encourage reaching a quota of dollars saved, Black Belts certified, and projects completed. If one does not, one is in trouble.*

9. Break down barriers between departments. People in research, design, sales, and production must work as a team, to foresee problems of production and in use that may be encountered with the product or service.

Lean principles *fully support an organization that is built for the betterment of the process and the elimination of waste that inherently occurs between departments.*

Lean practice *in the United States most often results in no organizational changes or restructuring for the betterment of the process. Departments still exist the way they used to, all-inclusive of their departmental objectives and politics, which creates more waste. Many lean efforts result in optimizing the flow within a department, sometimes to the detriment of the overall process.*

Furthermore, there are now new lean departments that have created even more new barriers.

10. Eliminate slogans, exhortations, and targets for the work force asking for zero defects and new levels of productivity.

    Lean principles *do not address this point one way or the other.*

    Lean practices *in the United States are promoted using all of the Japanese words, which act as slogans. If* kaizen *means continuous improvement, why can't we call them "continuous improvement events"? Because it does not sound as cool? No one would show up for a Continuous Improvement Event, but everyone wants to be part of a Kaizen Event! And so we use words like lean, value stream mapping, kaizen, 5S, kanban, jidoka, and muda.*

    If muda means waste, is it not muda-ful to have two words that mean the same thing?

11 a. Eliminate work standards (quotas) on the factory floor. Substitute leadership.

    b. Eliminate management by objective. Eliminate management by numbers, numerical goals. Substitute leadership.

    Lean principles *support not having production quotas for the workforce. Daily production boards are encouraged as a means not to blame employees but rather as a means of getting the team leader and supervisor involved with ensuring the availability of resources, supporting the people, and problem resolution on a real-time basis.*

    Lean practices *in the United States have resurrected new quotas and management by objectives to save thousands of dollars on kaizen events.*

12. Remove barriers that rob people of pride of workmanship.

    Lean principles *support active involvement of and respect for the people.*

    Lean practices *in the United States are somewhat successful at this when there are successful 5S (sort, set in order, shine, standardize, sustain) and TPM (total productive maintenance) efforts. The problem lies in sustaining these efforts. For the most part, all companies have a difficult time sustaining their lean 5S and/or TPM efforts because they have not worked on developing the lean culture to support them and the leader standard work that is a major part of ensuring that the efforts will be sustained.*

13. Institute a vigorous program of education and self-improvement.

    Lean principles *support this point by ensuring involvement of all people in the improvement processes as well as by the mentoring process of the gemba walk.*

    Lean practices *in the United States support only lean experts receiving additional education.*

14. Put everybody in the company to work to accomplish the transformation. The transformation is everybody's job.

    Lean principles *support active involvement of and respect for the people.*

    Lean practices *in the United States support only the lean experts who will accomplish the transformation. The CEO is not necessary, the engineers, the operators, and line workers are not necessary to be involved in the transformation.*

    The lean experts will be the heroes that the entire workforce will look up to when it comes time to do a kaizen event. Kaizen events will not or can not occur unless the expert is deeply involved. This is not true of lean and will not help a company to truly and continuously improve.

LEAN SIX SIGMA

This section addresses only the combination of lean and Six Sigma, not the individual topics, since they were addressed above.

The George Group, based in Dallas, Texas, states on its Web site, "We were the first to combine lean and Six Sigma." The George Group is a consulting and training company. From many perspectives, they have been wildly successful in merging two improvement processes to form a juggernaut of improvement tools that, one would think, would undoubtedly lead to tremendous improvement for any company that chooses to employ its services. Other consulting and training companies began to copy the combination of lean and Six Sigma, and why wouldn't they?

With the combination of two (lean and Six Sigma) boatloads of tools to consult and train people on, the billable hours would skyrocket for *their* business. Other trainers and consultants and practitioners attempted to get jobs with the George Group, including yours truly. (I made it to the final interview in Dallas and was rejected. I believe I was rejected because I said that I preferred to be a part-time subcontractor, rather than a full-time employee, but I will never know for sure though I attempted to find out why several times). Today, I am thankful that I did not subcontract my services to the George Group. Though the security of work would have been a great benefit, the real negative would have been that I would have been teaching something I had deep-rooted feelings against, but at that time the reasons for my feelings were not yet clear to me.

The main point is just this. Lean comes from Toyota. Six Sigma comes from Motorola. Lean Six Sigma comes from a consulting/training company trying to sell as many suckers out there as possible more of their services to increase billable hours and fatten their bottom line.

And many companies have fallen for it!

Lean Six Sigma—An Oxymoron

Lean and Six Sigma are based on contrary principles.

Where lean is based on *continuous improvement,* Six Sigma is based on adherence to specifications and project-based, *continual* improvement activities.

Where lean is based on the respect for and involvement of all the people, Six Sigma is based on the involvement of Belts in an elitist system that makes some people feel special and others stupid.

Where lean is simple, Six Sigma is complex.

Two systems can not cohabit within the same organization without the watering down and disintegration of one or both sets of practices. This is the biggest negative. Lean Six Sigma has withered away the values and principles behind lean and the principles of the Toyota Production System as well as the principles of Dr. Deming.

From page 135 of *The Toyota Way* (2004, McGraw-Hill), Jeffrey Liker writes:

> *Six Sigma has brought us roving bands of Black Belts who attack major quality problems with a vengeance, armed with an arsenal of sophisticated technical methods.*
>
> *At Toyota they keep things simple and use very few complex tools. The quality specialists and team members have just four key tools:*
>
> - *Go and see*
>
> - *Analyze the situation*
>
> - *Use one-piece flow and andon to surface problems*
>
> - *Ask "Why?" five times*

Six Sigma Is Anti-Lean

Once again, from *Quality Digest* magazine, in a "Last Word" article published in 2000 and entitled "The Emperor's New Woes, Revisited," an anonymous trained GE industrial engineer writes:

> *It used to be that I (a trained industrial engineer), in the normal course of my day, would observe quality or process problems and take appropriate action to analyze and correct them. I could often do this very rapidly so that we would enjoy the benefits of the changes immediately. But with the introduction of Six Sigma, such a logical system is no longer possible.*
>
> *With Six Sigma, if you don't run the gantlet of Six Sigma paperwork (charts, reviews, critiques, etc.) for every little thing, you're wasting your time. You see, now at GE, the litmus test for any employee is Six Sigma credit, a fact that I noticed while completing one of my first Six Sigma projects in order to earn my Green Belt certification.*
>
> *One part of my Six Sigma project process is enduring a conference call with a bunch of younger people who are supposed to "critique" the project. (This amounted to them telling me how I could change the fonts or add different bullets and colors to my PowerPoint presentation to make it more appealing.) I rolled my eyes, muttered, "Wow, thanks for your input," and went on.*

I have experienced this feeling, along with so many other Black Belts, that when completing a project for credit, the most important thing to do was to use as many tools and forms as possible within the Six Sigma arsenal so that those who evaluate your project will be blown away.

When, in fact, many of these tools, forms, methodologies, and analyses are completely wasteful. I can remember doing many simple designed experiments and root cause analyses that were many times more effective *and* efficient than many of today's Six Sigma projects.

Six Sigma encourages added waste in the principle-based lean approach and waters down lean's effectiveness.

Lean Six Sigma is wasteful and it is an oxymoron.

Lean Six Sigma Training—Another Oxymoron

Think about it. Who would ever say that the process of training employees and embarking on a Six Sigma program within the company is a lean effort? After all, the training usually encompasses a very long lead time and is very expensive. And yet, Lean Six Sigma is the catchphrase of the decade, and all training and consulting companies are jumping on the bandwagon, because it is the "in" thing, and so many unsuspecting clients can be booked for so many consulting/training days.

OK, so it is understood that Lean Six Sigma is really meant to be lean *and* Six Sigma and that *lean* is not an adjective for Six Sigma, but by having the two adjacent to each other, it does look very ironic and it makes one think. Well, it made me think at least . . . .

There is so much waste in Lean Six Sigma training itself. Again, anyone who has been through Lean Six Sigma Black Belt training should ask themselves, what percentage of what I learned have I used? More about this coming up soon . . . .

Is Ishikawa Turning Over in His Grave?

How soon we forget what one of the great quality gurus, Dr. Kaoru Ishikawa, taught us. He believed and tried to teach us that 90 percent of all problems can be solved through the use of the following simple tools, a.k.a "the seven tools of quality":

1. Cause-and-effect diagrams

2. Check sheets

3. Flowcharts

4. Histograms

5. Pareto diagrams

6. Run and control charts

7. Scatter diagrams

These seven tools can easily be taught to a group of practitioners in about 16 hours, or when needed. Can you imagine resolving 95% of your problems with 16 hours of training, rather than embarking on a Six Sigma training program, which typically consists of 160 hours of training over a four-month time period and costs tens of thousands of dollars? One might say, "Well, we don't want to solve only 95% of our problems, we want to solve 100% of our problems." I say, show me a company, even a company who has been doing Six Sigma for years, that has resolved 95% of their problems, and I'll eat my Black Belt, unless I've already sold it. Does one even know of a company that has resolved 50%, 40%, or 30% of their problems?

What Role Does Lean Have in Training and in Improvement Processes?

Lean is all about ridding the environment of excessive waste, including unnecessary:

1. Defects

2. Overproduction

3. Waiting

4. Not using employees' minds/skills

5. Transportation

6. Inventory

7. Motion

8. Excess processing

Without analyzing each type of waste, I ask the reader to review the level of waste in the Lean Six Sigma training received by your company.

Types of questions one might ask (notice the wasteful terms used):

1. Was there an "overproduction" of training given?

2. How much of what was learned was actually used?

3. What percent of the time spent in training was put to use?

4. How much "inventory" of quality tools do you have (stored as knowledge in your brain, in paper form in the manuals given to you in training, and in hard drive space on your computers containing the statistical software), and how much has never been used?

5. How long did you "wait" for the training to be completed? How long did you "wait" for the "processing" of initial results?

6. Is the "process" of a Black Belt analyzing the results taking too much time and is it holding up our actual improvement efforts?

7. What percent of the functions in your statistical software have been used?

8. Has the "lean department" grown?

9. How much "motion" or "transportation" was wasted in obtaining the training? (For example, travel costs of the trainer or trainees.)

10. How often have erroneous decisions (defects) been made because of an incorrect analysis?

11. How often have improvement efforts been stalled due to "analysis paralysis"?

12. If a trained person who doesn't use what was taught is considered a "defect," how many "defects" have there been in the form of Green Belts and Black Belts leaving the company after receiving their belt or never using what they learned?

13. How many people were totally confused by the training, so that it served "no value"?

14. How many "extra process" steps did you take to reach the same conclusion you would have by using a little common sense?

15. How many "people's minds and skills are not used" at all?

16. How long does it take your organization to "wait" for a Black Belt's assistance?

In general, has the process of learning Lean Six Sigma been *lean?*

Is Lean Six Sigma an oxymoron . . . and are we just morons?

Also, are the hundreds of thousands of dollars claimed to have been saved a result of instituting Lean Six Sigma or is it primarily the result of the Hawthorne effect? Are the hundreds of thousands of dollars claimed to have been saved partially influenced by the fact that the person responsible for instituting the program has a personal need to claim to have saved thousands of dollars, after spending thousands of dollars in training, and thus the results may be a little fudged?

The Hawthorne Effect or the Lean Six Sigma Effect?

When people know you're measuring something, they try to make the measurement turn out "right." When Wall Street measures corporate performance on a daily basis, many executives make decisions that favor short-term profits over the company's long-term well-being, and some actually fudge the figures.

The "Hawthorne effect" comes from early work done on organizational measurement at the Western Electric Hawthorne Works plant in Cicero, Illinois, in which the end result was that worker productivity improved with every adjustment of light level (whether up or down) because they were aware of the study. This is the same plant Dr. Deming worked at during his collegiate years.

By providing focus on a target area, improvements will result, regardless of the technique or methodology. It has happened before with quality circles, TQM, and reengineering. It's not the technique or methodology that matters most, it's the focus that matters most.

Are the thousands of dollars claimed to have been saved by embarking on a Lean Six Sigma journey due to the methodology, or were the savings going to be present regardless of the methodology because focus was provided?

What's more, the main driver behind a Lean Six Sigma initiative knows that he or she is being measured on performance and savings resulting from Lean Six Sigma efforts because of the huge investment in time and training dollars. Is the main driver behind Lean Six Sigma also ensuring that the measurements turn out "right"?

If so many companies are experiencing such great success with their Lean Six Sigma efforts, why are profits not going through the roof? Why are automotive plants and other facilities still closing down? Why does Toyota outperform the Big Three in all categories and trounce the Big Three in profits, when the Big Three has been trying to emulate the Toyota Production System, the "father of lean," for over 20 years?

Master Lean Six Sigma Black Belt Challenge

I find it interesting that, at least to my knowledge, there has not been a statistical analysis of whether the reported millions of dollars companies have saved after having embarked on a Lean Six Sigma program is *statistically significant or not*. Were these same companies not enjoying savings, via productivity gains, in the years prior to going Lean Six Sigma? Is there truly a statistically significant improvement in cost savings from improvement efforts made pre–Lean Six Sigma when compared to post–Lean Six Sigma? How does the return on investment (ROI) of a Lean Six Sigma program compare to the ROI of offshoring, new technologies, products, and processes, ISO 9001, lean (by itself), or other past continual improvement processes like TQM or reengineering?

A quick look at real GDP growth in the United States (Figure 4.1) does not seem to reveal any out-of-control points—at least not on the high side—demonstrating an unforeseen condition due to a special cause, like Lean Six Sigma, from the 1990s on . . . .

If a company were able to prove that that there was a statistically significant improvement in cost savings between two time periods, then the next challenge would have to be to determine what factors were statistically significant in contributing to this result, and of those that were determined

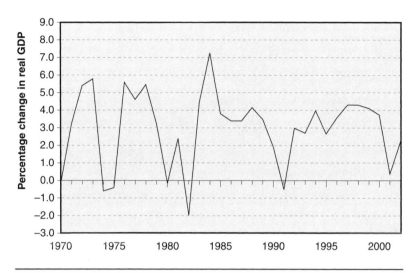

Figure 4.1 Annual percentage changes in real GDP (1970–2002).
Source: "A Case Study: Gross Domestic Product," EconEdlink, National Council of Economic Education, August 2003.

to be significant, which factors were the most significant. We assume that Lean Six Sigma is the reason for these improvements (because this is what we are told), but has it been proven?

One problem is that the Lean Six Sigma training and projects are confounded with another factor—employee empowerment of some individuals. Is it possible that the success this company experienced with statistically significant cost savings was due to empowerment—only? Or was this change due to some combination of empowerment and Lean Six Sigma? Would that company have enjoyed the same success if they had combined empowerment with a different continual improvement program (for example, Skinny Seven Sigma, re-re-engineering, ISO 9001, Appendix B of ISO 9004, or some internally developed program).

The point is that we just don't know. The truth is, the successes that a company claims that they've gained when comparing pre–Lean Six Sigma years to post–Lean Six Sigma years, if statistically significant, *may be attributed to any combination of the following factors and/or two-factor interactions:*

Lean

Empowerment

The Hawthorne effect

Six Sigma

ISO 9001

Noise factors (economy, market conditions, competitive issues)

Offshoring (as several of the Six Sigma pioneers are pursuing)

Top management personnel commitment and support

Involvement incentives

Cost consciousness and just thinking about eliminating waste

My challenge to Master Lean Six Sigma Black Belts is to perform some of the above or similar studies.

Understand Simple Root Cause Analysis First

In my line of work, I see many quality management systems. The effectiveness of any continual improvement effort, be it Six Sigma, lean, and/or an ISO 9001–based corrective/preventive action system, can be easily observed in a couple of different areas. Since the results of any continual improvement effort need to result in a control method (that is, the "C" in DMAIC), one should see changes in the quality management system. Therefore, one way to receive an indication of permanent improvements in a company's operations and processes and the success of its improvement efforts is to observe the number of revisions to the quality management system.

I have seen many companies who have been certified to an ISO 9001–based quality system for years, who have embarked on Lean Six Sigma programs, and who have not changed any or most of their procedures, systems, work instructions, or forms for years.

I challenge all employees within a company to review the change history of their quality management system to determine the effectiveness of its continual improvement efforts.

Additionally, when auditing, assessing, or just observing the results of documented corrective and preventive actions, I always review the Root Cause section first. Once again, I have seen many companies who have been certified to an ISO 9001–based quality system for years, who have embarked on a Lean Six Sigma program, and who still blame operators, engineers, designers, customer service reps, or machines for the errors, rather than the system.

Too many people within companies, including "Lean Six Sigma" companies, still do not understand how to get to the "root cause" of a problem and the simple tools (that is, five whys, cause-and-effect [Ishikawa] diagram) that could be used to determine the true root cause. The resulting documented "root cause" in these companies oftentimes is a mistake made by a person or machine or tool—not a bad system.

This formal name of this process is *root cause analysis*. Analysis is the same "A" as the one in DMAIC. If companies can not understand how to determine a simple root cause, how are they going to use the myriad of statistical tools in Lean Six Sigma? Perhaps we should consider a return to KISS (Keep it simple, stupid).

I challenge you all to review the root causes documented in your corrective and preventive action system and determine if this basic but most important concept is understood within the organization and, if not, consider a return to the basics.

When Did KISS Change from "Keep It Simple, Stupid" to "Keep It Six Sigma"?

Is it just me, or does one hear references to the phrase "Keep it simple, stupid" far less often these days than when it was a common business cliché in pre–Lean Six Sigma days?

Did the KISS pendulum swing to the other extreme of "Keep it Six Sigma," after "Keep it simple, stupid" ran its course? Are we going to return to the other extreme again one day with a new methodology and acronym, like "Business for Idiots"?

Lean Six Sigma's popularity is no different than was the popularity of *Men Are from Mars, Women Are from Venus.* They are both a repackaging of methodologies and philosophies that have existed for years, but now they sound "cool," and a number of people are making a lot of money from them—but are they needed? By the way, how many companies or processes have actually achieved 3.4 defects per million opportunities? Of those that have achieved 3.4 DPMO, how many have really achieved it and how many are victims of the Hawthorne effect?

Statistics Is Only a Quantification of Common Sense

Does one need to do a statistical analysis to determine if a baseball player with a career batting average of .333 is better than a player with an average of .250? Or does one just know this instinctively?

Does one need to perform a statistical analysis to determine if a 10-point decrease from 11,000 to 10,990 on the Dow Jones Industrial Average in one day is significant? Or if a 600-point swing in one day is due to a special cause?

Does one need to perform a statistical analysis on whether a process really improved when its before state had a standard deviation of 900 and its after-improvement state had a standard deviation of 300?

Some things are just obvious. You may have felt the same when reading the "Master Black Belt Challenge" section above and wanted to say, "Mike, come on, it's obvious, Lean Six Sigma is successful at our company. Why are you throwing this stuff in our faces?" I hope this is not your thinking; otherwise I might have to accuse you of making decisions just like top management did during the pre–Lean Six Sigma days.

I once attended four days of Minitab training and I really did enjoy it. It's a great package and can be very helpful. The training contained lots of examples, which is always a good thing. What struck me as most interesting was that in almost every example, the determination of whether or not there was a statistically significant difference, or the determination of what factor was statistically significant, was obvious prior to statistically analyzing it. Common sense gave you the answers. The software was not necessary.

In the case of a designed experiment, oftentimes the most significant factor (or two) is quite obvious, and those factors that have no effect on the result of interest are also quite obvious. It is the factors or interactions in the middle, the gray area, that we are not sure about, and they require statistics to help us determine what side of the fence they fall onto—the statistically significant side or the insignificant side.

However, the most important factors, those that are obviously and blatantly important without the use of statistics, are the ones we will concentrate on anyway to make improvements. The obviously insignificant factors are the ones in which there are no opportunities to save money since they had no effect. Since the factor is insignificant and has no effect on the result of interest, one chooses the least expensive of the factor levels experimented with. The gray factors in the middle we oftentimes do not take action on anyway, so why do we need to statistically analyze them for significance? And the obviously important and unimportant factors—why do we need to statistically analyze them if they are obvious?

Perhaps we can just use one of Ishikawa's seven tools—the Pareto chart—for a simple analysis of results, along with factor and interaction plots (which are similar to simple scatter diagrams—another Ishikawa tool), and be able to resolve 95 percent of our problems.

In fact, I'm not sure why one of the statistical software companies has not yet developed a simple statistical software package based solely on the seven tools of Ishikawa and sold at a much lower price that would be attractive to many more users.

Years ago, I taught a DOE class for a group of engineers at a high-tech medical device company. They had internally developed a very powerful design of experiments statistical software program but discovered that many designed experiments were getting bogged down by the fact that engineers were waiting for data analysis assistance from the internal statisticians. (These were the Master Black Belts of today's era.) There was a huge bottleneck in the *process improvement process* at the analysis phase, and the efficiencies that were suppose to be gained by performing a fractional factorial experiment were lost due to this bottleneck. It was my first exposure to what I now refer to as "Lean Six Sigma—An Oxymoron." As it turned out, this company hired me to teach a very low-tech, hands-on, Taguchi-based DOE class in which there was no exposure to software and all of the calculations were done by hand. This was done to transform control of the experiment from the statistician back into the hands of the experimenter in order to gain efficiency and become more lean.

Taguchi, Ishikawa, and Deming promoted and believed in putting the experiment into the hands of the people closest to the process.

So, if statistics is truly just a quantification of common sense, why do we feel the need to rely on it so much? Is it because we, as a society, lack "common sense," because perhaps we are so influenced by other factors (that is, politics, winning, making ourselves look good) that we do not know how to employ "common sense."

Do we rely on Lean Six Sigma because it makes up for our "common sense" shortcomings? Is common sense common? If it is, do we just not know how to deploy our common sense?

LEAN AND GREEN

In 1990 Jim Womack and colleagues had published *The Machine That Changed the World* as a description of the Toyota Production System, and coined the term *lean*.

The term "lean and green" did not come into prominence until the mid '00s. Why was there such a long delay?

This delay is probably best told through a story.

Back in 1987, as a Saturn employee, I headed a small group of Saturn employees to visit the NUMMI plant in California. NUMMI was the

GM–Toyota joint venture plant that GM'ers could have used much more to their advantage by learning the Toyota Production System firsthand.

As we were walking down the assembly line, I noticed the overhead fluorescent light fixtures running down the middle of the assembly line. On one side was a lighted bulb and on the other side was reflective aluminum foil. I had asked our guide why that was and he stated that it was an employee's idea to reduce energy consumption and save money.

Toyota is principle based. Many American companies are tool based. If the principle by which a company lives is the constant focus on eliminating waste, then that would mean that all waste, including the waste of resources, would be targeted for reduction. It makes perfect sense that the Toyota plant and its people would have looked for ways to reduce energy consumption.

But why hasn't *not wasting natural resources* been natural for American companies going through the lean process, and why does a newer term like "lean and green" need to be invented for us to focus on getting greener? The answer is simple and it's been the theme behind this entire book. American companies did not buy into the entire principle of eliminating waste. American companies bought into the elimination of *process* waste, not all wastes, because Americans were taught about value stream mapping, kaizen, 5S, and TPM, which are all tools focused on the elimination of process waste.

If American companies had bought into the principle of elimination of waste, of *all* waste, they would have naturally focused on the elimination of natural resource waste instead of inventing a new term called "lean and green." We can expect that more and more consultants/trainers will be coming out with new cutesy terms specific to other forms of waste removal, such as:

Lean and mean (the elimination of office politics)

Lean and beans (the elimination of fatty foods in the cafeteria)

Lean and clean (the elimination of filthy language in the office)

Lean and blue jean (the elimination of waste from not dressing properly)

Lean and queen (the elimination of playing solitaire on one's computer)

Lean and Charlie Sheen (the elimination of following the escapades of stars at work)

Lean and excessive e-mail elimination (sorry, no rhyming word)

Lean and lean (the elimination of waste in the lean process)

LEAN ACCOUNTING

Another new term has surfaced that, had American companies embraced the principles of Dr. Deming and lean, would probably not have been necessary.

In Chapter 3 of *Out of the Crisis,* Dr. Deming lists the *diseases* and *obstacles* to transforming the Western style of management, including:

> *Disease #5: Running a company on visible figures alone (counting the money)*

Dr. Deming wrote:

> *But he that would run his company on visible figures alone will in time have neither company nor figures.*
>
> *Actually the most important figures that one needs from management are unknown or unknowable (Lloyd S. Nelson, p. 20), but successful management must nevertheless take account of them: Examples:*
>
> 1. *The multiplying effect on sales that comes from a happy customer, and the opposite effect from an unhappy customer.*
>
> 2. *The boost in quality and productivity all along the line that comes from success in improvement of quality at any station upstream.*
>
> 3. *Improvement of quality and productivity where the management makes it clear that the policy of the company will henceforth be to stay in business suited to market; that this policy is unshakable, regardless of who comes and goes.*
>
> 4. *Improvement of quality and productivity from continual improvement of processes; also from the elimination of work standards, and from better training or better supervision.*
>
> 5. *Improvement of quality and productivity from a team composed of the chosen supplier, the buyer, engineering designs, sales, customer, working on a new component or redesign of an existing component.*

6. *Improvement of quality and productivity from teamwork between engineers, production, sales, and the customer.*

7. *Loss from the annual rating on performance.*

8. *Loss from inhibitors to pride of workmanship of employees.*

Furthermore, Dr. Deming wrote:

> *He that expects to quantify in dollars the gains that will accrue to a company year by year for a program of improvement of quality by principles expounded in this book will suffer delusion. He should know before he starts that he will be able to quantify only a trivial part of the gain.*

So then I wonder, especially given the above paragraph, is lean accounting even needed, or is it once again just putting a band-aid on an old wound? Lean accounting is defined on Wikipedia.org, as:

> *Accounting for the lean enterprise. It seeks to move from traditional cost accounting to a system that measures and motivates good business practices in the lean enterprise.*

Does Toyota use lean accounting? No, it doesn't have to because it operates under a different set of principles. By modifying our cost accounting practices to be more supportive of lean enterprise, we are compromising our lean practices because lean practices are not based on making decisions based on financial targets.

As H. Thomas Johnson, professor of business administration at Portland State University wrote in his December 2007 article titled "Management by Financial Targets Isn't Lean" and subtitled, "American Industry Must Erase Lean Accounting Before It Destroys Lean Management" (*Manufacturing Engineering*):

> This is what W. Edwards Deming meant *when he said many years ago that managers should not use financial targets to control long-run financial results. Instead, they should manage the system of relationships that produces those results. In other words, "the means are the ends in the making." Long-term financial results (the ends) can be no better than the system of relationships (the means) that is designed to produce them. Managers who strive to improve financial results by encouraging people to chase financial targets will invariably achieve poorer results than those who help the organization improve the system of relationships that generates the results. Deming's warning about targets remains unheeded to this day.*

As a small business owner, I have an accountant who comes to my house every quarter and produces income statements, profit and loss statements, and balance sheets. I never review this data. The only data I look at is cash flow, and this is how my small business decisions are made. As a homeowner, you too could look at income statements and balance sheets, but you most probably don't. You are probably making most of your decisions based on cash flow into and out of your household.

You might think "so what, we are nothing when compared to the large companies of this world . . . ."

On page 184 of *Rebirth of American Industry*, Waddell and Bodek (2005, PCS Press) wrote:

> *Taichi Ohno said in language that cannot possibly be any plainer, "All we are doing is looking at the time line, from the moment the customer gives us the order to the point when we collect the cash. Are we reducing the timeline by reducing the non-value-adding waste?" Ford said the same thing, that the only number that really mattered was the change in the bank balance from one week to the next. He was getting at the same point when he said that "Profit is the inevitable conclusion of work well done." To the man who believed that manufacturing is a function of quality, flow, and synchronization, "work well done" meant following along Ohno's time line at a pretty good clip.*

They also wrote:

> *Perhaps Americans are so focused on the dollars and cents of business, so intent on being "bottom line" managers, that it is impossible for them to give much weight to any number without a "$" in front of it. However, Ford and Toyota did discover the magic bullet to controlling manufacturing—cycle time. This apparently nonfinancial number is actually the key number they used to drive just about all of their financial numbers in the right direction.*

If cycle time is the key number to drive all decisions, then why is lean accounting even necessary? Is it to appease our current short-term focused cost accounting systems without asking business leaders to really change? I think so.

Is lean accounting allowing us to take our focus off of managing relationships and redirecting our focus to managing toward financial targets and ignoring Deming's principles once again? I think so.

I remind the reader of the story in Chapter 3, Point #14, in which I describe the ROI justification process I was put through to justify getting rid of subassembly machines and incorporating their operations right into the main assembly machine of aerosol valves, eliminating inventory, required storage space, part numbers, more scheduling, defects, transportation, waiting, and so on. I always felt that my very intelligent boss always knew that it made sense to make the changes I was making for the good of the process and the company, but he was trying to get me accustomed to working in the real world of financial justification and measuring financial results by chasing financial targets. In other words, my boss was doing exactly what all of the proponents of lean accounting are doing—trying to allow for lean to occur within the current confines and assumptions of Western management practices rather than *radically transforming* Western management thinking and practices as Dr. Deming and now I are encouraging.

ISO 9001 (AND ISO/TS 16949, ISO 13485, AS 9100, TL 9000)

Dr. Deming wrote on page 39 of *Out of the Crisis:*

> *How does a supplier qualify? Almost every company has a manual by which to "qualify" vendors. Military Standard 9858A (the predecessor to ISO 9001) is an example. Teams of unqualified examiners visit suppliers to rate them.*

Clearly, Dr. Deming did not care for the idea of unqualified third-party auditors examining and rating a facility's operations. Why? Because:

1. Who knows better of the actual or potential problems and defects that result from a supplier's processes than the customer himself?

2. Who knows the customer's requirements and critical characteristics better than the customer?

3. By having a third party audit a supplier's processes, the customer is outsourcing a relationship. There is a missed opportunity to further build a long-term supplier relationship based on loyalty and trust. There is a missed opportunity to resolve problems together. There is a missed opportunity to communicate and get to know each other.

4. A third party (that is, a registrar) is more concerned about maintaining the business of its clients (that is, your supplier) than the true improvement of its client's processes. To maintain the business of its clients (your suppliers), the third party realizes that it must meet the unspoken demands of its clients (your supplier),

which are oftentimes determined to be a piece of paper on the wall and as few nonconformities as possible.

When referring to what Dr. Deming's viewpoint on ISO 9001 would be, the issue needs to be broken into two parts—the ISO 9001 standard itself and the registration process.

What Might Dr. Deming Think of ISO 9001?

Dr. Deming would likely not have a problem with the principles upon which ISO 9001 is based:

1. Customer focus

2. Leadership

3. Involvement of people

4. Process approach

5. System approach to management

6. Continual improvement

7. Factual approach to decision making

8. Mutually beneficial supplier relationships

Who can argue with these principles? They are sound. However, in some cases there is no meat to them. A principle-by-principle analysis of ISO 9001 and the degree to which they are aligned with Dr. Deming's principles is given below.

Principle 1: Customer Focus

The ISO standard covers this principle fairly well in clauses 5.2 Customer focus, 7.2 Customer related processes, and 8.2.1 Customer satisfaction, of ISO 9001.

Dr. Deming would not have a problem with this—at least not for the present day. In other words, Dr. Deming talked of how quality should be the aim for the consumer, both present and future. What's lacking, though, is that ISO 9001 is restricted to the present day and doesn't consider the needs of the future customer.

When defining Point #1, *Create constancy of purpose toward improvement of product and service,* Dr. Deming states on page 25 of *Out of the Crisis*:

Problems of the future command first and foremost constancy of purpose and dedication to improvement of competitive position to keep the company alive and to provide jobs for their employees.

Innovation, the foundation of the future, can not thrive unless the top management have declared unshakable commitment to quality and productivity.

ISO 9001 would fall short in focusing in on the customer of the future. It only addresses customer requirements and customer satisfaction of the present-day customer.

Principle 2: Leadership

Dr. Deming stressed the need for leadership in Point #7, *Institute leadership*, as well as Point #2, *. . . take on leadership for change* and Point #11, *Substitute leadership.*

Though ISO 9001 claims leadership to be one of the principles upon which it is based, there is absolutely no evidence that it is part of the standard. Section 5 of ISO 9001 is entitled "Management responsibility." This has nothing to do with leadership as is evidenced by the lack of leadership driving continuous improvement and reduction in variation at ISO 9001–certified companies.

Leadership qualifications and actions are nonexistent in ISO 9001. A micromanager, the opposite of a leader, would be looked upon just as favorably, if not more favorably, by a registrar auditor.

Principle 3: Involvement of People

Dr. Deming would of course be a strong supporter of involving people as is evidenced by Point #6, *Institute training on the job,* Point #8, *Drive out fear,* Point #12, *Remove barriers that rob people of pride in workmanship,* Point #13, *Institute a vigorous program of education and self-improvement,* and Point #14, *The transformation is everyone's job.*

ISO 9001 falls far short in encouraging involvement of the people. Clause 5.5.3 of ISO 9001 requires "Internal communication" so that the people know how well the company is performing. Clause 6.2.2 of ISO 9001 requires that employees receive the necessary training, and so on, to ensure that they are competent to do their jobs, and it requires that "personnel are aware of the relevance and importance of their activities and how they contribute to the achievement of quality objectives."

Nowhere does ISO 9001 require the active involvement of employees to improve the processes of which they are a part. Though the standard claims involvement of people as a core principle in ISO 9001, there is no meat to this claim.

Principle 4: Process Approach

Again, Dr. Deming would have been a big fan of this principle as evidenced in Point #9, *Break down the barriers between departments.*

Clause 0.2 of ISO 9001 provides a great definition of the process approach in stating:

> *For an organization to function effectively and efficiently, it has to identify and manage numerous linked activities. An activity, using resources, and managed in order to enable the transformation of inputs into outputs, is considered as a process. Often, the output of one process directly forms the input to the next.*

This is true and Dr. Deming would have most likely agreed with this definition and the accompanying diagram within the ISO 9001 standard, shown in Figure 4.2.

Dr. Deming would have liked the model and its consistency with the Shewhart cycle, as he referred to it, or the Deming cycle, as so many others refer to it.

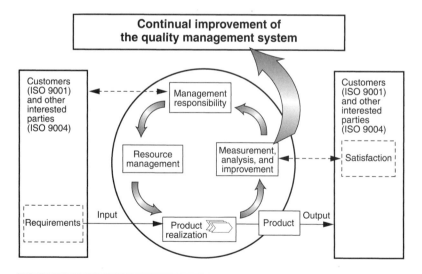

Figure 4.2 Model of a process-based quality management system from ISO 9001.

ISO 9001 does go further to support the process approach principle in 4.1 General requirements, 4.2.2 Quality manual, and 8.2.3 Monitoring and measurement of processes. The standard does attempt to address a process-oriented approach.

The problem lies in the fact that many ISO 9001–certified companies really are not process oriented, despite what their pretty flowcharts demonstrate, but rather they are still department oriented, with departmental objectives, and experience just as much infighting and politics as before ISO 9001 certification.

It is seriously doubtful that many companies would claim that ISO 9001 has minimized the politics within their company.

Deming would have been disappointed with the implementation of process orientation within companies, but not the standard's attempt to get companies to be more process oriented.

Principle 5: System Approach to Management

This principle is very much related to Principle 4 of ISO 9001, just at a higher level. It addresses the identification and management of interrelated processes as a system and how it contributes to the organization's effectiveness and efficiency in achieving its objectives. Therefore, the same comments made above in Principle 4 relate to this principle as well.

Principle 6: Continual Improvement

Dr. Deming would most probably state that *continual* improvement does not go far enough. Deming's Point #5, *Improve constantly and forever,* is more synonymous with *continuous* improvement and the true interpretation of kaizen as used in the Toyota Production System. True kaizen is not project oriented, as would be a Six Sigma project, a five-day kaizen event, or a corrective/preventive action performed whenever there is a periodic customer complaint or internal audit finding. True kaizen is about *constant* or *continuous* improvement—small improvements, made every single day, by everybody.

Clause 8.5.1 of ISO 9001 is entitled "Continual improvement" and it lists the many different sources from which continual improvement projects can be initiated, but it does not require that they be continuous, every day, with the involvement of all employees. (Annex B of ISO 9004 does a good job of defining "small-step or on-going process improvement," but then this is not part of ISO 9001 and, therefore, not a requirement and, therefore, does not get read.)

Principle 7: Factual Approach to Decision-Making

Section 8.4 "Analysis of data" of ISO 9001 states that an organization shall, "determine, collect and analyze appropriate data . . . . to evaluate where continual improvement of the effectiveness of the quality management system can be made." This is good.

In support of his 5th Point, "Improve constantly and forever the system of production and service, to improve quality and productivity, and thus constantly decrease costs," Dr. Deming believed that statistical thinking is critical to improvement of a system. Only by use of properly interpreted data can intelligent decisions be made. But to depend only on the use of statistics is a sure way to go out of business. This is where Six Sigma fails.

Dr. Deming might have actually been pleasantly surprised and happy about this requirement, but not necessarily the compliance with the requirement!

Principle 8: Mutually Beneficial Supplier Relationships

This principle is in full support of Deming's 4th Point, "End the practice of awarding business on the basis of price tag. Instead minimize total cost. Move toward a single supplier for any one item, on a long-term relationship of loyalty and trust."

Dr. Deming would have been happy if this principle were supported within the text of the ISO 9001 standard. This principle is very similar to principle #2, Leadership, of ISO 9001 in that the principle itself is so much aligned with Deming's principle . . . but there is no meat or substance within ISO 9001 itself. There is nothing in ISO 9001 that supports this principle at all, not even in 7.4, Purchasing. Companies continue to treat many suppliers as suppliers of commodities. A relationship based on loyalty and trust is not even a thought.

And we wonder why ISO 9001 companies continue to offshore, outsource, and make purchasing decisions based on price tag alone? The standard does nothing to discourage this behavior in spite of the 8th principle it claims to be based on.

So Who Is Responsible for Improving the Effectiveness of the Registration System?

The registration system is broken, people, and no one is fixing it!! The grand experiment is not working!

In theory, the third-party audit system was supposed to allow for completely objective audits performed by a company outside of the normal supply chain of conducting business. Ideally, a registrar could provide a completely unbiased audit to an ISO standard and not care whether the audited organization is happy with the results (for example, a rejected certification, placing a company on "probation") or not, because the audited company represents such a small amount of business to that registrar that the auditors can be completely objective.

Well, it's not working, as documented by these respondents to my Fall 2004 article published in *Quality Management Forum* entitled, "Easy Audits—the Downfall of ISO 9001:2000":

> *Our registrar doesn't give us the value I desire to get from them: the incentive to improve. The rest of my management group thinks we are so good because after every audit there are just some minor obscure things to fix. The problem I see with the registrar we use (and some of it for sure is the competency of the auditor) is that they really don't look at the bigger picture and actually determine if the processes we are following are actually meeting the intent of the standard and causing the company to improve.*
>
> —Alan E. Schneidewent,
> Corporate Quality Director

> *A group that conducts assessments of suppliers recently visited a new supplier who was asking to be qualified to supply on contracts. Their assessment was that the company had made an enthusiastic beginning, and with sustained effort should be ISO 9001:2000–compliant within a year. Two weeks later they received a successful ISO 9001:2000 registration audit. When I questioned the lead auditor who said that, "they've made a good start and we wanted to encourage them to continue," he fully admitted that they were not fully compliant and begged me not to make a fuss. Too late— the customer is already making a fuss!*
>
> *I've had several clients who have dropped their certification because they see no value and a lot of aggravation from their registrar auditors.*
>
> —David Jenkins

I received many more responses of a similar nature, from all over the world.

So who will take action? Will ANAB (ANSI–ASQ National Accreditation Board), who receives payments from the registrars to conduct said audits, or the IAF (International Accreditation Forum, www.iaf.nu), of which it is a member? In this there is a conflict of interest.

Will the companies who receive certifications, many of whom care only about the receipt and maintenance of said certificate?

Will the registrars, who are mostly concerned with obtaining surveillance audit business from other registrars and who appear to be primarily concerned with short-term profits rather than meeting the needs of their true customer—the ISO 9001 standard?

Who will step up to take action before the demise of ISO 9001? At this point, it is in no one's best interest to take real action, with the exception of those who truly believe and live by the spirit of ISO 9001, those who follow Deming's principles, and those who truly believe that quality of product or service is more important than short-term profit.

In my own experience, I have made the following observations, in *five different certified* companies. There are many more putrid examples of *certified* organizations that should not be certified:

1. Two internal audit findings and no preventive actions in five years

2. No registrar surveillance audits for 10 years

3. 110 open corrective actions; two closed during the last year

4. No proof of root cause determination (it's not on their corrective action form), no internal audits, no management review for two years

5. An obvious design-responsible company that claimed an exclusion to 7.3 Design and development, and has been allowed to do so for three-plus years

Are these not major nonconformities? Should these companies not be decertified or, at least, be placed on "probation"?

Two Separate Entities: ISO 9001 and the Registration System

ISO 9001: *pretty good!* Registration system: *bad!*

These are two separate entities, which unfortunately are perceived by many to be one and the same. Because it is so easy to maintain an ISO 9001 certificate, and therefore not driving real change to affect the bottom line, many people may think that ISO 9001 does not work. It's not the standard that does not work. It is the registration system that does not work because it no longer drives improvements.

This linkage is an unfortunate calamity because if top management chooses to live by the principles and spirit of ISO 9001 (as further defined in ISO 9004), they will find that it is a great foundation and structure with which to truly improve business operations and the bottom line.

So what is the root cause of an ineffective registration system? Let's use the five whys to find out:

1. The registration system is ineffective because the registrars perceive that what the client really wants is a certificate and as few nonconformities as possible, so the auditors provide easy audits. *Why?*

2. Registrar auditors perform easy audits because they are directed to do so by their top management. *Why?*

3. Registrar top management directs auditors to perform easy audits in order to maintain whatever business they can and to cease further erosion of the registration business due to clients jumping ship to the easiest registrar. *Why?*

Examples:

> *I have worked as a contract lead ISO 14001 auditor for two different registrars. One of the two registrars instructed me to spend most of my time on the paper system and got upset when I found too many issues out in the plant (I have stopped working for them). They actually certified a plant that had three major nonconformances, sending another auditor when I refused to pass them in time for the plant to meet an auto industry deadline.*
>
> —Randy Roig

> *I also have had lead assessors tell me they have to be easy on the customers to avoid criticism from their management.*
>
> —Frits Verdonk

From here, there are two paths in which we can proceed (a and b)

4. a. Registrars perform easy audits because they *can* do whatever they want because the checks and balances system is ineffective and there is currently no effective manner of evaluating the *effectiveness* of the audits that they provide. *Why?*

5. a. It is not in anyone's best interest to challenge the system—in the short term. The overall system is truly not built upon the principles of a long-term focus, process focus, and system focus.

4. b. Top management of registrars tells the auditors to provide easy audits because their focus is on meeting short-term results at the expense of a watered down registration system that will have no viability in the long-term. *Why?*

5. b. Long-term focus is not one of the principles of the registrar.

As we all know, when performing root cause analysis there can be many branches or paths to go down. Starting from the same point, another path could be:

1. The registration system is ineffective because the registrars perceive that what the client wants is a certificate and as few nonconformities as possible, so the registrars give the client what it wants. *Why?*

2. Registrars perceive this because the client does not tell them what they want from the audit—they just sign the registrar's contract. Clients do not follow 7.4 (Purchasing) of ISO 9001 for purchasing of registration services, so registrars follow 7.2.1.b and determine "requirements not stated by the customer . . ." *Why?*

3. Clients do not follow 7.4 because they do not want to put in writing that they only want a certificate and they are only doing it to maintain or gain business. *Why?*

4. Client top management does not believe in or does not understand continual improvement. *Why?*

5. Client top management does not understand that increased quality leads to decreased costs and more profits in the long run. They do not understand the spirit of ISO 9001. They do not understand the Deming cycle, which states that improved quality leads to increased productivity, which leads to decreased costs. Continuous improvement is not a principle of the company.

The root causes of all three paths relate back to a lack of principles in the overall system. This is exactly the reason why so many other companies fail in their improvement endeavors—the endeavors are tool based, not principle based.

The Leggett & Platt Story

(Contributions made by Steven W. Willis, staff VP quality systems, Leggett & Platt, Inc.)

Leggett & Platt (L&P) *has* done something about the lack of value they were receiving from initial and surveillance audits conducted by certain registrars.

L&P, a Fortune 500 company, has just over 300 sites worldwide and at one point had 69 sites certified to an ISO 9001–based quality system. L&P had contracts with 20 different registrars and they were unhappy with the value and variation they were receiving, so L&P decided to take two major actions:

1. Sites *not* mandated to be ISO 9001 certified by a customer would not employ the services of an outside registrar. L&P would develop an internal certification process at the corporate level (ensuring auditor objectivity by not allowing certification audits to be performed by site employees). If these sites passed the audit, they would be termed *LP 9000 certified.*

2. The remaining sites would be certified by one registrar who would receive the business only after L&P performed an in-depth selection and evaluation process of the current registrars.

The short-term results:

1. 77 sites have been certified to LP 9000, with an additional 30 targeted in the next two years (as of 2007).

2. Significant savings per annum by choosing one supplier of registration services.

3. Because of the leverage they now possess with the remaining registrar, they have met with the top management of the registrar and better defined L&P's expectations for audits: more value-added time spent auditing and more identified corrective and preventive actions. Finding a good registrar and establishing expectations is key to getting the value out of third-party certification for the 69 ISO-certified locations and future sites.

The long-term results:

1. At some point in the future, L&P will perform an evaluation and comparison of effectiveness between ISO 9001 and LP 9000.

What Can Smaller Companies Do?

Leggett & Platt is a large company and they can afford to take the above actions because of the number of sites they have. What can smaller companies do?

1. Top management needs to obtain training regarding the principles and spirit of ISO 9001 and how it can and should be used as a *business* management system, not just a quality management system, and they need to see how an effective QMS will affect profits.

2. Top management must dissect the principles behind ISO 9001 and build a robust quality system around those principles rather than just look for minimal compliance. They should integrate and combine ISO 9001 principles with Deming's principles and then build a culture and internal practices to support these overall principles.

3. The management representative should define the company's requirements and expectations of the registrar on the purchase order or other document, including what deliverables it wants from the audit and in what format (including perhaps the use of your internal forms).

4. The company should evaluate the performance of the auditor and the registrar based on defined criteria and provide that information to them as a means of improvement. The registrar is, after all, the company's supplier!!

5. The company should issue corrective actions to the registrar when the registrar does not meet the company's requirements, and preventive actions when its performance is ineffective and could lead to a potential issue.

6. The company should follow Leggett & Platt's lead, if possible, depending on customer requirements and the size of the company. Even if a customer(s) requires ISO 9001 certification, maybe a better plan can be pursued?!

7. Top management must also learn that if their company is involved with lean or Six Sigma, these need to be fully integrated into a company's ISO 9001–based business management system (BMS), as a subset of the BMS, in order to be truly effective.

8. The company should still assess supplier's facilities and not depend on a registrar auditor's assessment so as to strengthen the relationship and work on problems together.

What Should Quality Purists Do?

1. Set up a meeting with an ASQ Section, an association, industry group, or a panel of ISO 9001–certified companies to study, discuss, and determine the effectiveness of the ISO 9001 registration business with the goal of developing suggestions to ensure that the integrity of the ISO 9001 principles are upheld and that the ISO God is happy.

2. Complain directly to ANAB by logging on to www.anab.org and clicking on "Complaints."

3. Develop suggestions for radical change to the system and present them to ANAB, including elimination of the current registration system, as it stands today, and the development of one organization to perform said audits with the same fee structure for all companies. Learn from the weaknesses and strengths of the FDA.

4. Speak up, present papers, write articles, complain to ANAB and/or IAF, complain to your registrar, develop other internal options for auditing or certifying companies to ISO 9001!!

Dr. Deming would have approved of the principles upon which the standard is said to be based; he would not have approved of how the standard ensures adherence to these principles, and he definitely would have not have approved of the registration system.

ISO 9001:2008 and ISO 9004:2009

In 2008, ISO 9001:2008 was released. It contained very minor revisions and clarifications. A golden opportunity was missed at truly "continually improving the effectiveness" of the ISO 9001 standard.

Instead, TC 176, the writers of the quality system standards, focused on improving ISO 9004, a guidance standard that virtually no users really know anything about. There is no more incentive for users to refer to ISO 9004 than there was before. Countless hours were spent improving a product that has no market. Somebody should have done root cause analysis on why virtually no one reads ISO 9004, but instead the decision to improve it was made. This is no different than your company haphazardly changing the design of a product or service without knowing the root cause of the problems. The writers of the quality standards themselves do not practice what they write.

Meanwhile, no real drastic improvements were made to the registration system. Then again, there is no reason to or incentive to in the short term. There is no constancy of purpose for maintaining the business of ISO 9001.

OFFSHORING

Perhaps one of the biggest movements today is that of *offshoring,* defined as the relocation by a company of a business process from one country to another, and the United States is doing this at enormous levels, much more than ever before. In *Out of the Crisis,* Dr. Deming gave us Point #4:

> *End the practice of awarding business on the basis of price tag. Instead minimize total cost. Move toward a single supplier for any one item, on a long-term relationship of loyalty and trust.*

And yet just a couple of decades later we are making many more unwise purchasing decisions based on price tag alone, due to such events as:

> The passage of the North American Free Trade Agreement (NAFTA)

> China's entry into the World Trade Organization (WTO) in 2001

> India's technical progress in telecommunications

(but primarily due to)

> Corporate short-term greed!

> Shortsightedness and unwise decisions!

Before offshoring really took hold in the United States, stupid purchasing decisions were being made almost cyclically. The pattern of developing supplier relationships followed by aggressive cost-cutting, only to repeat, was probably never better played out than at General Motors from the late '80s (the Deming influence) to the early '90s (the Ignacio Lopez influence).

GM, Saturn, and Purchasing Chief Ignacio Lopez

When I worked for the Saturn Corporation of General Motors between the years of 1985 and 1988, there was a great deal of focus on developing and nurturing supplier relationships. When we chose a supplier, even an equipment supplier, we went through an exhaustive analysis of the strengths and weaknesses of the potential supplier base and determined how well each supplier matched up to our needs and our defined criteria. As mentioned previously, I was in charge of the design and procurement of the majority of fluid fill equipment in the General Assembly operations of Saturn. The fluid fill equipment consisted of the different pieces of equipment that would fill each vehicle with Freon, power steering fluid, engine coolant, gasoline, windshield wiper, transmission, and brake fluids.

There were three main suppliers to choose from. We chose the supplier based on how well they met our needs of partnerability, ease of working with, technical capabilities, and a number of other factors, only one of which was initial cost.

The Deming influence was definitely apparent at Saturn, perhaps due to Saturn's leadership consisting of many former Pontiac Motor Division managers who were, at the time, highly influenced by Dr. Deming's one-on-one consultation. However, it seemed that the Deming influence of not making purchasing decisions based on price tag alone was also spreading throughout General Motors, as there was greater and greater focus on developing and promoting strong customer–supplier relationships.

Any relationships that were built during those years and thereafter came to a crashing halt in 1992–1993, when Ignacio Lopez was GM's purchasing chief and gained a reputation of aggressive cost-cutting and an antagonistic attitude toward suppliers. Depending on one's point of view, Lopez was either a hero, saving $4 billion in short-term cash, or a devil. He was a hero to top management, shareholders, and Wall Street, because all they cared about was the short term, which suited Lopez's tenure perfectly, as he left GM tumultuously after just one year of destruction. To the suppliers and to the eventual customers, Lopez was the devil. Long-term partnerships and relationships, which had taken years to develop and were still developing, were thrown out the window as Lopez mandated that every part was subject to be sourced to the lowest bidder, regardless of quality.

Relationships suffered tremendously, and quality levels dropped. It takes years to build a community and a neighborhood, but a tornado can destroy all of that in seconds. Lopez was the tornado; he came, he destroyed, and he left, eventually hurting GM's reputation even more in the marketplace.

This is one more example of a company that is not based on principles. Lopez got out before the ramifications of his tactics were felt. One might say that, in his own very selfish and greedy way, Lopez was smart, and GM leadership was stupid for hiring Lopez and paying for his stupid decisions in the long run. GM leadership hired a man who had no principles. GM got what they deserved. A man with no principles will always be a man with no principles. Lopez left GM after one year with a briefcase full of GM trade secrets and a pending costly lawsuit with GM.

A company that does not learn from its past mistakes will make them once again.

GM's quality hurt for years after Lopez left the company. Yet, here we are again, offshoring in record numbers as we seek the lowest bidder, regardless of quality. History repeats itself as Ignacio Lopez has reincarnated himself in the form of American purchasing czars across the country.

Offshoring Is Full of the Eight Wastes

Thomas Jefferson, once again, said,

Be flexible in style, and unwavering, like a rock, in principles.

Oftentimes, Americans are just the opposite and practice

Be flexible in principles, and unwavering, like a rock, in style.

In other words, many companies stick with their Six Sigma and lean methodologies through thick and thin. These methodologies are their styles, and the leaders are unwavering, like a rock, in supporting them.

However, with regard to the principle of *constant focus on the elimination of waste*, a core lean principle, many organizations are *flexible* in standing by this principle, as they are the same organizations who practice lean *and* offshoring. Offshoring is riddled with waste. A quick examination of the how the eight wastes are increased and supported by offshoring follows:

Defects. The possibility of so many more defects exists for a couple of reasons: 1) Different quality standards exist in different countries. As we have seen in recent years, there have been numerous examples of large batches of defective product, including toys with lead-based paints, contaminated dog food, contaminated fish products, and help desks where you can not understand the person you are speaking with. 2) Because of the great distance between supplier and customer, oftentimes the customer has no choice but to receive defective products and find a way to sort through them or rework them because otherwise it would take too long to make and ship new product. The final product is compromised.

All too often, organizations have to accept defective products because they've given up the leverage they may have once had in the past by paying for the product as it leaves port in China or India.

Overproduction. Product is made far in advance of when it is needed because of the great distance between the two countries. This leads to possible obsolescence and loss of material flexibility, in turn increasing reliance on the wasteful and inaccurate "band-aid" process of forecasting.

Waiting. There is, of course, waiting for the product to be delivered. But there also is waiting for answers, waiting for quotes, waiting for translations of verbal or written communication, waiting for approvals, waiting for employees sent overseas to work on quality issues, sourcing issues, or governmental issues, and the long wait for—if they are ever to be delivered—good root cause analyses and corrective actions.

Not Using the Minds and Skills of the Employees. Bill Waddell and Norm Bodek stated, in their book entitled *Rebirth of American Industry*:

> *Outsourcing is not lean manufacturing. It is quitting.*

Dr. Deming said on page 53 of *Out of the Crisis:*

> *The greatest waste in America is failure to use the abilities of people.*

American skills and minds are not used when a company decides that it can not compete. If employees were told that the likelihood of product being offshored was imminent unless wastes and costs were taken out of the current process, while improving quality levels, and these same employees were given the training and the culture that would allow them to make changes, I am sure that the necessity to offshore would be much less than what it is.

At least the American employees would be given the opportunity to go down with a fight, by allowing them to use their minds and skills, rather than having the decision makers quit on them.

Once product is offshored, the ability to use the minds and skills of those doing the work in a different country is tremendously diminished. In fact, in many cases, American companies do not even know of the facility in which their once internally manufactured product is being made, much less the people, as brokers shop for the lowest prices within their countries.

A relationship based on loyalty and trust is nearly impossible unless many, many more dollars are spent developing this relationship to counter the opposing forces of different cultures, different values and principles, and different languages. But then that would cut the savings, and since it is not necessary in the short term, "why do it" is the prevailing thought process.

Transportation. This is obvious with the massive amounts of product being shipped daily over the turbulent seas. But, what may not be as obvious is the fact that there is even more transportation that is added as brokers in China and India go even further inland to find cheaper prices as wages increase by 15 percent a year near the largest cities near the coast.

We must also not forgot the additional transportation and movement of product (and the accompanying possibilities of more damaged or lost product) once the product is received in the United States, moved around on docks, moved through customs, in and out of various warehouses, and finally transported to its final destination.

We also must not forget the excessive transportation costs of the many employees taking month-long trips to China and India to work on problems.

Inventory. Of course, the necessity to increase inventory exists because of the long lead times in waiting for product to be delivered. There's also the necessity to keep extra inventory in case there are unforeseen issues in dealing with another country and culture so far away.

In 2008, Beijing, China, held the Summer Olympics. For three weeks all manufacturing operations in surrounding areas came to a halt so that the Olympiads could breathe and so that China did not look so bad to the rest of the world. (It didn't work!)

Many companies were hurt by this three-week stoppage of manufacturing operations in China, and many of their customers were severely impacted by late deliveries, except for, of course, those companies that had kept huge amounts of inventory as part of their contingency plan.

The wasteful were rewarded. The lean learned their lesson and will never be so dumb as to not hold bunches of inventory again. (This is a sarcastic comment.)

One of my ($40 million) clients was hurt by this very event. They lost the sale of a $500,000 order and boatloads of additional business because they could not receive castings in time from China for product that would have gone into the Panama Canal. A lead time of 24 weeks was given. The castings were received after 28 weeks and the order was lost and the customer will not deal with my client again.

Many other companies were hurt tremendously during the longshoreman strike of 2002.

Again, this goes to prove that the longer the supply chain, the more chance for errors and problems, and the more inventory one will need to maintain.

Motion. The difference between transportation and motion is quite simple. Transportation involves all the waste when going from point A to point B. Motion involves all the waste in movement once you've reached point B. One might think that there is not much in the way of motion waste due to offshoring, but there is, including the following motion wastes:

- Reading, deciphering, and translating documents, including technical and contractual requirements

- Inefficiencies in communicating requirements and problems due to language and cultural barriers

- Once overseas, senior executives dealing with managers, suppliers, or government officials on contentious issues

- Reworking out-of-tolerance product

Excess Processing. There's plenty of excess processing when it comes to offshoring, and so much of it is very difficult to put our arms around. Here are some of the many examples of excess processing when offshoring:

- Expediting orders due to late shipments

- Dealing with product recalls and warranty issues with out-of-tolerance product

- Additional QC incoming inspection costs

- Obsoleting goods or scrapping stock due to carrying higher levels of inventory

- Completing additional shipment papers

- Translating documents

Other Major Wastes. Of course, there are major wastes that are not covered by the above generally accepted wastes such as the costs of "out-of-stock" and lost sales caused by transportation mishaps, engineering changes, long lead times, material replacement, and disruptive forecast changes. In extreme cases, we have also experienced and witnessed an even worse waste—the loss of the entire company by the offshore vendor becoming the competitor and launching new or similar products to compete against you.

Goodbye to an American Icon—Schwinn Bicycle Company

Taiwanese bicycle manufacturer Giant saw the Schwinn Bicycle Company turn to Japanese manufacturers in 1972 as demand outpaced Schwinn's Chicago plant at the outset of the American bicycle boom. Giant began courting the biggest name in bikes the following year. An order from Schwinn would legitimize the startup. It took four more years. Giant produced its first Schwinn World ten-speed in 1977, and Schwinn was impressed with the quality.

By the beginning of the 1980s Giant was manufacturing 100,000 bicycles per year for Schwinn. When Schwinn's workforce went on strike in the fall of 1980, Giant shipped Schwinn 80,000 bikes in five months. Production returned to normal after the strike, but Schwinn's aging manufacturing capabilities were not being upgraded. Giant could produce chrome-moly frames. Chicago Schwinn could not. *The American company became increasingly reliant on the Taiwanese manufacturer, sharing both manufacturing and design expertise.* In the fall of 1982, Giant shipped 130,000 BMX Schwinn Predators, Schwinn's first successful BMX entrant. By the end of the year, Schwinn shifted most of its production to Giant and closed the Chicago plant.

In 1985, Giant produced one million bikes, most of which went to Schwinn. By 1986, Schwinn depended on Giant for 80 percent of its inventory.

Meanwhile, the Giant label was on very few of the bikes the company was turning out. They had a reputation for quality within the industry, but actual riders did not demand a Taiwanese-built Giant. As early as 1981, Giant's management began fostering the Giant brand name. It was launched in Europe in 1986. In 1985, the unimaginable occurred. Schwinn and Giant began negotiating the terms of a Schwinn–Giant joint brand. The deal was outlined, but never came to fruition. It did, however, mark a major turning point. Giant was now the equal of Schwinn.

The tide had turned. Schwinn knew it and began evasive maneuvers. In 1987 the American cycle company struck a deal with China Bicycles that gave Schwinn a one-third equity stake and promised to shift the majority of its manufacturing to the new company. But it was too late. Giant could put out one million bicycles in a year. Schwinn could barely sell that many in 1987. Giant put all of its brunt behind the Giant brand and went head-to-head with Schwinn on its own soil. *By 1991, Giant was selling 300,000 branded units, a little more than half as many bicycles in America as Schwinn, who would declare bankruptcy the following year.*

In the mid 1990s Giant fully lived up to its name. At $380 million in annual sales, Giant was the largest bicycle manufacturer in the world. Schwinn had $0 million in annual sales.[16]

Obviously, Schwinn's demise was precipitated by ignoring Deming's 4th Point, but perhaps more importantly, Schwinn ignored Point #1:

> *Create constancy of purpose toward improvement of product and service, with the aim to become competitive and stay in business, and to provide jobs.*

BALANCED SCORECARD

From wikipedia.org:

> *The underlying rationale (behind the balanced scorecard) is that organizations can not directly influence financial outcomes, as these are "lag" measures, and that the use of financial measures alone to inform the strategic control of the firm is unwise. Organizations should instead also measure those areas where direct management intervention is possible. In so doing, the early versions of the balanced scorecard helped organizations achieve a degree of "balance" in selection of performance measures. In practice, early scorecards achieved this balance by encouraging managers to select measures from three additional categories or perspectives: "Customer," "Internal Business Processes," and "Learning and Growth."*

It is further stated:

> *Although it helps focus managers' attention on strategic issues and the management of the implementation of strategy, it is important to remember that the balanced scorecard itself has no role in the formation of strategy. In fact, balanced scorecards can comfortably coexist with strategic planning systems and other tools.*

So, if balanced scorecards (BS) can comfortably coexist with strategic planning systems and other tools, it means that BS can coexist with an ISO 9001, Six Sigma, or lean system. It would supplement these strategic systems and tools with a way to measure the success of the systems and tools. But, it's still management by objectives, and management by objectives is wrong and will never work. Managers who strive to improve financial or any other results by encouraging people to chase financial or any other targets will invariably achieve poorer results than those managers who help the organization improve the system of relationships that generates the results. Dr. Deming's warning about targets continues to remain ignored to this day with the popularity of BS.

Wikipedia.org further provides examples of typical performance measures for three of the four categories such as:

Financial:

- Cash flow

- Return on investment

- Financial result

- Return on capital employed

- Return on equity

- Residual income

- Economic value added

Internal business processes:

- Number of activities

- Opportunity success rate

- Accident ratios and environment compatibility

- Overall equipment effectiveness

Learning and growth:

- Investment rate

- Illness rate

- Internal promotions percent

- Employee turnover

- Gender ratios

There are countless examples that one can find by performing a search on the Web. I have seen numerous balanced scorecards at a variety of different companies. One critical measurement and area of focus that is blatantly missing from the above example and many other examples is quality. And in those companies that might have a quality metric, oftentimes it is a metric like customer complaints, PPM, or internal rejects. There is nothing regarding the reduction of variability. BS does nothing to provide focus on the continuous improvement of quality and productivity.

Since we have already agreed that a BS is not a set of principles or a strategy, rather that it is intended to be a way to measure the success of different strategies, we could analyze each of Deming's 14 principles and show how the BS does nothing to promote every single principle. But then why go through this exercise if BS does nothing for every single principle.

I would rather list the Deming principles that are directly violated by the use of a BS:

1. Create constancy of purpose toward improvement of product and service, with the aim to become competitive and stay in business, and to provide jobs.

2. Adopt the new philosophy. We are in a new economic age. Western management must awaken to the challenge, must learn their responsibilities, and take on leadership for change.

5. Improve constantly and forever the system of production and service, to improve quality and productivity, and thus constantly decrease costs.

7. Institute leadership. The aim of leadership should be to help people and machines and gadgets to do a better job. Leadership of management is in need of overhaul, as well as leadership of production workers.

8. Drive out fear so that everyone may work effectively for the company.

11. b. Eliminate management by objective. Eliminate management by numbers, numerical goals. Substitute leadership.

12. b. Remove barriers that rob people in management and in engineering of their right to pride in workmanship.

TRAINING WITHIN INDUSTRY (TWI)

Why Did TWI Die in the United States in the Late '40s and Will It Happen Again?

Training Within Industry (TWI) could easily die again within American companies if a company's structure, systems, and practices are not based on principles that will support and sustain the principles behind TWI.

Again, it is time to evaluate and question a company's principles before another good tool comes and goes, again, just as it did in the late '40s. So why did TWI go away the first time?

TWI Was Born out of a Crisis

The U.S. government created the TWI service in August of 1940 as a means of supplying the Allied Powers with the arsenal to defeat Hitler's forces. At this time, the United States was just exiting from the Great Depression. Unemployment was still high and production capability was low. Supervisors and lead men were in short supply because they were enlisting or being drafted into the military. The world was in a crisis, and yet most Americans did not want to enter into the war because of the country's own weaknesses.

The purpose of TWI was to increase productivity by training hundreds of thousands of new workers in the three modules of Job Instructions, Job Methods, and Job Relations and allow the United States to become, as Franklin Roosevelt referred to it, the "arsenal of democracy." This, he thought, would win the war without having to enter the war. Of course, the United States did enter the war, and by 1942 approximately 6000 new workers were entering the U.S. workforce every day to supply the required arsenal for all the Allied forces, including those of the United States.[17]

In 1945 the crisis was over. The United States had the strongest and largest production facilities in the world. The U.S. government disbanded the TWI service when the war ended.

The companies themselves had no incentive to keep to the ideals and practices of TWI, or at least they *saw* no incentive. After all, TWI was developed out of a crisis, not for internal reasons. TWI was not part of the company's makeup. It was not based on the *company's* principles and culture, rather it was based on TWI service's principles—and the TWI service was now disbanded. If companies had adopted the principles and culture on which TWI was based for their own sake, for the sake of their own profitability and long-term survival, then perhaps TWI would have survived within these organizations and would have existed to the present day without having to be reborn again as it has in recent years.

TWI Moves to the Next Crisis

The United States had exited from a crisis in 1945 and was at the top. Japan had exited World War II at the bottom. *Japan* was now in a state of crisis. Several members of General MacArthur's staff were intimately aware of the benefits of TWI and thought it would be beneficial to teach it to Japanese industry. However, they were not just interested in teaching the *tools* of TWI, but also the democratic *principles* behind TWI, such as "Treat people as individuals." There was an ulterior motive to what General MacArthur wished to do. By helping the Japanese become more productive and improve their economy, it could also teach the *principles* of TWI and democracy and thus reestablish Japan as a democratic nation.

An Organization's Principles and Practices versus TWI's Principles and Practices

An organization must determine its principles first before rolling out a new tool or methodology for two reasons: 1) to determine if the new tool or methodology supports its principles, and 2) to give the new tool or methodology a fighting chance to survive.

This book has encouraged organizations to begin by adopting the Deming principles:

Principles 1st, Culture 2nd, Practices 3rd, Tools 4th!

Ideally, prior to learning the methods of TWI, a company should have determined its principles, established its culture, ensured that its business practices support both, and then developed its own tools or found the tools that support all of the above.

After establishing and communicating its principles, an organization's management must ask itself, "Do our organization's practices support our principles? Are our principles and practices aligned with the principles and practices of TWI?" If not, TWI will die another death, at least at this organization.

When determining an organization's principles, it is important to understand that "principles" are fundamentally accepted rules of action or conduct that are generally inarguable depending on one's purpose or goal, such as raising a family, playing a sport, or building a business.

Dr. Stephen Covey, in his landmark book, *The 7 Habits of Highly Effective People,* wrote:

> *Principles are guidelines for human conduct that are proven to have enduring, permanent value. They're fundamental. They're essentially unarguable because they are self-evident. One way to quickly grasp the self-evident nature of principles is to simply consider the absurdity of attempting to live an effective life based on their opposites. I doubt that anyone would seriously*

consider unfairness, deceit, baseness, uselessness, mediocrity, or degeneration to be a solid foundation for lasting happiness and success.[18]

There are many practices that one lives by that are in violation of principles. Hitler was a prime example of this. Practices in the business world can be in direct violation of good business principles.

What Are the Principles behind TWI?

Deming points (principles) that are also TWI principles:

Point #5: Improve constantly and forever the system of production and service, to improve quality and productivity, and thus constantly decrease costs.

Point #6: Institute training on the job.

Point #7: Institute leadership. The aim of leadership should be to help people and machines and gadgets to do a better job

Point #11a: Eliminate work standards (quotas) on the factory floor. Substitute leadership.

Point #12a: Remove barriers that rob the hourly worker of his right to pride of workmanship.

Point 13: Institute a vigorous program of education and self-improvement.

By far, the greatest benefit of TWI is that it supports supervisors and other top managers in *how to be a leader* by forcing the supervisor to know the process, know the work, lead by example, coach, involve all people, respect and involve the individual, and continuously improve the process, and ensuring that the supervisor will be there at the process.

Internal Practices That May Not Support TWI

The benefits of TWI and lean itself and the all of its tools (that is, 5S, value stream management, quick changeover, work cells, TPM, *and* TWI) will never be sustained within an organization unless the company adopts the principles, culture, and supporting practices behind lean. Lean principles (which are also aligned with Deming principles), such as "respect for and involvement of all people" and "process focus rather than department/objective/goal focus," need to be in place.

In other words, if a *culture* of blame exists, and the *practices* of employees being chastised, written up, or evaluated poorly because of defects "they" caused are in effect, then lean improvements and TWI benefits will not be sustained because the culture and practices do not support the *principle* of respect for the people.

Or, if a departmentally focused *culture* exists and the *practice* of establishing departmental objectives and rewarding departments for meeting their own goals is in place, then lean improvements and TWI benefits will not be sustained because the culture and practices do not support the *principle* of process focus.

The following practices are symptoms of principles and a culture that *are not aligned* with the principles of TWI and of Deming and will eventually lead to TWI dying within your organization:

1. Performance evaluations

2. Employees being chastised, written up, or dinged for defective product ("operator error" causes)

3. Departmental objectives, organization, and focus

4. Hiding problems (from auditors and management)

5. Problem solving by Green and Black Belts, not by the people

6. Egotistic management

7. Supervisors at all levels managing by numbers, rather than being "at" the process

8. No monitoring/watching of TWI training; no feedback on the process

9. Micromanagement style versus leadership

10. Hiring kids out of college to be production supervisors

11. Supervisors not working the job for an extended period of time before training others

12. No TWI or any training during the last week of the month or year due to an order from above to ship as much as possible (short-term thinking)

13. Mass inspection by another department (QC)

14. Buying materials, components, gages, tools, equipment from lowest bidder, regardless of quality and *total* cost

15. *Continual* improvement activities (that is, once-a-month kaizen events/blitzes) rather than *continuous* improvement activities (that is, every day, by everybody)

16. Supervisors not ensuring standard work is being completed

17. Layoffs

18. Excluding certain people from improvement activities

19. Production quotas

20. No preventive maintenance of equipment, and so on

21. No allocation of training resources or time

You Could Have Developed TWI

How many times on a corrective action report have you seen the "root cause" of the problem being "poor training"? Normally, the action taken as a result of this "root cause" is "retraining," which of course does nothing for the long term, and the problem reoccurs. Why? Because the system did not change! Essentially, a person was blamed again—the trainer. The action is to have the trainer train again, probably the exact same way he or she did before.

If an organization had performed a good root cause analysis in the first place and kept asking why the training program was ineffective, it might have found out that some of the root causes may have been:

- No allocation of training resources and time because it's not important.

- Trainers not knowing how to train because there is no system.

- Trainers do not see trainees do the job effectively.

- Work instruction format is too complex.

- Many trainees are learning-disabled, dyslexic, or speak another language, and the written and verbal words are not enough to help them understand.

- There is no training plan.

- There is no follow-up plan.

- Trainers are not held accountable for their training actions.

- Trainers are not given feedback.

- Trainers only show how to do something once.

- Trainees do not understand the importance of each major action because it is not recorded anywhere on the work instruction.

TWI's Job Instruction module addresses all of these root causes, and does not blame the trainer or trainee.

If any organization had done root cause analysis well, it could have developed its own TWI process and called it whatever it wanted to call it.

"Getting to the root causes of problems" is perhaps the most important principle of all!!

5

Knowledge versus Certification

Dr. Deming said six very powerful words on many occasions:

There is no substitute for knowledge.

CONTINUOUS SELF-IMPROVEMENT THROUGH KNOWLEDGE GAIN

As we go through the journey of life, we should all be gaining more knowledge and improving ourselves. We make dumb mistakes along the way, we learn from them, we change our minds, our beliefs, and perhaps even our principles. If we are not getting smarter and more knowledgeable as we grow older, we are wasting our minds.

I've never understood why, when politicians running for office are asked why they said or did something or voted for something that is completely different than what they are proclaiming or doing or voting on in the present day, they try to defend or cover up what they said or did previously.

Granted, sometimes politicians change their minds, positions, or beliefs because if they do, they will receive something greater in return than if they did not change . . . or they are just liars.

However, I do believe, or perhaps I want to believe, that sometimes a politician has gained more knowledge and simply has changed his or her mind. I've often wondered why politicians feel that they can not just admit that at one time in the past they believed a certain way, they got smarter, and they changed their mind. This is continuous improvement! This is a good thing! I would rather a politician simply state that he or she believed a certain way when they were younger, then something happened that changed their outlook or their beliefs and they simply changed their mind than feed us a line of bull and try to talk circles around us defending what they said and what it really meant. Tell us the truth and save us from the crap that you get away with in court.

WHY GET A BLACK BELT?

Early in my consulting career in the mid '90s, training companies in statistical tools such as design of experiments (DOE), statistical process control (SPC), and failure mode and effects analysis (FMEA) was my bread and butter. Shortly thereafter, this type of work dwindled as becoming certified to ISO 9001 and ISO 9002 (at the time) became more of a priority with companies. I reached a point in my consulting career in which my work evolved into more than 95 percent of sales being related to developing quality management systems for a large variety of companies. This was quite a good ride for a while, until new work and clients wanting to get certified or recertified to ISO 9001 began to spiral down after 2003.

About that time I wondered to myself, "Why have I not performed any DOE, SPC, or FMEA classes for companies in such a long time?" I realized that as I was so busy helping companies build effective quality management systems, I had fallen further behind the Six Sigma bandwagon that was racing years ahead of me. I attempted to tell clients that throughout my career as an engineer with the Saturn Corporation and then with Seaquist-Perfect Dispensing in Cary, Illinois, I had experience in 90 percent of what a Six Sigma program taught people anyway. It didn't matter. They wanted to know if I had a Black Belt, as if the Belt was the only thing that mattered.

I had resisted attempting to get a Black Belt for so long. Perhaps I was just stubborn and felt that I didn't need a "Belt" to prove to people that I could do what I've been doing effectively for so many years in my career.

So, I bit the bullet, and as discussed earlier, I practiced taking tests well enough to pass the test. For the most part, I gained no additional knowledge, but I was a Black Belt.

Any system, educational or business oriented, that focuses on grades or certification or belts and not gaining more knowledge is a bad system and can actually be detrimental to the actual learning process and knowledge gained.

As an independent consultant, I could not really earn a Black Belt within my company because there was no program within my two-person company. (Actually, I could have if I was a scoundrel. I could have proclaimed myself to be a Black Belt or Master Black Belt or Super-Duper, Triple Wide, Master Black Belt based on my own set of criteria, since there is no set of standard criteria anyway. Who would be able to question my credentials?)

I could not do this though. It just seemed too scummy to me. I could though, take the American Society for Quality (ASQ) Certified Six Sigma Black Belt exam, perform a small Six Sigma project with one of my clients, and become an ASQ Certified Black Belt, which is exactly what I did.

The ironic part of all of this is that part of the actual exam was lean oriented, filled with lean questions. If those who profess Six Sigma only realized how un-lean the Six Sigma process and training can be, they would realize the mockery of how one completes a Six Sigma project.

By passing the exam and having my project accepted, I was now an ASQ Certified Six Sigma Black Belt in 2004, complementing my previous ASQ certifications of Quality Manager, Quality Engineer, and Quality Auditor.

Developing typical Six Sigma materials for me to teach other Green and Black Belts would be a monumental task, so I decided to evaluate previously developed materials being sold on the market. I chose a supplier of materials, updated my business cards and Web site, and began to sell my Six Sigma services, a little late in the game, but in the game nonetheless.

I had received a Black Belt for the sake of personal gain and sustaining my consulting career, not for the sake of gaining more knowledge. This is no different than all those employees who have gone through Six Sigma training, understanding very little of what was being taught, but nonetheless placing the "Belt" on their resume and leaving the company for another that would pay them more handsomely for all of their "knowledge."

Gaining a Green or Black Belt is little more than a resume builder.

This was all before I changed and realized how wrong Six Sigma was. This was only after I got myself much more acquainted with Dr. Deming's teachings than ever before. This was before I gained more knowledge and improved myself.

WHAT PART OF CERTIFICATION DO YOU NOT UNDERSTAND?

Earlier in the book, I talked about a woman who had called me from St. Louis asking me to provide Black Belt *certification* training for her and her five direct reports.

I told her that since all six people had earned Green Belts from six different sources, the training that they had received was probably completely inconsistent (because there was no standard for training materials). I told her that this could be a problem because Black Belt training should build on what one learned from their Green Belt training. They should really receive new Green Belt training for consistency in what they all learn and to build a more effective Black Belt training class.

She objected. She obviously wanted to get the Black Belt with as little money or time investment as possible and without regard to effectiveness.

I provided her with two written proposals: 1) Black Belt training by itself and 2) Black Belt training with a shortened Green Belt training session preceding the Black Belt material. Both proposals included my cost for purchasing the materials from a third party.

We talked about a week later. Option #2 was out. Option #1 was still too expensive. I then asked her, "What topic is it that you and your people are most interested in gaining more knowledge of? I have a lot of my own material for topics such as design of experiments, statistical process control, and many other topics. I could provide the specific training and knowledge you wish to have at a much lower cost using my own materials." At this she abruptly cut me off and said,

"What part of certification do you not understand?"

The conversation died soon after this. We hung up the phone and I sat stunned at what just happened because I knew it was happening all over the country. Knowledge was not important, it was the Belt that everyone wanted so they could build their resume and get more money, oftentimes with a new employer. With these personal incentives, are companies really benefiting from Six Sigma, I wondered. Was this all just a big scam created by my larger training and consulting counterparts?

LEAN SIX SIGMA IS AN OXYMORON AND MANY MORONS ARE BUYING IT

Lean came from Toyota. Six Sigma came from Motorola and GE. Lean Six Sigma came from training/consulting companies. Consulting and training companies work to increase sales, just like any other company. The best way to create sales is to increase the number of training days, and one way to do that is to combine lean and Six Sigma into one big package. By doing so, companies do not have to struggle with the decision of going the lean route or the Six Sigma route. They can get it all in one big, gigantic *batch*.

The problem, though, is that in principle lean and Six Sigma are essentially different in many respects, including the following:

1. Lean tools, and so on, are taught as you go, as a need arises, ideally just in time. Its tools offer possible solutions to root causes of problems and should be used as such. Six Sigma is taught in batches, one full week at a time, filling the brain with large inventories of techniques, tools, and analyses.

2. Lean teaches us "respect and involvement of all of the people." Six Sigma is elitist in that the Belts do all the figuring, defining, analyzing, and improving of other people's processes. This is not respectful to the experts of the systems and processes.

3. Lean follows the plan–do–check–act (PDCA) cycle, or as Dr. Deming referred to it, the Shewhart cycle, or as everyone else refers to it, the Deming cycle. It is cyclical—never ending. Six Sigma teaches us the define–measure–analyze–improve–control (DMAIC) process, which means that once you control the improvements, you are done, and you move on to the next project.

4. Lean encourages us to build a system of "continuous improvement," little improvements made every day by everybody, in single-piece-flow fashion. Six Sigma encourages us to do big projects in which hundreds of thousands of dollars would supposedly be saved. It teaches us about "continual improvement," not "continuous," in which improvements are made in batches. The irony of doing Six Sigma projects on a monthly or otherwise periodic basis (and for those companies that do monthly-only kaizen events or blitzes) is that they are doing batch processing of improvement activities to get rid of batch processing.

5. Lean is about reducing *mura,* the Japanese term for variation in everything, whether it is production scheduling, model mixing, or service and part variation. Six Sigma is about achieving a number below 3.4 defects per million opportunities (DPMO) whether this is done by defining an ever-increasing number of opportunities, thus reducing DPMO, or opening up the specifications, thus reducing the number of defects and DPMO. Another way is to truly reduce variation, but this is only one option.

REAL SIX SIGMA STORIES

    1. "The Emperor's New Woes, Revisited: What Has Six Sigma Done for General Electric?"[19] This is the story told earlier about the GE Industrial

Engineer who, after mentioning that he had made some process improvements outside of the typical Six Sigma Project format, was told, "If you didn't do it in Six Sigma, then it didn't happen." Her metric of preference was dollar savings from Six Sigma projects. It's not the knowledge and improvement that matter most, it's the Belt and the number of projects a Belt does that matter most.

2. *Training waste.* This was the story of the Six Sigma executive of a large manufacturing company who told me that his company had trained and certified 800 Black Belts, five percent (40) of which were practitioners. Of the 40 practicing Black Belts, each used about five percent of the materials that they were taught during the extensive Black Belt training sessions, or the equivalent of two Black Belts fully utilizing all of what they were taught.

Effectively, two Black Belts out of the 800 trained Black Belts were fully using all of the training received, and 798 Black Belts were not. That's 0.25%. If that's not wasteful, and sinful, I do not know what is.

3. *Overburdening statistics and comments made by different individuals.*[20] The typical Six Sigma syllabus is riddled with multiple heavy statistical techniques, but to what benefit?

> *"I've been a BB for three years, and I've never used a designed experiment!"* *"Mmm, me neither!"* (Overheard in a men's bathroom.)

> *"I can't remember the last time I calculated a* p-value!*"*

> *"We know of people who have been taught this range of statistical techniques in a rote manner, plugging the numbers into Minitab and being given a screen of very precise numbers from which conclusions are to be drawn. And yet we have heard skilled statisticians remark that they are unconvinced that the people drawing these conclusions are confident that they know what the numbers really mean."*

Is this not considered wasteful?

4. *Too much training.* In a typical Six Sigma Black Belt training syllabus, there might be 30 or more days, often split into six separate weeks. You might want to consider the cost of this in training fees, let alone the cost of having high-caliber people missing from the workplace for so long.

5. From a Black Belt:

> *My training must have been very expensive. I did five weeks worth of training in the center of Berlin! There were two Brits,*

one Swede, one Italian, one Indian, one Austrian, one Dane, one American, and five Germans, all being taught in English by two Canadians.

For the last week of the training we were joined by three other Master Black Belts who took us through mind-numbingly boring statistics and tools (hypothesis testing, sigma values, and so on), which became a very slow process with obvious language barriers.

In all, we went through around 2500 slides!

How about getting out of the classroom and learning near the process?

6. From another Black Belt:

Why are you doing this Six Sigma project?
Answer: To get my BB accreditation to add to my resume.

What's more important—knowledge or the BB?

7. *Six Sigma cost savings.* I've heard many stories along these lines, but here is one e-mail that sums it up very well:

I have no beef with Six Sigma per se—the problem is the management policies that go with it. Departments have been told that any cost saving or improvement plan must be a Six Sigma project. Managers are evaluated, in part, by how many projects they sponsor. You actually get in trouble by saving money by doing obvious things—because you are now required to start a SS project so that savings can be counted. Management prefers to delay the benefits for several months and to invest thousands of dollars in time to reach the obvious answer.

Quotas don't work. Try leadership, Deming would say.

8. *Leadership* (from another e-mail):

The fact that we were one of the world's most prominent Six Sigma users is hardly recognizable when you closely look at how it was led and introduced. Our senior managers were taken through three or four days of the same style of training as I had received— death by PowerPoint. They could barely stay awake or contain their contempt for the material, although some of them clearly felt embarrassed for the new trainers who tried to present the methods and tools that were going to be used. The business we were in was highly political and full of blame culture. The senior managers were reluctant to sanction any projects because they would have to admit there was something wrong in their department.

> *Consequently, the ones that did get approved tended to be insig-*
> *nificant and solely contained within a single department to avoid*
> *cross-functional confrontation. There was great pressure applied*
> *to agents to find evidence to support the senior managers' pet*
> *theories.*

Sounds like what is missing are many of Deming's principles!!!

9. *Ranking Black Belts.* The great Jack Welch said in an annual GE shareholder letter, "A company that bets its future on its people must remove the lower 10 percent and keep doing it every year." I know at least one company that was doing just this with its Black Belts, and yet another company that was giving people the choice of studying to become a Black Belt or being made redundant! Another company confined all their Black Belts in a conference room, for a whole day, to work out how they were going to rank themselves performance-wise so that the appraisal rewards could be handed out.

Again, grades and ranking do not work. Competition sets in. The focus is on the competition itself, not process improvement. Knowledge of Deming's principles would have helped this person as well.

10. It takes *so* long:

> *Six sigma is alive and well—but takes too long. I prefer shorter*
> *projects. Our project on xxxx is a good example. We started it*
> *January '04 (it's now April '05)—we are in the middle of improve*
> *phase! As there have been so many changes to the xxxx plan since*
> *we started, if we fix what was in our original scope we may not see*
> *a great improvement as something else now has become broken.*
> *And new things can not be added into the project at this stage—*
> *they must be treated as a new project entirely. It is not flexible*
> *enough to reflect the changing nature of (our service).*
> *. . . Then the wheels came off the Six Sigma project. Because*
> *we had taken so long to get to this point (about three months in*
> *total) and Six Sigma projects had a target time scale to com-*
> *plete within three months, we were told to stop the project. I was*
> *annoyed and disappointed but hopeful that common sense would*
> *prevail and the cross-functional team we had worked with would*
> *continue the work we had begun.*
> *Sadly they didn't. The functional silos became entrenched yet*
> *again. Senior managers carried on playing political games with*
> *each other, pointing fingers and blaming others. And some of the*
> *middle managers who felt that the Six Sigma project was imposed*
> *upon them wouldn't continue with it.*

I was later told that people were also reluctant to help because, apart from upsetting their bosses, they felt it was unfair that I would have received a financial bonus for completing a Six Sigma project and they would get nothing. (I could honestly say I didn't want the bonus and in fact turned down simple, meaningless projects that would have paid me a bonus—this was baffling to some of my colleagues.)

In short, no leadership, no genuine desire to improve, plenty of empty words (but no real focus on the customer), and treating people disrespectfully resulted in even more waste and a further drop in morale to the point where people left.

Is this not just a repeat of examples of not following Deming's principles?

11. Comments from a sampling of "Black Belt for Sale" readers:

"I came out of Motorola where Six Sigma was taught tool by tool as part of every employee's annual training. All were trained, starting with the seven basic tools, sometimes Shainin, . . . Six Sigma was embedded in the quality system and had equal status to cycle time reduction (also taught tool by tool and mostly to one another rather than in a formal class setting). I was at the beginning of the Six Sigma consulting explosion with AlliedSignal, GE, and a bunch of others but exited in 1998 when I became disgusted with what it was becoming—watered down and fraught with paper and structure."

"I am a long time Motorolan, where Six Sigma was invented. I was in the first group of Black Belts back in '93, when Mikel Harry was heading it up in Motorola's Six Sigma Research Institute . . . . Certification is a joke as you clearly understand."

"When I was with Motorola we were very careful not to hand out Black Belt certifications willy-nilly (I never liked the name, but I think we're stuck with it). When I left for consulting in 1998 it quickly became obvious that there would be consultants of the kind Deming would call "hacks," and that they were in the process of watering down the recognition. I have seen people claim to be Master Black Belts whose depth and breadth of quality expertise couldn't fill a thimble. A child's thimble."

"I put much of the blame on corporate management who themselves do not know what it takes to run a business. They want quick fixes and silver bullets, and have little patience for those

of us who advocate hard work and detailed analysis. While I list MBB as an accomplishment, I am first and foremost an engineer. I learned the tools that evolved into DFSS because I had real problems to overcome in developing products. For me, the certification was an acknowledgment of achievement, not an end in itself (as has become the case for far too many). We have a director and VP of CI who have no clue on what it takes to embed good problem prevention and solving methods in the company. They put up their primary metric—number of people trained—and only count "hard dollar savings" which really means people out the door. Our organization is becoming known as the precursor to headcount reduction, and nobody wants us around. My company is on a tear (like so many) to send production to low-labor-cost countries and then are flabbergasted that the products produced have numerous problems. No evaluation of capabilities at these other sites is done ahead of time, the only analysis that seems to be performed is a wage rate analysis."

"As one who was around as Mother Motorola began the birthing process for Six Sigma, I fully agree with your evaluation. In the years since, I have noted many organizations, projects, and similar that made no real gains except on paper. It seems to me that all the quality tools and statistics are a waste when most people trying to use them do not have any understanding of the process. They take data from what seems to be a good point (spelled "easy" in most cases), spend hours (sometimes days) evaluating, and then come up with a new plan that is different but really no better. Understand the process and you will likely note the real problem areas. Analyze the problem area and you will likely determine what data are required (and it never seems to be the easy data you thought!). The folks at Mother M were adamant about implementing a Six Sigma project in our area (linear final test) where the result that made them happy was a nice chart. The chart was 'pretty' but provided no useful information. But it did prove that we were using the tools!"

"I was forwarded this article by my company president because of a recent customer visit. The customer first gave his presentation, which stated their expectations from their suppliers, and #2 on the list was Six Sigma. I then gave my presentation that showed not only DFSS tools but some from the automotive industry, namely PPAP, 8D, and mistake-proofing, and he looked at me with the

biggest expression of surprise on his face and point-blank asked, 'Why aren't you a Black Belt? You obviously understand all the components.' Yes, I do understand and have a good working knowledge of all the components, but I explained to him that I learned all these tools in a facility that practiced Toyota management and therefore did not issue any Black Belts. His response to that? 'If you had told me that you were a Black Belt, I wouldn't have questioned your quality system!' In other words, it didn't matter that I knew what I was doing, it only mattered that I owned a Black Belt. Now my boss is asking if I should go and get certified so that our customers can be impressed. It never ends . . . ."

KNOWLEDGE AND LEADERSHIP

A degree, certificate, or Belt does not mean one is competent, knowledgeable, qualified, or a leader. It only means they passed a test.

Dr. Deming frequently referred to the silliness of young girls and boys, fresh out of college, being thrust into a supervisory role over employees who have perhaps worked for 20 or 30 years in a particular role. These kids would have no experience, no knowledge of the process, and not necessarily any leadership qualifications. They did have a degree, though . . . and that's it.

Can you imagine being an employee working in a particular area and all of a sudden you have a new boss—a kid half your age—and he or she begins to bark out orders to you, just because of their title, which is predicated on the fact that he or she has a degree from some prestigious university. What does the employee feel is appreciated at this company? Is it knowledge? Is it leadership? Is it experience? Is it creativity?

The employee knows that this will be short-lived. The new supervisor will be moved out in about six months. She's seen it before. New supervisors come and go through a revolving door. Either they don't like the job, can't handle the people, get promoted, switch companies, or transfer to a new role. It becomes something of a challenge to see how fast we can get the new guy to quit. Resentment on the part of the long-term employee has built up over the years because his or her talents are not appreciated by the company. So she or he tries, along with other employees, to find ways to make sure the new supervisor fails in the new role. There is no teamwork . . . just finger-pointing, competition, attacks, and counterattacks . . . all because the company values a degree over knowledge and leadership.

Sounds silly, does it not? It happened to me though. I bring this up at the many presentations that I give, and many people say that it still happens today.

MY STORY AS A POTENTIAL SUPERVISOR

This was the story of how I was recruited out of college to be a manufacturing supervisor for Seaquist Valve in 1985.

I've never really admitted to not wanting to be a supervisor fresh out of college because it seemed weak. And yet, I wanted to eventually get into management. That's what I dreamed of. I mean, I was really more of a business major–type person (it was my "secondary field") than an engineering major–type person in the first place. I thought it would be smart to get a degree as an engineer and stand out as a different type of engineer with business qualifications.

And yet even with this desire to eventually manage, I felt I was unqualified to supervise people because I had no knowledge of the process, manufacturing, the equipment, or for that matter, how to lead. So I took my dream job as an engineer with Saturn.

Several years later, as an engineer with the Saturn Corporation, the decision would need to be made again. Would I go into management and run part of an assembly line? Most of my cohorts, with now a couple of years of engineering experience, were going in this direction as it seemed to be the typical route. Even though my knowledge of the process I was responsible for was high (because I ran so many designed experiments in the prototype facility to optimize the process), I still had no leadership experience, and it did not appear that it would be taught. Fortunately, or unfortunately, I did not have to make that decision because, for personal reasons, I had to move back to Illinois and leave Saturn, which I definitely did not want to do.

WHAT TO DO?

Dr. Deming would have been ticked off about the continuing focus on degrees, certificates, and belts and the lack of focus on knowledge and leadership.

We need to teach employees how to lead, coach, and mentor. Leadership does not come natural to many people. This is a skill that can be taught and encouraged within an organization. An organizational culture can be developed to support leadership qualifications. This includes spending much less time running the organization on metrics, objectives, and goals from a conference room, office, or database, and focusing more on living with the process.

At the same time, the organization needs to encourage supervisors to *not* micromanage. Micromanagement is the opposite of leadership. Micromanagers do not see themselves as micromanagers, rather they see themselves as controlling the process. Striving to achieve quotas and short-term goals encourages micromanagement. These need to be abolished and replaced with leadership.

The knowledge of the workers needs to be harnessed and allowed to flow into process control and process improvement. The creativity of the workers needs to be encouraged. A culture of continuous improvement needs to be developed. Knowledge for everyone needs to be continuously expanding, and the culture must encourage this.

The 9th and 10th principles from *The Toyota Way* are:

1. Grow leaders who thoroughly understand the work, live the philosophy, and teach it to others.

2. Develop exceptional people and teams who follow your company's philosophy.

These are employee-focused and knowledge-growing principles and they are so consistent with Dr. Deming's principles. The methods and cultural aspects that could help to support these principles and support employees gaining more knowledge (as opposed to a certificate or belt), include:

- Leader standard work

- Daily accountability meetings

- Gemba walks

- Leadership discipline

- Set-based approach to decision making

- Visual management

- Quick and easy kaizen

- The A3 process of mentoring and leading

- Training Within Industry

Or, perhaps even more importantly, your company could and should develop its own culture, methods, tools, style, and processes based on the principles of Dr. Deming.

6

Why Root Cause Analysis Sucks in America

In recent years, I have been asked to provide root cause analysis training more than ever before in my 15 years as an independent quality/lean consultant. I find this interesting in this age of Six Sigma, especially since "analyze" is the heart of DMAIC (define, measure analyze, improve, control). I further find this interesting in this age of lean, in which the lean tools that are taught to so many people should only be used after performing root cause analysis on a defined problem. I (further) further find this interesting in this age of so many companies being ISO 9001 certified for so many years, when the essence of continually improving the effectiveness of the quality management system lies in performing good root cause analysis.

So, I began to wonder, "Why does root cause analysis suck in America?" and I came up with the following possible, *and somewhat sarcastic*, root causes. It's up to you to decide which ones apply to your company by asking "why" somewhere around five times until you find the systemic reason(s) as to why root cause analysis sucks within your company.

Drum roll please . . .

10. *It's more fun to blame people.* There is no greater thrill than to find out who caused the problem and blame them even though that person had no control over the situation. The situation is also easy to rectify, because all one has to do is to counsel, retrain, talk to, and convince them that they need to pay more attention—or better yet, fire their butt. Fixing the system is way too boring and takes way more time than blaming someone anyway.

9. *Top management does not want to find out they are to blame.* What if Dr. Deming was right? What if 94 percent of root causes are due to common cause variation and only top management can control this type of

variation? What if employees all understood what Dr. Deming was really telling us? Then top management would have to attend root cause analysis training along with other supporting functions (such as sales, engineering, production planning). Management might even have to change their ways from micromanaging to leading—this would absurd. It's easier to send only manufacturing personnel to training and make them feel that they are the root causes, and ensure they feel the fear of making another mistake.

8. *I was told to shut up after asking "why" one time.* Children naturally ask "why," but sometimes they ask too many questions, so it's best to shut 'em up now before a parent has to admit that he/she does not know the answer to a question and before the kid gets too comfortable asking "why" multiple times. Example:

Five-year-old: *"Daddy, why do we have to die?"*

Daddy: *"So we can go to heaven?"*

Five-year-old: *"Why do we have to go to heaven?"*

Daddy: *"So we can live with God and other good (insert faith here—Catholic, Muslim, Orthodox, Jewish, Buddhist) people forever."*

Five-year-old: *"Why do we have to live with God?"*

Daddy: *"Shut up, kid, and go watch TV."*

This dad allowed way too many "whys." He's an inexperienced young dad and will learn to shut the kid up after one "why," thus properly preparing the kid for the working world.

7. *We don't have the time to think long-term . . . right now.* "Maybe next month we will. Right now, we have to make the numbers for the quarterly report. The shareholders, Wall Street, or owners need to see that we met their predictions this quarter or else. We need all our people focused on making as much product as possible, shipping as much as possible during the last week of the month, and storing as much inventory as possible before the end of the year. We'll get to root cause analysis next month, or next year, and really resolve some problems." They never do.

6. *Fixing root causes is too expensive.* The Jefferson Memorial was degrading.

Why? Use of harsh chemicals.

Why? To clean up after pigeons.

Why so many pigeons? They eat spiders, and there are a lot of spiders at the monument.

Why so many spiders? They eat gnats and there are lots of gnats at the monument.

Why so many gnats? They are attracted to the light at dusk.

Why are the lights on at dusk? Because the timing of the lights going on does not change with the change in the time of sunset throughout the year.

Solution: Turn on the lights at a later time for now, and develop a system to change the "lights on" setting every week depending on the date and amount of sunlight. Automate.

In the above example, one would typically stop asking "why" after the answer of "harsh chemicals" was given, and a solution might have been to use less harsh chemicals more often. Expenses would have gone up. After getting to the real root cause of this problem, the solution is actually a cost savings. This less expensive solution is not just typical of monuments, but of the many problems within your operations as well, once the root cause has been determined. The perception that only expensive solutions are possible once the true root cause has been determined is simply not true.

5. *"My peeps can't do root cause analysis and I'm a micromanager."* "And yet, I do not have the time to do RCA the right way, so I'd better not encourage root cause analysis at all. I would rather give them the fish than teach them to fish. I've made it this far in my career because I am smart. My peeps obviously are not smart and they need me. I love to get my hands into everything, and even though this slows up decision making we are assured of the right answers, and this is best in the long run, right? Leadership and coaching are overrated. They are the opposite of micromanaging and they do not work."

4. *It requires thinking.* Who needs to think when they have their degree, their Master Blaster, Double Thick, Triple Wide Black Belt, the title of Sensei, and they and their company are Certified? We are in a competitive world in which quick movement and decisions are most important. Thinking is for the professors at university where nothing real ever gets accomplished anyway. We need to get product out the door now. I only think—I think—when I'm in the classroom.

3. *Why do root cause analysis training when we can buy all the solutions anyway?* It's much easier to buy 5S, value stream mapping, kaizen,

TPM, quick changeover, all of the Six Sigma tools, and an ISO 9001 certificate than to go through the hassle of determining root causes. Many people do not understand that "tools" like 5S are only by-products developed by Toyota after doing proper root cause analysis. No one ever taught Toyota how to do 5S.

What came first—root cause analysis or 5S? Root cause analysis of course. Perhaps one day there was a product defect. An engineer went to ask the operator what happened. After blaming himself, the operator and engineer studied the process, and the operator realized that when the defect was created he had used the wrong tool. The engineer asked why?

Because the right tool was not available. Why?

Because the right tool could not be found. Why?

Because the work area is so unorganized. Why?

Solution: Sort out the stuff that is hardly used in the area and create clearly identified spaces for everything that does belong so that it becomes obvious when something is missing. These are the *sort* and *straighten* steps of 5S.

If a company wishes to copy Toyota, it should copy how it does root cause analysis, not 5S. That company may come up with a different "tool," or "style," that varies from the 5S style.

As Thomas Jefferson said, "Be flexible in style, but unwavering, like a rock, in principles." Getting to the root of a problem is the principle; 5S is the style.

Top managers would rather buy styles than develop their own.

2. *We don't practice it at home, so why should we do it at work?* Over 25 percent of our children are on antipsychotic drugs, antidepressants, Ritalin, and other ADHD drugs under the banner of "mental health." Anti-anxiety drugs are rampant, and there has never been any proof that they have ever cured anyone of anxiety. To quit smoking, we can chew gum, buy a patch, get hypnotized, or take drugs. To lose weight, we can go on a myriad of diets, some claiming that exercise is not necessary, or we can just get our stomachs stapled via a gastric bypass operation. To get us out of an economic slump, our government issues us checks or bails out entire industries with taxpayer money. If our marriage is in disarray, we get a divorce. If we do not get along with other countries, we go to war. We rarely get to root causes at home, in our neighborhood, or in our country. We are not accustomed to it. So we go for the quick fix—the new drug. This gets carried over to work, and we continue to buy the latest drug at work—ISO 9001, Six Sigma, lean tools, and products from India and China.

1. *Getting to the root cause would require us to work with other kingdoms.* When one asks "why" so many times, the systemic reason as to "why" a problem exists will more than likely exist within the confines of another "kingdom" or department. Understanding this would require true process orientation or value stream management. Most companies do not have true process orientation—they only talk of this during an audit, a kaizen event, or a Six Sigma project.

Most companies' organizational structures are still based on departments, or kingdoms, no matter what they tell others. Most still have departmental goals and are evaluated on meeting these goals, so they continue to suboptimize, no matter what the effect is on other kingdoms. This makes root cause analysis even more difficult, if not impossible. It's easier to blame another department rather than continue on digging deeper for the root cause, which always exists in another department despised by the department doing the root cause analysis. It's easier to fight!

THE ROOT CAUSES LIE IN THE LACK OF THE IDENTIFICATION OF CORRECT PRINCIPLES

In example #3 above, "Why do root cause analysis training when we can buy all the solutions anyway?" we never really did get to the root cause of the problem and why there was such a lack of organization in the company. We basically got to the point of cleaning up and organizing the area, or *sort*ing and *straighten*ing the area, the first two S's of 5S.

So the engineer continued on.

Why was the plant not organized? The operator had a difficult time answering this question. He simply said he did not have to because he was not told to. We know now that we are getting close to the root cause because we now have to go up the chain of command and ask a manager. Effective root cause analysis must allow us to go up the chain of command and/or must allow us to investigate other department processes, otherwise we will never uncover the true root causes and will have to apply band-aids.

The plant manager was then asked, "Why is the plant not organized?" His answer was that there was no system of organization. So they began to develop 5S. They already had the first two S's. They added *shine* to develop a method of cleaning and inspecting all equipment and process areas and methods to prevent dirt/contamination buildup in the first place. They wished to implement the process in all areas, so they developed *standardize* as the fourth step to ensure consistency throughout, and finally they added *sustain* as a means of ensuring that their work was sustained throughout all areas every day. In short, they blamed the system and developed the system with 5S.

There's no reason your company couldn't have done the same thing and developed its own process, and called it 6Q or 12D or FaQ or whatever, by simply applying effective root cause analysis.

In this story, it appeared that the engineer was done with the root cause analysis, but he wanted to dig even deeper. He then asked, "Why was there no system of organization in the first place?" The plant manager could not answer that because the answer was a deeper issue that was beyond his control. The engineer asked the president. The president said that the identification and elimination of waste was not one of the principles of the company, nor was blaming the system through root cause analysis, which had everything to do with not respecting the people.

The president (granted, this is an *ideal* president in this made-up story), developed *company-wide principles,* upon which the *culture of the company* would be based and fostered. The president documented and announced the following principles, among others:

The constant focus on and elimination of waste

Respect and involvement of all people in a no-blame environment

Voracious efforts in determining and eliminating root causes

ROOT CAUSES OF TOYOTA'S SUCCESS

The irony lies in that as so many American companies try to become more like Toyota, they are actually becoming less like Toyota. Many lean practitioners do not realize that one of Toyota's often unstated principles is being *self-reliant.* If we were truly trying to be more like Toyota, we would be developing our own way, our own style, our own methodologies, our own equipment, our own technology. Instead, we copy Toyota's ways because they are proven, we don't have to think, and it's easier to do. No person ventured into Toyota years ago and taught their people tools like 5S, TPM, quick changeover, or value stream mapping. These were the styles that Toyota developed based on the principles they lived by, as defined above, and as Dr. Deming taught them years ago.

I saw this principle of Toyota being self-reliant in practice as a young engineer working for the Saturn Corporation when I witnessed how Toyota designed and built its own equipment, while the counterparts at GM, yours truly included, purchased equipment to meet the same needs. Toyota engineers designed and built their own equipment, unlike all of the other dozen or so automotive plants I had visited. They were self-reliant with their equipment as they were with their improvement methodologies. They developed their own ways, their own equipment, and their own styles.

Once again, Thomas Jefferson said:

Be flexible in style, but unwavering, like a rock, in principle.

If one is to copy anything from Toyota, copy its principles and develop your own style. Or, copy Dr. Deming's principles, build a culture around his principles, and develop your own style, much like Toyota did.

Dr. Deming wrote on page 129 of *Out of the Crisis,* "It is a hazard to copy. It is necessary to understand the theory of what one wishes to do or make. Americans are great copiers . . . ."

Dr. Deming also identifies on page 127 that, "The supposition that solving problems, automation, gadgets, and new machinery will transform industry" is one of the great American obstacles to true transformation.

Americans seem to think that root cause analysis is only done when bad things occur (for example, customer returns of defective products). However, root cause analysis should also be done on good things that happen (like a successful product introduction within your company).

If companies would only attempt to do root cause analysis on Toyota's success they would discover that the root causes are not tools like 5S and TPM, rather they are the principles by which Toyota lives and which Dr. Deming taught us.

EXPENSIVE BAND-AIDS

GM, like so many other companies, was not very good at performing root cause analysis (RCA). When RCA is not done well, the company has to do something to prevent the problem or defect from getting to the customer, so the norm is to add multitudes of band-aids, including inspection, inventory, and extra processing. This is exactly why "lean" is so popular today—we have accumulated so many band-aids over the years because of not doing RCA well.

In my particular case at Saturn, I was a manufacturing engineer, responsible for designing, purchasing, and testing the fluid fill equipment for the General Assembly facility. I was advised by experts from the GM Technical Center and other GM plants of what I needed to purchase and the number of items to purchase. As I was supposed to do, I would benchmark other facilities (mostly GM, but also Honda, Chrysler, and Nissan) to find out how they processed the fluid fill operations and what equipment they had.

In one particular example, I was told by many people that I needed to buy two transmission top-off units at about $85,000 each. The second machine was a backup, which was the GM norm, but, as I was told by many, the second unit was there primarily to hold spare parts for the first unit. The machine would require one-half person to operate each shift.

The transmission top-off unit was always located after final assembly and test. The machine, when attached to the transmission, would sense the level of transmission fluid, and if there were too little, it would dispense in what was needed. If there were too much, it would suck out the excess.

At one point, I organized and led a group of about five people to the NUMMI GM–Toyota joint venture plant that produced Toyota Corollas and Chevrolet Novas (or "No Go" in Spanish—"no va"). I brought my long list of benchmarking questions to California and received a lot of good information. I finally asked our tour guide if I could see their transmission top-off equipment. He asked me what it did. I told him the purpose of the unit and how it performed. He said they did not have anything like that. I told him that he must be mistaken (I was after all 25 years old and had already visited many plants, so I knew). I offered to take him to the end of the assembly line where the equipment would be located. We looked everywhere and could not find the top-off equipment. It was at that time that I realized that transmission top-off units were just band-aids, put into place because the root cause as to why the plant could not dispense an accurate level of fluid into the transmission in the first place was never determined. And it was an expensive band-aid, too: $170,000 in equipment and lot of labor to cover up a wound made much earlier in the process.

I wondered how many other band-aids Saturn was buying . . . .

When a new plant is built, the typical statement made is that the new plant will receive the best of everything. Unfortunately, without any focus on the elimination of waste, that also means the company will buy the best band-aids.

When I returned to Saturn headquarters, I gave up the $170,000 budgeted for this particular equipment because I took it to heart that my processes should be as good or better than Toyota's (few people really did). People thought I was nutty for doing so, and some would say that one should never give up money in his or her budget just in case something unexpected happens. I took it as a challenge, assembled a team, and started a failure mode and effects analysis (FMEA) on the initial transmission fill process (so that a top-off would not be necessary).

It is my belief that Saturn bought a lot of waste and broken processes from other GM plants. We could, though, because we could afford to buy waste. We had $1 billion dollars to spend, and spend we did. We also did not have company-wide principles like "constant focus on the elimination of waste" and "getting to the root causes of problems" to live by, so we did not. The lack of the right principles was the beginning of the end for Saturn.

ROOT CAUSE ANALYSIS AND DR. DEMING

If one were to do a search of root cause analysis in the index of *Out of the Crisis,* one would not find any references. A quick scan of Dr. Deming's 14 Points does not reveal any references to root cause analysis. So did Dr. Deming believe in root cause analysis?

Of course he did. He just explained it using different terms than we use today.

Probably the one Point of the 14 Points that comes closest to referencing eliminating root causes would be Point #12: "Remove barriers that rob people of pride in workmanship." These barriers, or root causes (or getting close to root causes), include:

- The annual rating of performance

- Merit ratings

- Unclear standards for acceptable performance

- Instruments and gages out of order

- Supervisors pushed by top management to meet a daily quota or a new monthly record for shipments

- Substandard equipment in need of repair

- Cheap materials purchased from China because Purchasing was directed to do so by top management

- Cheap tools

Dr. Deming also gave us Point #10 as he wrote on page 24 of *Out of the Crisis,* "Eliminate slogans, exhortations, and targets for the work force asking for zero defects and new levels of productivity. Such exhortations only create adversarial relationships, as the bulk of the causes of low quality and low productivity belong to the system and thus lie beyond the power of the work force."

Dr. Deming also gave us Point #9, "Break down the barriers between departments." The barriers between departments are, in fact, what prevents us from reaching the root causes of so many of our problems.

The point is that even though Dr. Deming did not refer to the term root cause analysis, our lack of following his 14 Points is the root cause of poorly run businesses.

Let us not forget that Dr. Deming proclaimed on page 315 of *Out of the Crisis*, "I should estimate that in my experience most troubles and most possibilities for improvement add up to proportions like this:

94% belong to the system (responsibility of management)

6% special."

In other words, a full 94% of the *root causes* to our problems reside in poor management systems, which are controlled by management. This is why Dr. Deming told us that Western management must change, and leadership must be instituted!!

7

Dr. Deming As the Early Pioneer of Lean

Let us not forget, Dr. Deming constantly talked about removal of waste in all of our processes. Many people associate Dr. Deming with the quality movement and fail to realize that he played a major role in today's lean movement, because both movements really are one and the same.

I know of companies that are very much involved in a lean initiative and yet the lean leaders are still in constant battles with the quality people, just as they always have been. They use all the tools of lean, including kaizen events, 5S, and TPM, but they still do not see the relationship between quality and productivity. They are *using lean* to do what they've always done—increase the production numbers at any cost and meet new production goals. They still do not understand that the way to higher production and lower costs is through decreasing variability in quality and production scheduling. The way to increase production and decrease costs is by making products more uniform around a nominal or target value and concerning themselves less with just meeting specifications.

> *Those companies that use lean to drive up production numbers with no concern for improving quality are practicing fake lean.*

I believe that it is very important to give credit to whom credit is due. This is one reason why I have written this book. I also think it is important to rally around Dr. Deming's principles as a central point of concentration because he is the one person that truly understood and brought together for the first time how quality and productivity move in the same direction. If quality goes up, so does production. If quality goes down, so does production.

> *Dr. Deming deserves much of the credit for today's lean movement.*

As Dr. Shoichiro Toyoda, founder and chairman of the Toyota Motor Corporation, said:[21]

> *Every day I think about what he meant to us. Deming is the core of our management.*

Dr. Deming wrote on page 12 of *Out of the Crisis:*

> *A. V. Feigenbaum estimated that from 15 to 40 percent of the manufacturer's costs of almost any American product that you buy today is for waste embedded in it—waste of human effort, waste of machine time, nonproductive use of accompanying burden. No wonder American products are hard to sell at home or abroad.*
>
> *In some work that I did for a railway, study showed that mechanics in a huge repair shop spent three quarters of their time waiting in line to get parts.*

And on page 53, he wrote,

> *The greatest waste in America is failure to use the abilities of people.*

Those who have learned about the *7 process wastes,* which were then later modified to the *8 process wastes* with the addition of underutilization of employees' minds and skills, will now know that the "newest" waste was the same waste that Dr. Deming wrote about in his book in the '80s.

Lean is also known as the Toyota Production System. *The Toyota Way* describes the Toyota Production System as 14 principles and, as seen earlier in this book, there is a very strong correlation between the principles defined in *The Toyota Way* and the principles defined by Dr. Deming.

CONTINUAL VERSUS CONTINUOUS IMPROVEMENT

Dr. Deming gave us his 5th Point: Improve constantly and forever the system of production and service, to improve quality and productivity, and thus constantly decrease costs. What is meant by "constantly"?

Constantly implies happening all the time.

Continuous means extending uninterruptedly in time, as in a continuous procession of cars. It is more synonymous with the term *single-piece flow,* as opposed to doing things in *batches.* Continuous improvement involves the little improvements that take place every day, by many people, throughout the company. Continuous improvement activities don't happen once a week or once a month or just when a customer complains. They happen every day. This is the same as constant improvement.

On the other hand, *continual* implies recurrence at regular or frequent intervals. For example, if one was to continually improve his or her dancing abilities, he or she would continually practice, perhaps by going to a dance class once a week. (On the other hand, if one was to *continuously* improve his or her dancing, he or she would never quit dancing.) *Continual* is more synonymous with *batch processing*. It is more project oriented. When a company schedules a once-a-month kaizen or Six Sigma project, that company is practicing continual improvement, not continuous improvement. Big useful changes to a system or a value stream can take place, but it is not the end-all, and it is not continuous improvement.

The literal translation of *kaizen* is *continuous* improvement, not *continual* improvement. When a company performs once-a-month kaizen events, they are not really doing kaizen because they are only improving once a month. The term *kaizen event* is really an oxymoron.

The irony in conducting once-a-month kaizen events, in which a team of perhaps five to eight people do nothing for three to five days except work together on improving an area or a process, is that *the team is doing batch processing of improvements to get rid of batch processing!!*

Continual improvement activities and continuous improvement activities are both of value. The challenge, though, for a company is to evolve itself into an organization that is involved in continuous improvement, or as Dr. Deming stated *constant* improvement, with many people involved on making many changes and improvements, every day. This is where the true benefits are achieved. Developing a culture that allows for continuous improvement is absolutely necessary for an ever-improving company in an ever-changing world.

A company that relies on once-a-month kaizen or Six Sigma events, run by experts, will never experience the benefits of continuous improvement. Dr. Deming said that the transformation is everyone's responsibility. It should not be in the hands of a few experts. When everyone is involved with improvements every single day, this is the best way to demonstrate respect for all of the individuals, and this is the essence of lean as it was initiated by Dr. Deming.

DR. DEMING LIVED LEAN

As mentioned previously, when Dr. Deming was a young boy he and his brother Bob would run around the farm in Wyoming all summer long. The Demings were poor people and had very little in material possessions. Mrs.

Deming made each boy two one-piece jumpsuits. They were pajama-like and they were very practical for two active boys growing up on a farm. Each day, Mrs. Deming would wash the outfits from the previous day and the boys would get dressed in the outfit cleaned the previous day. Today, we would call this single-piece flow of the laundry process, as mother would wash one piece at a time rather than batch processing the laundry as we all do today.

Single-piece flow of the laundry process in the Deming household was developed out of necessity because they had very little in the way of inventory (of clothes) and there was no other choice. And yet, the product—cleanly dressed boys—was still of high quality. Dr. Deming saw what can be accomplished with little and he, like so many of our elders who lived through the Great Depression, saw the vast amounts of waste we have created over the years because we could afford to be wasteful, or so we thought. We have vast amounts of inventory and other assets. We could afford to be wasteful, and so we are. Each succeeding generation becomes more wasteful than the preceding generation until a crisis occurs. The crisis might be another depression, war, running out of natural resources, global changes, or the negative impacts of offshoring all of our manufacturing capabilities. All of these are happening to some extent in today's world. The question to ponder is, are any of these crises or potential crises large enough to make us less wasteful as a society?

Toyota nearly went bankrupt in the late '40s. They had to eliminate waste in the process so that they could get paid for manufactured vehicles prior to paying their suppliers for the materials and components that went into those vehicles, in order to manage cash flow. They were poor, and the lean mentality was born, once again, out of necessity. The difference is, though, that Toyota was able to sustain the lean mentality as it became a wealthy company, primarily because of the deep-seated principles upon which the company is based and is run.

On the other hand, as American companies became wealthy, they also became increasingly wasteful. And instead of doing the hard work of getting rid of the waste, Americans outsourced their processes to other countries, thus increasing the waste even more.

During World War II, Dr. Deming was asked to use his skills in training supervisors to run production efforts in the United States to support the war effort. One of the key principles he taught the supervisors was how to eliminate waste through reduction of scrap and rework. Any elimination of waste of scarce raw materials was the equivalent of finding great deposits of those same raw materials. After the war, U.S. companies were no longer interested in reducing waste, improving quality, and the teachings of Dr. Deming until market share began to drop due to relatively low levels of quality when compared to Japanese products, some 30 years later. Where the United States abandoned Dr. Deming's teachings after the war, the Japanese picked them up. He then took the message of waste reduction to a country that had very little in the way of natural resources, and they listened and responded.

Dr. Deming experienced life as a person who abhorred waste in all that he did and practiced. Up until the time of his death at the age of 93, he kept up a consulting and teaching schedule that would tire people a quarter of his age. His secretary recalls Dr. Deming watching television on only four occasions; he believed that it took one away from useful work.

8

From Grades . . .
to Pay for Grades . . .
to Pay for Performance . . .
to Pay to Play

A client of mine awards one lucky employee an Employee of the Quarter award and money four times each year. When I talked to some of the employees, they said that most times a group of employees will get together to nominate one employee, and that when he or she wins, the group splits the money. This is very similar to employees pooling their money together to buy lottery tickets and split any proceeds. This is why I referred to the "lucky" employee who wins. The other option that had been used was that the decision makers who choose the Employee of the Quarter oftentimes would award the prize to the employee who complained the most as a means of appeasing that employee and perhaps getting him or her to shut up. This was at least the perception of many of the employees. Whether it was true or not did not matter. What mattered most is that the employees knew how to work the system, either by pooling their votes together or complaining a lot, so that they could win the prize. They also knew that the prize really had nothing to do with being an outstanding employee and had everything to do with manipulating the system.

What was meant to provide an incentive for employees to be better employees, as if they had control over that, turned out to be an incentive to cheat the system, and provided no focus at all on continuous improvement.

Dr. Deming taught us in *The New Economics* that the rewards based on extrinsic motivation (money, gold stars, grades, belts, certificates) do not work. Organizations should be based on intrinsically motivating employees and students. People naturally want to do a good job for the company; children naturally want to learn all there is to learn. Grades are a demotivator. They put the focus on obtaining a good grade rather than on learning as much as possible.

My seven-year-old daughter has such a strong desire to learn. She absolutely loves going to museums and she wears out Mom and Dad as she wants to see everything within the museum. She *naturally* wants to learn. She also hates going to school. It's too slow for her. It slows her down. Are grades really going to motivate her to learn more? No, she's already motivated to learn, but the school system is inadequate in allowing her to learn.

School is getting in the way of education.

If a company feels that it has an unmotivated workforce, adding incentives such as Employee of the Quarter, pay for performance, or other financial stimuli are only band-aids on a much bigger problem that involves the management system and the culture of the company. As such the band-aids will only work for a very short time, if at all, until the employees learn how to manipulate the system as we saw in the above example.

NO CHILD LEFT BEHIND

The No Child Left Behind Act of 2001 (Public Law 107-110), often abbreviated in print as NCLB and sometimes shortened in pronunciation to "nicklebee," is a United States federal law (Act of Congress) that was originally proposed by President George W. Bush on January 23, 2001, immediately after taking office.

NCLB is the latest federal legislation (another was Goals 2000) to enact the theories of standards-based education reform, formerly known as outcome-based education, which is based on the belief that setting high standards and establishing measurable goals can improve individual outcomes in education. The Act requires states to develop assessments in basic skills to be given to all students in certain grades, if those states are to receive federal funding for schools. NCLB does not assert a national achievement standard; standards are set by each individual state, in line with the principle of local control of schools.[22]

From an article entitled "Pros & Cons of the No Child Left Behind Act," written by Deborah White of About.com, the following negatives are perceived by many people, especially the teachers' union.

Teaching to the Test

Teachers and parents charge that NCLB encourages, and rewards, teaching children to score well on the test rather than teaching with a primary goal of learning. As a result, teachers are pressured to teach a narrow set of test-taking skills and a test-limited range of knowledge.

NCLB ignores many vital subjects, including science, history, and foreign languages.

Problems with NCLB Standardized Tests

Since states set their own standards and write their own standardized NCLB tests, states can compensate for inadequate student performance by setting very low standards and making tests unusually easy.

Many contend that testing requirements for disabled and limited–English proficient students are unfair and unworkable.

Critics allege that standardized tests contain cultural biases, and that educational quality can't necessarily be evaluated by objective testing.

Failure to Address Reasons for Lack of Achievement

At its core, NCLB faults schools and curriculum for student failure, but critics claim that other factors are also to blame, including class size, old and damaged school buildings, hunger and homelessness, and lack of healthcare.

The most important con, as perceived by teachers and parents, is that once again teachers are learning how to teach students how to do well on a test. It is no different than companies learning how to pass an ISO 9001 audit or employees learning how to take a test to become a certified auditor, a Black Belt, or certified kaizen team leader.

Teachers are encouraged to do whatever it takes to ensure that the students do well on the test in order to ensure the flow of funds into the school. The joy of teaching and the joy of learning become nonexistent as high test scores become the focus. Alternative and interesting methods of teaching and learning are destroyed because the class has to work within the system and are not allowed to challenge the system, which is the only hope of improving the system. Math and English are the subjects of focus at the expense of science, history, the arts, and going to the museum to learn.

> *Many teachers are enraged by the law's reliance on high-stakes exams that lead schools like Blaine to focus relentlessly on boosting scores rather than pursuing a broader vision of education. More than 30,000 educators and concerned citizens have signed an online petition calling for the repeal of the 1100-page NCLB statute. Some offer comments like this one from a former superintendent of schools in Ohio: "NCLB is like a Russian novel. That's because it's long, it's complicated, and in the end, everybody gets killed."*[23]

Also, because of the reliance on passing tests, teachers do what they have chastised children about doing for years. They cheat on tests. My wife experienced this firsthand as she watched experienced teachers providing answers to children during tests and giving them more than the allotted time. What were the children learning from their teacher? They were learning the art of cheating.

THE RESULTS

The discussions and battles over whether or not NCLB is working continue. According to TIME magazine, the early results, as of May 2005, show:

> *Whether NCLB is achieving its objectives remains an open question. Fourth-grade reading scores on the National Assessment of Educational Progress (NAEP) rose sharply from 1999 to 2004, but most of the gains occurred before the law took effect. The achievement gap appears to be narrowing in some spots—fourth- and eighth-grade math scores for minorities, for instance—but not others. The gap between white and black eighth-graders has widened slightly in math, for example. Gains for eighth-graders in general remain stubbornly elusive.*

Newly minted education secretary of the Obama administration Arne Duncan spoke in early 2009 about the need to fix the Bush administration's No Child Left Behind law. His opinion of it:

> *I think we are lying to children and families when we tell children that they are meeting standards and, in fact, they are woefully unprepared to be successful in high school and have almost no chance of going to a good university and being successful.*

But Duncan is also interested in other people's opinions. He's meeting with the heads of the two national teachers unions and . . . he plans to travel the country to gather input from school officials and families about ways to improve the federal testing law. Duncan also says he is in the market for ideas to rename the law.[24]

Here's an idea for a new name: "Learning How to Pass a Test without Learning Anything—for Dummies"

Even if the NCLB goals are achieved, all that this means is that the children have learned how to take a test in a few limited areas focusing on English and math. They have not learned how to communicate, how to think, how to work with others effectively, how to problem-solve, how to problem-prevent, geography, history, the arts, and science. And, importantly, they have not learned how to learn. And even more importantly, they associate learning with a quantitative number, a quota, a bogey, and they have learned that there is no reason to learn more (for example, reading during the summer break) unless some reward for them or the school is the outcome. They have not learned the joy in learning and becoming more knowledgeable.

The debates that will ensue will be fruitless. The powers that be are missing the point. Even if some results show higher scores in reading and math, it does not mean that our students are more knowledgeable or more prepared for the world. It only means that they are more prepared to take and pass tests of very limited subject matters. They will grow up to learn how to manipulate a system for the benefit of recognition, grades, Black Belts, certifications, and yes, even money.

FROM GRADES . . .
TO PAY FOR GRADES . . .
TO PAY FOR PERFORMANCE . . .
TO PAY TO PLAY

Earlier in the book, I discussed how our new secretary of education Arne Duncan created a pay for grades program in the Chicago Public Schools system, and you can bet your bottom dollar he will try to do the same nationally.

From the September 2008 edition of the *Chicago Tribune:*

Earn an A? Here's $50.
(Eke out a C? That's Still Good for $20.)
A Chicago Public Schools pilot program will pay up to 5000 freshmen for good grades. Is that a smart idea?

By Carlos Sadovi
September 11, 2008

Up to 5000 freshmen at 20 Chicago public high schools will get cash for good—and even average—grades as part of a new, Harvard-designed test program that city education leaders are rolling out Thursday.

Students will be measured every five weeks in math, English, social sciences, science, and physical education. An A nets $50, a B equals $35, and a C still brings in $20. Students will get half the money up front, with the remainder paid upon graduation. A straight-A student could earn up to $4000 by the end of his or her sophomore year.

> *Parents have been rewarding children for stellar report cards for decades. Chicago Public Schools officials are nodding to that tradition and saying the idea is to get students to stay in school and do well while they're there.*
>
> *"The majority of our students don't come from families with a lot of economic wealth. I'm always trying to level the playing field," said schools chief executive Arne Duncan. "This is the kind of incentive that middle-class families have had for decades."*
>
> *Chicago is following the lead of similar programs in their infancy in New York and Washington. The district's plan, part of the "Green for Grade$" program, involves no taxpayer money— the $2 million over two years comes from private sources.*
>
> *Critics suggest that what amounts to bribing students to get good grades isn't the right lesson to teach.*
>
> *"It's a terrible idea, because you're getting people to do things for the wrong reasons," said Barry Schwartz, a Swarthmore College psychology professor who has written on the issue. "They'll do well in school, maybe, but they won't take any of it out with them. Instead of trying to cultivate an interest in learning, curiosity . . . you are just turning this into another job."*

This system is a double whammy of extrinsic motivation for education. Not only are children being rewarded with grades but on top of that are earning money for good grades.

Perhaps some day soon these kids will get wise and form a Student Union and begin demanding more money than a lousy $50 for an A. And what about a D? That's within specification of passing. Shouldn't a D be worth what a C is now worth? D becomes the new C. C becomes the new B. B becomes the new A, and an A should be worth $100 for all of their hard work. And if they don't get the increase, they won't go to school! Is this what we're heading toward?

Can you imagine the cheating that will now occur? It will be rampant! Bullying in school will now increase as big dumb guys demand that little smart guys do their homework for them and allow them to cheat off of their tests. Collusion, paybacks, schemes, blackmail, and bribes between students and teachers will increase, with the intent of increasing the pay of both student and teacher. And meanwhile, learning and gaining new knowledge will take a back seat to the almighty dollar.

Eventually, these kids might grow up to become Illinois governors and come up with schemes like bribes for truck drivers' licenses, which our former Governor Ryan—now in prison—supported until one of the unqualified truck drivers killed an entire family on an Illinois interstate. Or our kids might grow up to be like our latest ousted Governor Blagovech and try to sell a senate seat, vacated by the newly elected President Obama, to the highest bidder because they become accustomed to entitlements in the school system.

We wonder why we have so many crooked politicians. With programs like grading, paying for grades, standardized tests, performance appraisals, and merit pay for teachers, the dishonesty and greed will only get worse in government, business, and education.

WHAT DOES DR. DEMING HAVE IN COMMON WITH THE FOUNDER OF KINKO'S?

Paul Orfalea (founder of Kinko's) began his most excellent book entitled *Copy This! How I Turned Dyslexia, ADHD, and 100 Square Feet into a Company Called Kinko's* with:

> *Not many kids manage to flunk the second grade, but I did. I couldn't learn the alphabet. This code called reading, so easy for other students, I found difficult to break. They read as though angels whispered into their ears. They wrote in graceful curves and perfectly straight lines. I made chicken scratches. To me, a sentence was a road map with ink stains in all the critical places.*
>
> *Consequently, I became a goof-off. Of the eight schools my parents enrolled me in, four expelled me. In the third grade, my frustrated teachers sent me to a school for "mentally retarded kids" . . . . Fortunately, I was given an IQ test, scored 130, and rejoined the public school system. Still, things didn't get much better. I may not have been able to read, but I could find my way back to the principal's office blindfolded. My typical report card came back with two C's, three D's, and an F.[25]*

On the other hand, Dr. Deming graduated with a college degree from the University of Wyoming in 1921 in electrical engineering, a master's degree from the University of Colorado in 1925 in mathematics and physics, and a doctor's degree from Yale in 1928 in mathematics and physics.

So what could these two great individuals possibly have in common? They both taught (or teach) at the university level and neither gave out grades to their students.

In 2000, Paul Orfalea retired from his position as chairperson of the company he named in honor of his college nickname (after his kinky hair).

Paul teaches economics to college seniors at the University of California at Santa Barbara. He does not take roll. He takes a Polaroid of each student on the first day and writes their first name on the photo. On the rare occasion that he asks the students to complete writing assignments, he never expects more than a single page of clear and concise prose. He couldn't care less about grades and he gives almost all his students A's. Instead, he teaches them skills that have little to do with academics or test scores.

Why does he teach so differently? Because he has such a strong belief that straight-A types live in abject fear of failure. They rack up all these perfect grades and think they will die if they come home with a B or a C. That's no preparation for real life. Out in the real world, failure—and benefiting from it—is the name of the game. Straight-A types unaccustomed to failure enter the marketplace and take their first belly flops especially hard. That's why so many of them return to graduate school and the security it brings them. Paul further said:

Our schools are producing test takers, not creative thinkers.

and:

If George W. Bush ever succeeded with his "No Child Left Behind" program, I'd still be in the third grade.

It is understandable why Paul felt this way. He came out of a system that, had it not been for a strong family and strong parental guidance, would have made him a complete failure, and yet because of his inability to get good grades he was an utter success.

But then how did someone like Dr. Deming, a person who did not struggle in school, received good grades, and excelled within the system, come to the same conclusion as Paul did—that grades in school are detrimental to all students, even those who receive good grades. Dr. Deming studied human psychology and statistical theory and came to this conclusion. He did not experience the negative impacts of our current educational system as Paul did; he deduced the negative effects of our educational system and pay-for-performance systems through theory, and then verified his theories by listening to willing workers.

Dr. Deming did not give grades to his students. They all passed. He would read the papers that his students turned in, not to grade them, but:

1. To learn how he was doing as a teacher. In what ways was he failing? How could he improve his teaching?

2. To discover whether any student was in need of special help and to see that s/he got it.

3. To discover whether any student was extra well prepared and could receive benefit from extra work.

A student could take their time. They did not have to rush their papers. Meanwhile, the student received his or her grade, P for *pass*.

The first reason Deming listed above, to learn how he is doing as a teacher, is very consistent with Miyagi's message in the memorable film *The Karate Kid* in 1984:

> *No such thing as bad student, only bad teacher. Teacher say, student do.*

It is also very consistent with the Training Within Industry (TWI) credo, which many people say was the real beginning of the Toyota Production System and lean thinking:

> *If the worker hasn't learned, the teacher hasn't taught.*

TWI Services was created by the United States Department of War, running from 1940 to 1945 within the War Manpower Commission. The purpose was to provide consulting services to war-related industries whose personnel were being conscripted into the U.S. Army at the same time the Department of War was issuing orders for additional material. After the war, it was brought to Japan to teach personnel attempting to build up the industrial base, while it was forgotten about in the United States until very recently.

Dr. Deming taught that as two people play a game, there is a winner and there is a loser. He did not understand why that pattern of games continued on into grades in school, and on up through the university, the merit system, and ranking groups and divisions within the company. Grading and ranking produce artificial scarcity of top grades. Only a few students are admitted to the top grades and only a few workers are admitted to the top rank.

Dr. Deming claimed that this was wrong because there is no scarcity of good pupils and there is no scarcity of good people.[26]

Dr. Stephen Covey, author of *The 7 Habits of Highly Effective People*, could not agree more with Dr. Deming:[27]

> *People with a scarcity mentality tend to see everything in terms of win–lose. There is only so much; and if someone else has it, that means there will be less for me. The more principle-centered we become, the more we develop an abundance mentality, the more we are genuinely happy for the successes, well-being, achievements, recognition, and good fortune of other people. We believe their success adds to . . . rather than detracts from . . . our lives.*

Why can't we just learn without the pressure of grades? My seven-year-old daughter naturally wants to go to museums, planetariums, aquariums, zoos, and on expeditions, just for the sheer joy of learning. We, as parents, are not trying to entice her to these establishments of learning with money or gold stars—she just wants to go.

The want to learn is natural until we make it artificial with extrinsic motivators such as grades, gold stars, Black Belts, certificates, and/or money . . . in school, in business, in government . . . thus depriving ourselves of the joy in learning and the joy in becoming more knowledgeable.

9

I'm Sorry—the Recession of '07–'09 Was My Fault

OK, it is well understood by many of us that we should not blame people for systemic errors, and that given the recession of '07–'09, we have some real systemic errors. So why would I blame myself—a person—for these problems? I think that I, or we, as Deming advocates, should begin to take much more ownership in the downfall of our economy, including the downfall of our mortgage companies, financial institutions, and automotive industry. If Deming advocates, as a whole, had been doing a good job, we should have been much better prepared as a country in predicting and warding off a large portion of the economic mess of '07–'09. The state of the economy was one of low quality, and we should shoulder some of the blame in allowing it to get to this point. I feel that I have not done enough to promote true quality ideals and Deming principles in all industries and facets of life, and I would hope that many of you do, too.

Let's face it, Deming advocates and quality professionals—we are a weak bunch!! How many CEOs of any size company, whether a small, medium, or large company, in any type of industry, have a "quality" background? When was the last time you talked to a CEO, asked him or her what their background was, and he or she exclaimed that they had once been the quality manager or director of quality? I've worked with many different companies as a consultant and trainer for 15 years, and I have yet to meet one. I did find out from one of my readers that one Don Jackson, a former quality guy from Toyota, is now president of the new Volkswagen factory in Chattanooga, Tennessee. That's great, but it is far too uncommon.

Even large organizations *that promote quality* are oftentimes not run by people with any sort of quality background. I can remember listening to a panel discussion at a conference in which the three CEOs of the top three ISO 9001 registrars were speaking. One of them almost boastfully proclaimed, "I am not a quality guy." I think that statement actually had two meanings.

CHALLENGE #1

We must ask ourselves, why are we a weak bunch? Why do we not have more quality-type people and Deming advocates at the highest levels within a company? How can we promote quality ideals and Deming's principles at the highest levels? How can we get more *quality* people to run organizations? And then we must do something about it.

Create Constancy of Purpose in Improving Products and Services versus Greed

In the '80s, CEOs of major corporations began to truly listen to the virtues of quality primarily due to the fact that the United States was embroiled in a crisis of producing products of inferior quality, especially in comparison with what was being produced in Japan.

The first Point of Dr. Deming's once famous 14 Points is "Create constancy of purpose toward improvement of product and service, with the aim to become competitive and stay in business, and to provide jobs."

In today's world of business, as in 1980, if you were to ask American CEOs what the purpose of their business is, most would answer, "to make money." If you then induced a truth serum into the same American CEOs (this is a must) and then asked each one what the purpose of their life is, most would have the same answer.

This has been played out in the public eye, and to the detriment of thousands of employees, as we have watched one CEO after another fall to the temptation of greed and short-term thinking—the exact opposite of what Dr. Deming was teaching business and quality executives. We saw how Bernard Ebbers destroyed WorldCom, Dennis Kozlowski nearly destroyed Tyco, Joseph Berardino brought down Arthur Andersen Consulting, and of course, Kenneth Lay and Jeffrey Skilling blew up the once mammoth Enron.

If you were to ask the few CEOs of those companies who truly believe, breathe, practice, and live in continual improvement, quality, and waste elimination, they would provide such answers as, "improve society," "improve quality of life," "provide and maintain jobs," and "be competitive in the long run." The purpose of their being in business is one based on higher character, morals, and ethics, and it would benefit society, employees, community, and environment, and lastly themselves.

The *opposite* of Dr. Deming's 1st Point is indeed *greed*. I can't help but remember back to my grade school days and learning about the Seven Deadly Sins, one of which was greed. A quick check on Wikipedia states that greed includes:

> *Disloyalty, deliberate betrayal, or treason, especially for personal gain, for example through bribery. Scavenging and hoarding of materials or objects, theft and robbery, especially by means of violence, trickery, or manipulation of authority are all actions that may be inspired by greed.*

Does this not describe the actions of Bernard, Dennis, Joseph, Kenneth, and Jeffrey? Does this describe your own CEOs?

Freddie Mac, Fannie Mae, Constancy of Purpose, and Greed

Does this also not describe the actions of the government-sponsored home mortgage underwriters Fannie Mae and Freddie Mac as they began to extend home mortgages to individuals whose credit was generally not good enough to qualify for conventional loans? Freddie and Fannie, starting in 1999 and encouraged by both Democratic and Republican administrations, simply extended mortgages by relaxing lending standards, creating more false demand than the market could handle. Freddie and Fannie's risk was then spread across many financial and insurance organizations via the development of fanciful financial mechanisms to mask the major problems that could eventually occur one day.

As quality professionals and Deming advocates, if we had used what we've practiced all of our lives, we would have plotted average home prices on a control chart and realized that the housing industry was "out of control" as housing prices "trended" up for more than seven points (years) in a row. I knew this. Others in the quality profession knew this. But I didn't do enough to help shut down the process and address the special causes of variation (relaxed lending standards and fanciful mechanisms for spreading lender risk) before we began producing defective products (foreclosures). I apologize for not doing my part. I believe that all quality professionals should apologize for not doing his or her part. Dr. Deming would have!

As Jim Womack, a well-respected lean professional and founder of the Lean Enterprise Institute (www.lean.org), wrote so succinctly in his article entitled "Meg Mura Bubble Trouble":

> *Mega mura (variation) by contrast applies to large and lengthy shifts in total demand by external customers across the economy.*

> *Unfortunately, a boom in demand—caused in the current case by the surge in real estate prices fueled by low interest rates and relaxed lending standards—always leads to a bust. The sad part of these episodes—which are as old as market economies—is that they are almost never due to a fundamental change in consumer desires. Millions more Americans and Europeans didn't suddenly want to own a home or buy a bigger home in the years after 2001. They presumably had always had these desires but lacked the money to act on them. Instead the boom was caused by manipulation of the financial system—through cheap credit, relaxed lending standards, and fanciful mechanisms for spreading lender risk—to pump up the housing market for the short-term benefit of those doing the pumping.*

Freddie, Fannie, and all of the other investment banks and insurance companies involved in the process of falsely increasing housing demand focused on greed and increasing short-term profits at the expense of long-term stability of their businesses and their customer base. The purpose of their business was "to make money," not "Create constancy of purpose toward improvement of product and service, with the aim to become competitive and stay in business, and to provide jobs."

Without a doubt, they failed to hold to Deming's 1st point, and we failed to spread the word of Dr. Deming and stable systems and how control charts should have been used to defuse a special cause. Again, I apologize.

CHALLENGE #2

We must ask ourselves how we can be more proficient in spreading the word of quality, the word of Dr. Deming, and the word of stability in the markets, the benefits of control charts at all levels of *any* organization, state, or federal government, and the evils of greed and short-term thinking? And then we must do something about it.

Sending Wall Street to Jail

In an article entitled "Wall Street: It's Payback Time" written in the September 19, 2009 edition of *Fortune* magazine, I read in horror the following paragraph regarding the role of the prosecutors of Wall Street CEOs whose companies American taxpayers bailed out:[28]

> *The job of the prosecutors is not to ferret out the root causes of what went wrong with the economy. That's a task for historians.*

The prosecutors are to look for unambiguous, intentional wrong-doing . . . .

No wonder our government, judicial system, Wall Street, and CEOs are so screwed up. Essentially no one will ferret out root causes. As a result, new band-aids (laws) will be passed, and new CEOs will develop new schemes to work around the new laws, and new problems will occur. If there is no effort to get to the root causes of these major issues on Wall Street, we will never improve.

From the same article, a lawyer who advises corporations said anonymously:

The reality is, you've put your finger on one of the most difficult situations that will come up in counseling executives of corporations. You can't lie. You're trapped between serving the best interests of shareholders and the legal requirement not to lie. You need to thread the needle.

As an example from the same article, Matt Tannin, Bear Stearns hedge fund manager, wrote in an internal e-mail on April 22, 2007:

If we believe the (Bear Stearns internal report is) anywhere close to accurate, I think we should close the funds now . . . . If (the report) is correct, then the entire subprime market is toast.

On April 25, 2007, three days after writing this e-mail, he told investors:

So from a structural point of view, from an asset point of view, from a surveillance point of view, we're very comfortable with exactly where we are.

The system within which he is working encourages him and all the other CEOs to lie. The system sucks. Prosecuting CEOs, just as retraining an operator, is not going to improve or change the system. The system that encourages Wall Street's focus on the short term and encourages CEOs to lie must change *for the benefit of Wall Street* and all of its investors and employees. The system must encourage long-term focus and honest disclosure of problems without punishment. Is this not what we want within our own organizations?

Root causes must be determined, by asking "why" five times or more, for the following questions:

1. Why does the system encourage lying?

2. Why does Wall Street not know about or use root cause analysis?

3. Why are our judicial system and the public so focused on blaming people rather than fixing the problems?

4. Why do CEOs (and politicians) feel that they deserve more because of the position they hold? Why are they so greedy?

One possible answer to the fourth question is below.

Why Do CEOs (and Politicians) Feel That They Deserve More Because of the Position They Hold? Why Are They So Greedy?

It starts young. Perhaps the system within which we are educated is to blame—the system that makes some of us feel that we deserve more for just doing our job, and makes so many people so greedy.

A system that rewards children with gold stars or grades is a system that encourages children, and then grown-ups, to work for rewards and not to work for increasing their knowledge, not to learn for the sheer joy of learning, and not to increase the quality and profitability of a company. Our current system of awarding grades in school and performance evaluations and bonuses at work encourages focus on oneself and greed.

Dr. Deming's 11th Point or principle was "Eliminate work standards (quotas) on the factory floor. Substitute leadership. Eliminate management by objective. Eliminate management by numbers, numerical goals. Substitute leadership."

Dr. Deming warned us about the evils of performance reviews, grades in school, gold stars, and management by objectives, and we have ignored these principles and we have gone backwards. The future does not look any brighter. I also see no evidence that leadership will be substituted.

I am sorry I did not do more to educate more people about the evils of grading systems and performance reviews. I apologize because I did not see the evils of these systems because I was the type of person who looked forward to receiving my report card and I asked for performance reviews. I am a little weird.

CHALLENGE #3

We must ask ourselves, how can we educate those who establish our educational systems that grades (and definitely money) are not the means to encourage our youngsters to want to gain knowledge and learn for intrinsic reasons? Then we must do something about it.

The Automotive Industry and Constancy of Purpose

I can remember when I began my career with the Saturn Corporation of General Motors back in 1985. Saturn was going to be a new small-car company that would be profitable in its own right and compete head to head with Toyota and Honda. We were taught a little bit about the Toyota total development process, and some of us were taught that we should each be as good, if not better, than Toyota in the areas of responsibility that we controlled as engineers developing the manufacturing process. (Some of us took this seriously; most did not). Many of the Saturn leaders at that time were from the Pontiac Motor Division and had been tutored directly by Dr. Deming. Some of Dr. Deming's Points and principles were evident in the early years but they soon died out as Saturn became more and more integrated into General Motors.

For a short time, though, when Saturn was a reactive response to poor American car quality and a loss of the small-car market to Japan, it seemed that General Motors was at least looking to the future and embracing Deming's 1st Point:

> *Create constancy of purpose toward improvement of product and service, with the aim to become competitive and stay in business, and to provide jobs.*

Today, Deming's 1st Point, and for that matter, most all of his points, have long since been forgotten. Saturn became fully integrated into General Motors, and its survival outside of a bankrupt General Motors is up in the air. Saturn now produces cars of just average quality. Toyota and Honda already have a seven-year lead in the development of hybrid vehicles.[29] The Big Three focused most of their efforts on producing highly profitable SUVs and trucks while Peak Oil, the year that the most oil will ever be produced worldwide, occurred in 2005, some experts believe. As Peak Oil was being surpassed, worldwide demand for oil was increasing dramatically, gas prices were increasing exponentially, and the Big Three were once again not prepared, as they had not been three decades prior. Today, the leftovers of the Big Three have relatively few fuel-efficient options to offer the public, and though gasoline prices did subside in 2009 in concert with the recession, the price of gasoline will skyrocket once again with an improving economy. While all of this was happening over the last few decades, the Big Three had not addressed many of their other leadership and organizational issues, and as a result the CEOs flew to Washington in their private jets, tails between their legs, to request a bailout from the U.S. government and the taxpayers because they could not stay *"competitive and . . . stay in business, and . . . provide jobs."*

The shame of it all was that Ford and GM had spent a great amount of time learning from Dr. Deming but then soon forgot everything they were taught.

I worked in the automotive industry for about three years. I apologize once again for not doing my part and for not speaking up more as a quality professional about the shortsightedness of the automotive world.

ASQ's Code of Ethics

Why do I feel responsible for not doing enough? Because I know that as a quality professional and a Deming advocate, I, and we, are not doing enough to spread the word of "quality first" and the ideals of our quality God, Dr. Deming.

Additionally, I have the following certifications from ASQ: Six Sigma Black Belt (though I did try to sell my Black Belt), Manager of Quality/Organizational Excellence, Quality Auditor, and Quality Engineer. The ASQ Code of Ethics is located on the back side of each certificate. It states:

Fundamental Principles

ASQ requires its members and certification holders to conduct themselves ethically by:

I. *Being honest and impartial in serving the public, their employees, customers, and clients.*

II. *Striving to increase the competence and prestige of the quality profession, and*

III. *Using their knowledge and skill for the enhancement of human welfare.*

It is in the last two principles that I believe I am weak and we are very weak as a profession, and we need to change. We need to improve. We are not upholding these principles and the principles of Dr. Deming!

CHALLENGE #4

We must ask ourselves, how can we as quality professionals and Deming advocates, not just ASQ certification holders or members, better support and promote the above three principles throughout the highest levels of business, education, industry, healthcare, and government? And then we must do something about it.

10

Going Forward

This is a short chapter. Why? Because how to go forward was already written in Dr. Deming's *Out of the Crisis*.

Principles are timeless. Dr. Deming's 14 Points (principles) are as applicable today as they were in 1982, as they were in 1950, and as they were in the 1800s. They will be applicable in 2020, 2050, and 2200. They are not dependent on industry, technology, language, or geography.

As Dr. Stephen Covey stated in *The 7 Habits of Highly Effective People*:

> *Principles are guidelines for human conduct that are proven to have* enduring, permanent value. *They're fundamental. They're essentially unarguable because they are self-evident.*[30]

Most importantly, they have "enduring, permanent value." It's similar to the Bible: whether one believes in the stories in the Bible or not, the Bible has for many people over many hundreds of years provided enduring, permanent value.

Out of the Crisis is a business management system Bible. One can learn from it over and over again. There should be Deming preachers who speak from pulpits once a week referring to his many different passages. This is the reason why I began doing Dr. Deming impersonations some time ago. I wanted to teach people about what he taught us and to show people how far away we have veered from his path. We are business and governmental sinners who have veered away from self-evident principles.

We don't need a new scheme or program, even after ISO 9001, Six Sigma, lean, and balanced scorecards run their courses and become obsolete, just like TQM, reengineering, and benchmarking did before them.

Be flexible in style, but unwavering, like a rock, in principles.

—Thomas Jefferson

SOME POSSIBLE ACTIONS TO TAKE

1. Purchase and read at the least the first three chapters of *Out of the Crisis*. Discuss the implications of what was read as a management team and evaluate your company's practices against the principles of Dr. Deming. Determine the impact of establishing Deming's principles within your organization and what would need to change organizationally and structurally to support his principles.

2. Go to www.youtube.com and download some of Deming's speeches.

3. It all starts with the principles. Determine what your principles are first. If a company is to copy anything, it should copy Dr. Deming's principles, build a culture around those principles, and then make up its own tools. Are we not smart enough to develop our own tools and practices? Toyota did. Why do we feel this need copy other organizations' ways? Toyota did not. Why can't companies be their own organizations, based on sound business and ethical principles—the principles of Dr. Deming.

4. An alternative beginning that can be very eye-opening is to find someone who knows Dr. Deming's principles very well and ask that person to perform a very honest assessment of your facility, organization, leadership, buying practices, and continuous improvement activities in comparison to Dr. Deming's principles. Have that person present the results to top management and then have that person teach them Dr. Deming's principles.

5. From there, document your principles and proclaim to the organization that these principles will be the basis for the entire culture, which will be rebuilt from this point forward, and that only practices that support these principles will be put into place. Any new ideas, programs, or management philosophies will have to withstand the test to determine if they support the principles.

It's not too late. In these tough economic times, and with multiple crises occurring at the same time, including the depletion of and dependence on oil, loss of U.S. manufacturing capabilities, dishonest public and business officials, rampant greed, and a spiraling economy with debt piling up beyond control, *there's still hope.*

The hope lies in following the principles of Dr. Deming, one company/organization at a time, starting your company over again, changing your ways and becoming more humble, and then, once success has been reached, loudly proclaiming the virtues of Dr. Deming's principles once again so that they sweep the nation as they did in the '80s. It all begins with you!

Appendix

Are You a Member of S.A.D (Society of Anti-Deming)?

A sarcastic article published by *Quality Digest* magazine . . . .

Many of us in U.S. industry have forgotten the principles of our dearly departed quality guru, Dr. W. Edwards Deming, since his passing in 1993. Obviously, since he did pass, our quality levels as a country have grown somewhat, but not substantially. So we, at the Society of Anti-Deming (SAD), believe that if we practice the opposite of what He preached to us, we might do better.

Please evaluate yourself on each of the 14 points as follows:

1: I do not uphold this principle.

2: I sometimes uphold this principle, depending on the pressure from ownership.

3: This is great. I love this principle and abide by it all the time.

Add up your score to determine whether you meet the requirements to become a member of SAD. Though it would be sinful to do so, you may wish to read *Out of the Crisis,* the original twisted version of the 14 Points, from the teachings of Dr. W. Edwards Deming.

Point #1: Create inconsistency in purpose toward improvement of product and service.

Ensure that you *look* very competitive in the short term. Build up huge amounts of inventory and fire all supporting personnel like quality and maintenance. This all looks great on the balance sheet and financial statements produced each quarter. It doesn't matter if you plan on using the inventoried product in the future, because by the time the future rolls around, you'll have gotten the hell out of there, collected a huge bonus, and started with a new company to save their sorry butts, just like you did with this company. Screw the employees . . . I rule!

Score _____

Point #2: Adopt this philosophy.

Take on micromanaging, as you make delayed decisions from the golf course, even though you don't know anything about the business. It's all about control and having your people wait on you. You've earned it. Bilk the company for thousands of dollars. Long live Enron!

Score _____

Point #3: Institute 200% to 500% inspection.

You can never inspect enough! If you send a defect to the customer, tell them you'll add an extra inspector. If they're still not sure about your response, tell them you'll add a third inspector. They'll be so impressed that you are adding inspectors and are willing to bear such a burden at no cost to them. After the customer has stopped complaining for a few weeks, drop the inspection level to the pre-problem level by firing a temporary employee, and build profits once again!

Score _____

Point #4: Award business based on price tag alone.

Outsource to China and India!! Forget about the total cost of the product. Piece part cost is all that matters. Forget about the defects you have to live with because you have no leverage. Forget about paying for products weeks or months in advance and the abuse the products take in being transported across the world. Forget about the fact that you buy through a broker and that broker can buy from any one of hundreds of manufacturers, or from barns with dirt floors, and you have no idea where your products come from or what types of controls they have in place, but it's OK, because you buy from China, and that must be good. Forget about translating your requirements for the Chinese broker and his suppliers. These are commodity items and we're getting them cheap. Even if they send one right part out of 10, it's still cheaper, because all that matters is piece part cost. And while you're doing this, do lean (see next point).

Score _____

Point #5: Once in a while, improve the system of production or service.

Do this, especially after you've had a crisis resulting from a major customer complaint or product recall. Show the customer that you're committed to change by spending lots of money buying a prepackaged improvement process like Six Sigma or lean. After all, it worked in the past when you bought quality circles, TQM, benchmarking, quality education system, reengineering, and ISO 9001. Don't bother with developing your practices based on your principles. Hell, don't even bother with developing principles. This is supportive of Point #1. So, buy a program, tell everyone you support it, follow up a year later, and if things have calmed down with your customers, scrap this initiative and search for the new China.

Score _____

Point #6: Institute trial and error.

The greatest waste in America is using the minds of employees. We don't hire thinkers—we hire workers. So let them work! If they don't need to think, don't train them. In fact, the quicker you get them to work (say like within the first 30 minutes of their first day), the quicker they'll screw up, the quicker you can make them feel like a total idiot, and the quicker they'll learn from their mistakes. It's all about trial and error. That's why it's best to hire as many temps as possible. This way if they screw up a lot, you can just hire another worker within 30 minutes. Workers are just commodities, like nuts and bolts. It would be ridiculous to train nuts and bolts, although we do sometimes train nuts.

Score _____

Point #7: Adopt and institute micromanaging.

1. Treat everyone as imbeciles.

2. Let everyone know how tough your job is so no one will want it.

3. Do not participate in any improvements.

4. Maintain the highest level of dishonesty (that is, tell them the company's doing well when it's not).

5. Insist on mediocrity and let your people get away with missing deadlines.

6. Build competitiveness within the organization.

7. Show no confidence in your people. Maintain complete control. Micromanage (see #1).

8. Maintain a strong sense of "taking it easy."

9. Stay in your office with your door closed.

10. Stop learning—you know it all by now.

Score _____

Point #8: Drive home fear!

Ensure that all employees know that if they screw up, they can and will be fired. Ensure insecurity. Take advantage of lean. While getting rid of waste, let them all know that they could be the next waste to be thrown out. Take advantage of ISO 9001 registration audits. Let them all know that nonconformities are unacceptable, and if any are found, they will be fired. Encourage everyone to hide nonconformities or at least lie to the auditor so that you never lose the ISO 9001 certification. Let everyone know that the *root cause* to most problems is employee errors.

Score _____

Point #9: Build and protect your kingdom!

You are the manager of your department. This is your home, and a person's home is his/her kingdom. You have your departmental objectives by which you will be evaluated. The other departments have theirs. This is a competition. You must protect your kingdom, oftentimes at the expense of the performance of the other kingdoms. Screw them. You need to meet your objectives and achieve maximum bonus. Any time one of your subordinates is requested to work on a cross-functional team, this takes away from your chances of meeting your goals. Don't let them work in teams, outside of your department.

Score _____

Point #10: Promote slogans, exhortations, and targets.

Plaster them all over the walls in the production and office areas. In fact, for the conference rooms, buy the expensive nature and sports photos in the beautiful fake wood frames that display nice little thought-provoking phrases such as "Persistence," "Teamwork," and "Honesty." Customers and suppliers love these. Elsewhere, ensure that there are slogans about your Six Sigma, lean, and ISO 9001 programs. Ensure that everyone knows that our target is 3.4 defects per million.

Score _____

Point #11a: Institute production quotas.

Ensure that they all know that the numbers are the key. If there is a slower worker, he or she will feel the pressure to keep up, no matter what the cost. He or she will also see the faster workers standing around for the last 30 minutes, doing nothing, because they reached their quota (including the defects) early. This will be seen as a reward and will encourage people to work harder.

Point #11b: Institute management by objective.

Set arbitrary improvement percentages for managers, perhaps the same percentages that were set last year and the year before since they were not met. Do not set plans to achieve, because there's really no time to plan because we have to "make the numbers" this month. If you do make plans, at least keep them vague and in support of Point #5, like, "Save $400,000 through

5S and TPM." Also, make sure that you set a goal for 100 Black Belts trained and 1000 Six Sigma projects completed. This will look good to our shareholders, even if nothing good comes out of it.

Score (for a and b) _____

Point #12: Develop a culture in which people are not proud of their work.

Perform an annual rating of performance, or merit rating, for salaried employees. Merit rating rewards people that do well in your system. It's *your* system. You don't want people to actually try to change your system. You want them to suck up to you within your system.

Don't spend time on developing and communicating acceptable work-manship levels. Let employees come to you to make the decision on what to ship and what to scrap. Keep them off balance with your decisions, so that they don't know of the deep complexities of your decision-making process. This will keep them in awe of you and ensure you even more job security, which you don't really need, because you're working with a headhunter right now, but you never know . . . . Getting rid of quality and maintenance (as described in Point #1) will help promote a lack of pride since they will not be able to make good parts, but will still have to "make the numbers."

Score (for both parts) _____

Point #13: Discourage education and self-improvement for everyone.

We went to school in the past. But that's the past and it may have helped get us to the point where we are in life right now, but most of that stuff wasn't used anyway. So why waste time and money on it now? Besides, if it doesn't have some kind of certification behind it (such as Black Belt, ISO 9001, ASQ, and SME certifications), then it's worthless to get more education because people can not pad their resumes. Also, can you imagine actually encouraging driving waste out of our personal lives and actually trying to improve who we are, our marriages or relationships, our health, our society, our government, or our environment? I would rather watch TV!

Score _____

Point #14: Become the hero!

Bear the burden of any transformation of the company on your shoulders and reap the rewards and accolades. If the transformation was unsuccessful, then blame the culture you inherited, resistance, the industry, the owner, or a management coup. By now, your organization understands that the root cause of every organizational failure rests on the shoulders of one or some of the employees. If the transformation is successful, you can take full credit for the accomplishment. This is the time to take the next job and move on to reap even greater rewards, because the successful transformation is only short term. The company will soon begin to crumble.

This is your most important action! Get out now!

Score _____

Add up your score. The maximum number of points is 42 (14 × 3).

Total score _____

If you scored between 32–42, you can now say you're a member of SAD (Society of Anti-Deming). Someday, we may give you a Certificate, which makes it even more worthwhile!!

If you scored between 20–31, you need work. Perhaps fire someone and instill some fear in the others by instituting new numerical quotas.

If you scored less than 19, you're a *quality freak!*

Endnotes

1. www.answers.com.
2. W. Edwards Deming, *Out of the Crisis* (Cambridge, MA: Massachusetts Institute of Technology, 1982): 53.
3. Scott M. Paton, "Four Days with W. Edwards Deming," The W. Edwards Deming Institute, http://deming.org/index.cfm?content=653. (2000)
4. Stephen R. Covey, *The 7 Habits of Highly Effective People* (New York: Simon and Schuster, 1989).
5. Tony Burns, "Six Sigma: Lessons from Deming," *Quality Digest* (February 5, 2008).
6. "The Mortgage Meltdown: Cause and Effect," http://themortgageu.wordpress.com/2007/08/24/the-mortgage-meltdown-cause-and-effect/, 8/24/07
7. Jed Rothwell, "Lessons from the Enron Collapse," *Infinite Energy* 41 (January–Febuary 2002). Available at http://www.infinite-energy.com/iemagazine/issue41/enron.html.
8. Ernest Beck, "End of the Road for U.S. Automakers?" MSN Money, http://articles.moneycentral.msn.com/Investing/StockInvestingTrading/EndofTheRoadForUSAutomakers.aspx (August 15, 2008).
9. Roland Watson, "Peak Oil 2005?" Energy Bulletin, Published July 14, 2005 by New Era Investor. Available at http://www.energybulletin.net/node/7284. Accessed January 19, 2010.
10. Mary Walton, *The Deming Management Method* (New York: Dodd, Mead, and Co., 1986): 59.
11. Ibid., p. 60
12. Robert E. Scott, EPI Briefing Paper #188, Economic Policy Institute, http://www.epi.org/content.cfm/bp188, October 9, 2007 (revised—originally released May 2, 2007).
13. Some of these came from 2007 Manufacturer's Advantage Conference, "The Top Ten Hidden Costs of Outsourcing," presentation by Joe Petti of JP Associates.
14. Walton, *The Deming Management Method,* p. 66.

15. Art Smalley, "TPS vs. Lean and the Law of Unintended Consequences," Superfactory, http://www.superfactory.com/articles/featured/2005/ 0512-smalley-tps-lean-manufacturing.html. Accessed December 2005.

16. Judith Crown and Glenn Coleman, *No Hands: The Rise and Fall of the Schwinn Bicycle Company, an American Institution* (New York: Henry Holt & Co., 1996).

17. Donald Dinero, *Training Within Industry: The Foundation of Lean* (New York: Productivity Press, 2005).

18. Stephen R. Covey, *The 7 Habits of Highly Effective People* (New York: Simon and Schuster, 1989).

19. Anonymous, "Last Word," *Quality Digest* (2000) Available at http://www.qualitydigest.com/aug01/html/lastword.html.

20. Examples 3 through 9 are from experiences related to me by Nigel Clements of PRISM Consultancy International

21. *W. Edwards Deming: The Prophet of Quality,* video, CC-M Productions (1991), Films for the Humanities and Sciences, Princeton, NJ.

22. Wikipedia, Available at http://en.wikipedia.org/wiki/No_Child_Left_ Behind_Act.

23. Alex Tehrani, "How to Fix No Child Left Behind," *Time* (May 24, 2007). Available at http://www.time.com/time/magazine/article/0,9171,1625192, 00.html.

24. Eddy Ramirez and Kim Clark, "What Arne Duncan Thinks of No Child Left Behind," *U.S. News and World Report.com* (Posted February 5, 2009). Available at http://www.usnews.com/articles/education/2009/02/05/ what-arne-duncan-thinks-of-no-child-left-behind.html.

25. Paul Orfalea, *Copy This! How I Turned Dyslexia, ADHD, and 100 Square Feet into a Company Called Kinko's* (New York: Workman, 2007).

26. W. Edwards Deming, *The New Economics* (Cambridge, MA: Massachusetts Institute of Technology, 1994): 148.

27. Covey, *7 Habits*, p. 35.

28. Roger Parloff, "Wall Street: It's Payback Time" *Fortune* (September 19, 2009).

29. Clare Crawford-Mason and Robert Mason, "Geared for Happiness," *The Washington Times* (November 30, 2008).

30. Covey, *7 Habits*.

Index

Belong to the Quality Community!

Established in 1946, ASQ is a global community of quality experts in all fields and industries. ASQ is dedicated to the promotion and advancement of quality tools, principles, and practices in the workplace and in the community.

The Society also serves as an advocate for quality. Its members have informed and advised the U.S. Congress, government agencies, state legislatures, and other groups and individuals worldwide on quality-related topics.

Vision

By making quality a global priority, an organizational imperative, and a personal ethic, ASQ becomes the community of choice for everyone who seeks quality technology, concepts, or tools to improve themselves and their world.

ASQ is...

- More than 90,000 individuals and 700 companies in more than 100 countries
- The world's largest organization dedicated to promoting quality
- A community of professionals striving to bring quality to their work and their lives
- The administrator of the Malcolm Baldrige National Quality Award
- A supporter of quality in all sectors including manufacturing, service, healthcare, government, and education
- YOU

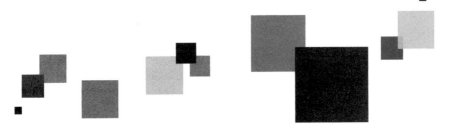

Visit www.asq.org for more information.

ASQ Membership

Research shows that people who join associations experience increased job satisfaction, earn more, and are generally happier*. ASQ membership can help you achieve this while providing the tools you need to be successful in your industry and to distinguish yourself from your competition. So why wouldn't you want to be a part of ASQ?

Networking

Have the opportunity to meet, communicate, and collaborate with your peers within the quality community through conferences and local ASQ section meetings, ASQ forums or divisions, ASQ Communities of Quality discussion boards, and more.

Professional Development

Access a wide variety of professional development tools such as books, training, and certifications at a discounted price. Also, ASQ certifications and the ASQ Career Center help enhance your quality knowledge and take your career to the next level.

Solutions

Find answers to all your quality problems, big and small, with ASQ's Knowledge Center, mentoring program, various e-newsletters, *Quality Progress* magazine, and industry-specific products.

Access to Information

Learn classic and current quality principles and theories in ASQ's Quality Information Center (QIC), *ASQ Weekly* e-newsletter, and product offerings.

Advocacy Programs

ASQ helps create a better community, government, and world through initiatives that include social responsibility, Washington advocacy, and Community Good Works.

Visit www.asq.org/membership for more information on ASQ membership.

*2008, The William E. Smith Institute for Association Research

ASQ Certification

ASQ certification is formal recognition by ASQ that an individual has demonstrated a proficiency within, and comprehension of, a specified body of knowledge at a point in time. Nearly 150,000 certifications have been issued. ASQ has members in more than 100 countries, in all industries, and in all cultures. ASQ certification is internationally accepted and recognized.

Benefits to the Individual

- New skills gained and proficiency upgraded
- Investment in your career
- Mark of technical excellence
- Assurance that you are current with emerging technologies
- Discriminator in the marketplace
- Certified professionals earn more than their uncertified counterparts
- Certification is endorsed by more than 125 companies

Benefits to the Organization

- Investment in the company's future
- Certified individuals can perfect and share new techniques in the workplace
- Certified staff are knowledgeable and able to assure product and service quality

Quality is a global concept. It spans borders, cultures, and languages. No matter what country your customers live in or what language they speak, they demand quality products and services. You and your organization also benefit from quality tools and practices. Acquire the knowledge to position yourself and your organization ahead of your competition.

Certifications Include
- Biomedical Auditor – CBA
- Calibration Technician – CCT
- HACCP Auditor – CHA
- Pharmaceutical GMP Professional – CPGP
- Quality Inspector – CQI
- Quality Auditor – CQA
- Quality Engineer – CQE
- Quality Improvement Associate – CQIA
- Quality Technician – CQT
- Quality Process Analyst – CQPA
- Reliability Engineer – CRE
- Six Sigma Black Belt – CSSBB
- Six Sigma Green Belt – CSSGB
- Software Quality Engineer – CSQE
- Manager of Quality/Organizational Excellence – CMQ/OE

Visit www.asq.org/certification to apply today!

ASQ Training

Classroom-based Training

ASQ offers training in a traditional classroom setting on a variety of topics. Our instructors are quality experts and lead courses that range from one day to four weeks, in several different cities. Classroom-based training is designed to improve quality and your organization's bottom line. Benefit from quality experts; from comprehensive, cutting-edge information; and from peers eager to share their experiences.

Web-based Training

Virtual Courses

ASQ's virtual courses provide the same expert instructors, course materials, interaction with other students, and ability to earn CEUs and RUs as our classroom-based training, without the hassle and expenses of travel. Learn in the comfort of your own home or workplace. All you need is a computer with Internet access and a telephone.

Self-paced Online Programs

These online programs allow you to work at your own pace while obtaining the quality knowledge you need. Access them whenever it is convenient for you, accommodating your schedule.

Some Training Topics Include
- Auditing
- Basic Quality
- Engineering
- Education
- Healthcare
- Government
- Food Safety
- ISO
- Leadership
- Lean
- Quality Management
- Reliability
- Six Sigma
- Social Responsibility

Visit www.asq.org/training for more information.